Statistics for Social Work with SPSS

Statistics for Social Work with SPSS

SERGE LEE

CALIFORNIA STATE UNIVERSITY, SACRAMENTO

Bassim Hamadeh, CEO and Publisher
Amy Smith, Senior Project Editor
Celeste Paed, Associate Production Editor
Jess Estrella, Senior Graphic Designer
Alexa Lucido, Licensing Manager
Natalie Piccotti, Director of Marketing
Kassie Graves, Senior Vice President of Editorial
Jamie Giganti, Director of Academic Publishing

Copyright © 2022 by Cognella, Inc. All rights reserved. No part of this publication may be reprinted, reproduced, transmitted, or utilized in any form or by any electronic, mechanical, or other means, now known or hereafter invented, including photocopying, microfilming, and recording, or in any information retrieval system without the written permission of Cognella, Inc. For inquiries regarding permissions, translations, foreign rights, audio rights, and any other forms of reproduction, please contact the Cognella Licensing Department at rights@cognella.com.

Unless otherwise noted, all software screenshots are from SPSS Copyright © by IBM Corporation.

Trademark Notice: Product or corporate names may be trademarks or registered trademarks and are used only for identification and explanation without intent to infringe.

Cover image copyright © 2009 iStockphoto LP/merrymoonmary.

Printed in the United States of America.

This book is dedicated to my most beautiful wife, Kia, and our four wonderful children: Pheng, Tou, Maly, and Chong Dylan.

Brief Contents

List of Figures xv
List of Tables xvii
Preface xxi
Acknowledgments xxiii

Chapter 1	Brief Introduction: Statistics and Research	1
Chapter 2	Variables, Variable Classifications, and Levels of Measurement	17
Chapter 3	Descriptive Statistics: Frequency Distributions	33
Chapter 4	Descriptive Statistics: Measures of Central Tendency and Variability	49
Chapter 5	Normal Distribution and Z Score	73
Chapter 6	Probability and Hypothesis Testing	93
Chapter 7	Inferential Statistics: Cross-Tabulation and Chi-Square	115
Chapter 8	Inferential Statistics: Correlation	137
Chapter 9	Inferential Statistics: The T-Tests	165
Chapter 10	Inferential Statistics: Simple Linear Regression	191
Chapter 11	Inferential Statistics: One-Way ANOVA	211
Chapter 12	A Snapshot of Qualitative Research	231
Appendix A	SPSS Instructions	249
Appendix B	Critical Values of F	263
Appendix C	Basic Foundations of Statistical Analysis	273

References 275
Index 279

Detailed Contents

List of Figures   xv
List of Tables   xvii
Preface   xxi
Acknowledgments   xxiii

Chapter 1   Brief Introduction: Statistics and Research. 1
    Overview   1
    Statistical Concepts   2
    You as the Researcher   3
    Types of Statistics   4
        Descriptive Statistics   4
        Inferential Statistics   5
    Evidence-Based Practice and Statistics   6
    Ethical Issues in Social Science Research   7
        Informed Consent   7
        Anonymity   7
        Confidentiality   8
        Sensitive Information   8
        Reliability and Validity   8
    Relationship Between Research Methods and Statistics   9
        Research Data, Hypothesis, and Statistics   9
    The Research Cycle   10
        Problem Identification   11
        Operationalization   11
        Methodology   11
        Statistical Analysis   12
        Statistical Package for the Social Sciences (SPSS)   12
    Summary   12
    Study Questions   13

Chapter 2   Variables, Variable Classifications, and Levels of Measurement. 17
    Overview   17
    What Is a Variable?   18

Variable Classification   19
Types of Variables   20
Two Types of Data   22
   Quantitative Data   22
   Qualitative Data   22
Levels of Measurement   23
   Nominal Variable (Nominal Data)   23
   Ordinal Variable (Ordinal Data)   24
   Interval Variable (Interval Data)   25
   Ratio Variable (Ratio Data)   26
Summary   27
Study Questions   28

Chapter 3   **Descriptive Statistics: Frequency Distributions** **33**
Overview   33
Frequency Distributions   33
   Frequencies   33
   Frequency Count and Percentage   36
   Graphs   37
   Bar Graphs (Bar Charts)   37
   Pie Graphs (Pie Charts)   37
   Histograms   38
   Frequency Polygons (Line Graphs or Line Charts)   39
Introduction and Data Entry Using SPSS   39
   Overview   39
   Data Entry Using SPSS   40
   Practice Example   43
Summary   44
Study Questions   44

Chapter 4   **Descriptive Statistics: Measures of Central Tendency and Variability** **49**
Overview   49
Measures of Central Tendency   50
   The Mean   50
   Trimmed Mean   51
   The Median   52
   The Mode   52
Effect of the Mean on Outliers   53
Measures of Variation   54
   The Range   54
   Quartile and Interquartile Range   55
   Properties of the Mean and Mean Deviation (MD)   56
   The Variance (SS^2)   58
   The Standard Deviation (SD)   59

    The Coefficient of Variation (CV)   60
  Using SPSS to Calculate Measures of Central Tendency and Variability   61
    Practice Example   64
    Answer to Practice Example   64
  Summary   67
  Study Questions   68

Chapter 5   Normal Distribution and *Z* Score 73

  Overview   73
  Background of the Normal Curve   75
  Properties of the Normal Curve   76
  Areas Under the Normal Curve   77
  Understanding the Z Score   79
    Practice Example 1   80
    Practice Example 2   84
  Additional Note About the Z Score   85
    Practice Example 3   86
  Summary   87
  Study Questions   88

Chapter 6   Probability and Hypothesis Testing 93

  Overview   93
  Population and Sample   94
    Population   94
    Sample   94
  Probability and Sampling: Distribution of the Mean   94
    Probability   94
    Sampling Distribution of the Means   95
    Hypothesis and Hypothesis Testing   97
  Types of Hypotheses   98
    The Alternative Hypothesis   98
    The Null Hypothesis   99
  Direction of the Hypothesis   99
    Directional (One-Tail) Hypothesis   100
    Nondirectional (Two-Tailed) Hypothesis   101
  Constructing the Confidence Interval (CI)   101
    What Is the Confidence Interval (CI)?   102
    Interpreting Results of Statistical Tests   104
  Constructing the Confidence Interval Using Z Score   105
    Statistical Rules on Converting Proportion Into a Z Score   105
    Practice Example 1 for Two-Tailed Hypothesis   106
    Practice Example 2 for One-Tailed Hypothesis   107
  Error in Hypothesis Test and Alternative Explanation   107
    Type I and Type II Errors   108
  Alternative Explanations   108

Using SPSS to Construct Confidence Interval   109
Summary   111
Study Questions   111

Chapter 7   Inferential Statistics: Cross-Tabulation and Chi-Square 115

Overview   115
The Meaning of Bivariate Analysis   115
What Are Cross-Tabulation and Chi-Square?   115
  Practice Example   117
  Constructing a Contingency Table   118
  Calculating Percentages   119
  Formula for the Chi-Square (χ^2)   120
  Calculating the Chi-Square   121
  Interpreting the Chi-Square Result   122
  Note About a 2 x 2 Study   125
Measuring the Strength of Association   125
  The Phi (Φ)   125
  The Cramer's V   126
  Practice Example 2   127
Using SPSS to Compute Chi-Square   128
Summary   133
Study Questions   134

Chapter 8   Inferential Statistics: Correlation 137

Overview   137
Introduction to Correlation   137
  What Is Correlation?   137
  Graphical Display of Direction of Correlation   139
  Is a Positive, Negative, or Zero Correlation a Better Coefficient?   141
  Value of the Pearson Correlation Coefficient (Pearson's)   141
  The Strength of the Correlation Coefficient Range   142
Correlation Is Not Causation   143
Usefulness of Correlation in Social Work and Behavioral Settings   143
Formula for Calculating the Correlation Coefficient   144
  Practice Example 1   145
What Is the Coefficient of Determination (r^2)?   148
Using r^2 to Determine Variation   148
Calculating Pearson's r Using an Unbiased Formula   150
  Practice Example 2   151
Understanding Kendall's Tau B, Spearman's Rho, and Partial Correlation Coefficient   154
  Kendall's Tau B and Spearman's Rho   155
  Partial Correlation Coefficient   155
Using SPSS to Calculate Pearson's r   156
Summary   159
Study Questions   160

Chapter 9 **Inferential Statistics: The T-Tests** 165

Overview   165
The Meaning of T-Tests   166
Three Types of T-Tests   167
  Various Statistical Assumptions About the T-Tests   167
  The One-Sample T-Test   168
  Practice Situation Using One-Sample T-Tests   169
  The Independent Samples T-Test and Its Relation to Social Work   173
  Formula for the Independent Samples T-Test   173
  Practice Example Using Independent Samples T-Test   175
  The Dependent Samples T-Test   176
  Practice Example for the Dependent Samples T-Test   177
The Correlation Effect Size and Cohen's d Effect Size   181
Using SPSS to Compute the T-Tests   183
Summary   186
Study Questions   187

Chapter 10 **Inferential Statistics: Simple Linear Regression** 191

Overview   191
The Meaning of Simple Linear Regression   193
The Meaning of Prediction in Health and Human Services   194
Statistical Requirements/Conditions for Simple Linear Regression   194
Computational Formula for Linear Regression   195
  Practice Example 1   196
  Practice Example 2   200
  Other Statistical Symbols (Notations)   202
SPSS Instructions on LRM   204
Summary   207
Study Questions   208

Chapter 11 **Inferential Statistics: One-Way ANOVA** .211

Overview   211
The T- Test and F-Ratio   212
  Statistical Assumptions   213
  Overall Meaning of the F-Ratio   213
Two Sources of Variability for ANOVA   214
  Variability for Between-Groups Means $(MS_{Between})$ 214
  Variability for Within-Groups Means (MS_{Within})   214
  Practice Example   215
Steps in Calculating the F-Ratio   216
  Calculating the Vignette   219
Tests of Statistical Significance   221
SPSS Instructions on ANOVA   222
Summary   225
Study Questions   226

Chapter 12 A Snapshot of Qualitative Research **231**

    Overview   231
    What Is Qualitative Research?   232
    Data Collection Justifications   233
    Fieldwork Versus Field Notes   234
        Fieldwork   234
        Field Notes   234
    Questionnaire Construction   235
    Qualitative Data Recording   236
    Narrative Data   237
    Types of Qualitative Data Analysis   238
        Discovering Patterns   238
        Content Analysis   240
        Semiotics   241
        Conversation Analysis   242
        Computer Applications and Online Resources   242
    Summary   243
    Study Questions   244

Appendix A SPSS Instructions **249**

    Overview   249
    Preparing the Data for Analysis   249
    Suggested Steps in Preparing the Obtained Scores for Analysis   249
    Introduction and Data Entry Using SPSS   250
        Data Entry Using SPSS   251
        Saving Data   255
        Practice Example   255
        Computing Descriptive Statistics   256
        Computing Inferential Statistics   257
        Recoding a Variable   258

Appendix B Critical Values of F **263**

Appendix C Basic Foundations of Statistical Analysis **273**

References   275
Index   279

List of Figures

FIGURE 1.1   The Research Cycle   10

FIGURE 3.1   Bar Graph for Gender From Table 3.1   37

FIGURE 3.2   Sample of Good and Not so Good Pie Graphs   38

FIGURE 3.3   Histogram Graph   38

FIGURE 3.4   Frequency Polygon on Age and Anxiety Level   39

FIGURE 3.5   Variable View Blank Screen   40

FIGURE 4.1   Annual Income Reported by Patients/Clients at a Local Hospital   53

FIGURE 4.2   The Property of Mean Deviation   58

FIGURE 4.3   SPSS Data Created From Table 3.2   62

FIGURE 5.1   The Normal Curve   74

FIGURE 5.2(A)   Positively Skewed   74

FIGURE 5.2(B)   Negatively Skewed   74

FIGURE 5.3   Normal Distribution With a High Peak or Kurtosis   76

FIGURE 5.4   Normal Curve With SD   76

FIGURE 5.5   Normal Curve With Correspondence Percentages   78

FIGURE 5.6   Likelihood the Couple Will Get Their Child Back Within 3 Months   82

FIGURE 5.7   SPSS Computation for the Normal Curve   85

FIGURE 5.8   CPS Case With a 97% Confidence Interval   87

FIGURE 6.1(A)   Prediction That Significant Differences Are Only Observed on the Left Side   100

FIGURE 6.1(B)   Prediction That Significant Differences Are Only Observed on the Right Side   100

FIGURE 6.2   Nondirectional Hypothesis   101

FIGURE 6.3   Z Score Needed to Construct 95% Confidence Interval (p value = .05)   106

FIGURE 6.4   Z Score Needed to Construction a 99.9% Confidence Interval (p value = .001)   107

FIGURE 8.1(A)   Sample Scatterplot With Positive Correlation for Table 8.1   140

FIGURE 8.1(B)   Diagram Depicting Positive Correlation   140

FIGURE 8.2(A)   Scatterplot Depicting a Negative Correlation   140

FIGURE 8.2(B)   Depicting Negative Correlation   140

FIGURE 8.3(A)   Scatterplot Depicting a No (Zero) Correlation   141

FIGURE 8.3(B)   Diagram Depicting No Correlation   141

FIGURE 10.1   LRM   206

FIGURE 11.1   Partitioning the F-Ratio   217

FIGURE A.1   Blank SPSS Screen   252

FIGURE A.2   The Value Label Column   253

FIGURE A.3   Data View Screen   254

FIGURE A.4   Chapter Data Bank   254

FIGURE A.5   Bar Graph for Gender   257

FIGURE A.6   Analyze Ribbon Showing Both Descriptive and Inferential Statistics   258

FIGURE A.7   Sample Help for Correlation Analysis   258

FIGURE A.8   Recode Variable   259

FIGURE A.9   Recode Old and New Variables   260

FIGURE A.10   Sample Recode Is Successful   261

List of Tables

TABLE 2.1   Age and Nationality of Research Subjects   19

TABLE 3.1   Sample Research Data   34

TABLE 3.2   Frequency for Sample Data on Gender and Anxiety Variables   35

TABLE 3.3   Formula for Percentage and Valid Percentage Calculations   36

TABLE 3.4   Frequency Count for the Variable Anxiety   36

TABLE 3.5   The Students' Anxiety Level   43

TABLE 4.1   Calculate Self-Care Scores From Table 3.1   56

TABLE 4.2   Calculating the Variance (SS^2) for the Self-Care Variable   59

TABLE 4.3   Measures of Central Tendency and Variability   63

TABLE 4.4   Summary of Descriptive Statistics   68

TABLE 5.1   Distance Between the Sample Mean ($\bar{x}$) and SD   78

TABLE 5.2   Calculating the Z Score and Converting to a Percentile   80

TABLE 5.3   Percentage Area Under the Normal Curve Between the Mean and Z   82

TABLE 5.4   Calculating the Z Score for the First College Student   84

TABLE 5.5   Solve the Z Score Formula to Get x   86

TABLE 6.1   Sample Two-Tailed Hypothesis and a New P Value   105

TABLE 6.2   The Four Possible Outcomes Associated With Hypothesis Testing   108

TABLE 6.3   Constructing a Confidence Interval Using SPSS   110

TABLE 7.1   Mindfulness Practice Is Good for Healthy Living   118

TABLE 7.2   Percentages State That Mindfulness Is Good for Healthy Living   119

TABLE 7.3	Hypotheses for Calculating the Pearson Chi-Square (χ^2)	120
TABLE 7.4	Observed Frequencies and Expected Frequencies for Mindfulness and Race	122
TABLE 7.5	Critical Value of Chi-Square	123
TABLE 7.6	Two-Parent Families Who Have Lost Parental Rights to Child in the District Juvenile Court	126
TABLE 7.7	Parental Perceptions on the Effectiveness of Ritalin on ADHD Kids	127
TABLE 7.8(A)	Students' Class Level * Gender of Respondent Cross-Tabulation	131
TABLE 7.8(B)	Chi-Square Tests	131
TABLE 7.8(C)	Measures on Strength of Association	132
TABLE 7.8(D)	Symmetric Measures	132
TABLE 7.9	Sample Chi-Square Tests When the Alternative Hypothesis Is Supported	133
TABLE 8.1	Relationship Between Years Spent in College and Hourly Wage	138
TABLE 8.2	Expanding Table 8.1 Into Segments for the Pearson's r Calculation	146
TABLE 8.3	Critical Value of r	149
TABLE 8.4	Domestic Violence Educational Training	153
TABLE 8.5	A Hypothetical Rank Correlation Using Kendall's Tau B and Spearman's Rho on the Use of Social Work Values and Ethical Practice.	158
TABLE 8.6	Rank Correlation Coefficient	159
TABLE 9.1	Critical Value of t	171
TABLE 9.2	Behavior Modification Treatment for Asian and Black Youth	175
TABLE 9.3	Youth Crime Prevention Success Training Program	178
TABLE 9.4	The Completed Breakdown Elements for Dependent Samples T-Test	179
TABLE 9.5	Correlation Coefficient of Effect Size	181
TABLE 9.6	Cohen's d Effect Size	182
TABLE 9.7	Paired Samples (Dependent) Statistics	185
TABLE 9.8	Paired Samples Correlations	186
TABLE 9.9	Paired Samples Test	186
TABLE 8.2	Expanding Table 8.1 Into Segments for the Pearson's r Calculation	198

TABLE 10.1   Self-Rated Socialization Skills Training to Improve Self-Esteem   200

TABLE 10.2   Expansion on Self-Rated Socialization Skills Training to Improve Self-Esteem   201

TABLE 10.3   Model Summary   206

TABLE 10.4   Coefficients   206

TABLE 11.1   Helpfulness of Life Coaching Methods   215

TABLE 11.2   Helpfulness of Life Coaching Methods Scores and the Sum of the Squares   220

TABLE 11.3   ANOVA for the Helpfulness of Life Coaching Methods   223

TABLE 11.4   Mean Difference Among the Groups   224

TABLE 11.5   The Mean Scores for All Five Groups (From Lowest to Highest)   225

TABLE 12.1   Example of Data Analysis Using the Magnitude Concept   239

TABLE 12.2   Example of Data Analysis Using the Semiotic Concept   242

TABLE A.1   The Students' Anxiety Level   256

Preface

Although the second edition is a complete overhaul, making it incompatible with the first *Statistics for International Social Work and Other Behavioral Sciences* (Lee et al., 2016), it continues with the same teaching and learning objectives. As an English learner, the author presents statistics using English as a Second Language and universally understandable statistical concepts. Thus, students from all backgrounds can use this book to help them understand statistics in ways that may be more helpful to them. The goal is to provide graduate and undergraduate social work students and practitioners—as well as those from other social sciences and behavioral sciences—a user-friendly, evidence-based, practical, quality textbook to enable them to make sense of, organize, analyze, and interpret data in modern-day educational training and practices. In addition, it incorporates one of the well-known software applications, the *Statistical Package for the Social Sciences* (SPSS 26, 2020), into every chapter to help students and practitioners integrate their statistical knowledge either manually or computerized. The book contents are organized pedagogically to mirror how the author has taught his students for over 29 years so students can see the progression of basic concepts and terms of complex statistical functions.

To make this book distinctly different, if not better than other social work statistics books, the author organized the learning contents in each chapter into four major learning styles: (1) the chapters' headings are clear with concise and simple explanations on terminologies, formulas, and calculations; (2) each chapter is accompanied with study questions and answers that enable learners and users to easily grapple with statistical results; (3) specific SPSS instructions on computerized computations are provided; (4) companion PowerPoint slides and practice questions are provided on student resources through Cognella Academic Publishing. More importantly, every chapter provides evidence-based practical examples for learners and practitioners to understand the chapters' everyday usage. Furthermore, the study questions and answers to the study questions should enable users to apply statistics to understand the globalization of our social world.

Acknowledgments

Throughout the years, I have crossed paths with so many amazing individuals on this earthly tile. From the time I was in school to the time I completed this second statistics book, some of these individuals mentored and guided me to be the person I am today. Most of them were named in my memoir, *From Earth to Elite: The Memoir of Dr. Serge Lee* (Lee, 2020). I am grateful that we know each other. The success of the first edition could not have been completed without the mentorship of my coauthors, Dr. Maria C. Silveira Nunes Dinis, Dr. Lois Lowe, and Ms. Kelly Louise Anders. Indeed, I owe a huge gratitude to Drs. Dinis and Lowe for their ongoing supports, mainly my writing issues. For my scholarly products, I am indebted to my best mentor, whom I also call "big brother," Dr. Francis K. O. Yuen, and a huge gratitude is extended to my editor, Houa Vang. This book could not have been possible without Houa's utmost editing skills. I also want to thank you Kassie Graves, Amy Smith, and Celeste Paed at Cognella, Inc. for the recommended changes to the text and the works you put to edit and design the book. Furthermore, I want to thank Dr. Curtis D. Proctor at Millersville University; Dr. Francis K. O. Yuen at California State University, Sacramento; and Dr. Megan Hicks at Wayne State University for their utmost review of the book. Each of them provided invaluable comments and suggestions for the final draft. Last but not least, this second edition could not have been completed without the Fulbright Distinguished Chair Fellowship awarded by the US Department of State for the entire 2019–2020 academic year to Hunan Normal University in the People's Republic of China. The fellowship enabled the manuscript to be completely rewritten for a new edition. And indeed, I am thankful to California State University, Sacramento for allowing me to take an academic year leave of absence when I had not yet qualified for another sabbatical leave.

CHAPTER 1

Brief Introduction
Statistics and Research

OVERVIEW

The Council on Social Work Education (CSWE) in the United States (CSWE, 2020) states that the purpose of the social work profession is to promote human and community well-being. It is guided by a person-in-environment, multicultural, and evidence-based framework. This framework is to focus on educating competent professionals at the bachelor's, master's, and doctoral levels; the conditions and functions of a global perspective; respect for diversity of human rights; and scientifically based inquiry. It states further that the accredited curriculum must include the person in the environment, diversity, social policy, research and statistics, and micro and macro practices that meet nine educational *competencies* that are consistent with four *policies* on social work mission and goal. A joint commission from the Educational Policy and Accreditation Standards (EPAS) has formed for the past 3 years to develop a more inclusive EPAS to be in place for US social work education institutions by 2022 (CSWE, 2020). The 2022 EPAS is to ally America's social work institutions of higher education with the international social work community to develop more uniform EPAS, such as the utilization of technology for evidence-based and translational social work (CSWE, 2020).

This chapter uses EPAS 2015 as a required education and knowledge-based standard to prepare students and practitioners to understand statistical concepts and their respective mechanics that will be/are used throughout the book. More importantly, the chapter introduces the relationship between research methodology and statistics as to how they correlate to evidence-based practice. First, let us begin with the term "statistical concept."

STATISTICAL CONCEPTS

There are two branches (types) of research: qualitative and quantitative.

The *qualitative research aspect is commonly used as an exploratory approach when one wants to gain understandings from societal situations and/or conditions* (see Chapter 12). This can be fulfilled by collecting data through observations and interviews because it is considered to have non-numerical meanings. An example of this is when a researcher conducts interviews through focus groups or individuals. Typically, when one goes this route and adopts this approach, the targeted sample size is usually small and manageable, and the results are not likely to be generalizable. Except for Chapter 12, this book is not about qualitative research.

On the opposite end, quantitative *research is used when one wants to discover facts about a social construct or phenomenon.* The result is more likely to produce good numerical values—meaning that the data set can be easily calculated and manipulated and likely be transformed into static statistics. The term *static statistics* means that the same data set from a particular research study will likely not change over time and hence the term *static*. This research branch encompasses very small to large sample sizes. One way to think about this is by looking at cities versus states versus the United States as a whole. Methods used to procure data collection are very structured, such as through surveys, rating scales, and self-administered questionnaires (i.e., Beck's Depression Inventory-II). Data can be manipulated to reflect purposeful research, and results are statistically generalized onto the population from where the sample was drawn. Except for Chapter 12, the focal point of this textbook will be on quantitative research and its important explorations. *Regardless of how data are produced, we commonly refer to them as statistical concepts.* In summary, results from large-scale quantitative research are considered to be rigorous and have scientific merits (Frost, n. d.)

In short, *statistical concepts* are guidelines that are typically meant to measure standards by researchers, and when data are compiled, it provides a deeper respect to justify the research topic. The goal is that it becomes universally understood, defined, and justified. An example of this concept is when we operationalize variables, such as defining and identifying variables that can be used to measure social, cultural, behavioral, and other related issues. Moreover, *social science concepts are often mental images that symbolize perceptions, motivations, opinions, categories, personality traits, ideas and thought processes, objects, and events.* Most of the time, the concept is coded (e.g., "1" for undergraduate students and "2" for graduate students, or "on a scale from 0 to 10, how would you rate your level of mindfulness?"). In some situations, the concept does not have to be coded (e.g., *"How old are you?"* or *"What is your racial background?"*).

In quantitative research projects, before collecting data, the researcher or research team critically appraises concepts and standards that will likely prove useful in finding solutions, explanations, and generalizations from the sample to the population, along with the project's research aims. The researchers begin to think about word phrases having both numerical and non-numerical meanings (details in Chapter 2). The word phrases enable the researchers to collect quantifiable data or categorical data to meet the research purposes. *Quantifiable data refers to data that is measurable, calculable, and computable.*

For example, a researcher wants to examine how freshman college students felt about leaving their parents' home for the first time. Categorical data are data that cannot be measured on the number line. For example, the categorical question could ask a group of college students for their current class standing.

In the quantifiable data question, the researcher will construct multiple questions and statements that are related to parent-child separation and the campus environment. Among the statistical concepts, a quantifiable question that can produce numerical score (data) is something like: "On a scale from 1 to 5, *how difficult is it to live alone without your parents?*" A sample quantifiable metric statement that can also produce numerical data can be something like: "Using 1 for '*Completely disagree,*' 2 for '*Somewhat agree,*' 3 for '*Agree,*' and 4 for '*Completely agree,*' choose one next to the statement '*I feel stress after arriving at my dorm or apartment after class in the evening.*'" And a quantifiable metric question that can produce non-numerical meaning can be something like, "*How is it like to live alone without your parents?*" The potential responses could be, "*I feel extremely lonely,*" "*I feel somewhat lonely,*" "*I feel lonely,*" and "*I do not feel lonely at all.*"

Depending on the numbers of freshman college students to whom the researchers intended to administer the questions and statements, the items/statements will produce enough *scores or data* for the study purpose. *Data are the numerical and non-numerical scores, words, or even tables and figures collected for a research project.* Data are used both in quantitative and qualitative research. The responses to the previous sample questions and statements are the statistical concepts (data). In simple terms, statistical concepts comprise *statistical data*. In this book, the terms *statistical concepts* and *statistical data* are used interchangeably.

YOU AS THE RESEARCHER

Social work students and practitioners often ask questions like the following: "*Why do I have to study statistics?*" "*Why do I need to know statistics in my field of practice?*" And, "*I will never become a researcher.*" The first response is that statistics is one of the foundation courses mandated by the CSWE—the accreditation body of social work. Specifically, the EPAS (2015) mandated that accredited programs must meet *Competency 4: Engage in practice-informed research and research-informed practice and Competency 9: Evaluate practice with individuals, families, groups, organizations, and communities.* All accredited bachelor's and master's social work programs must be reviewed every 8 years to make sure that the program remains compliant with this mandate. The second answer is that statistical concepts are used in everyday life and in professional activities (Lee et al., 2016).

When thinking about research and statistics, consider that laypersons, as well as social scientists, are constantly experiencing private matters, as well as interacting with others in public. *Private matters* include such things as the amount of time one spent on self-care per week, stress level, years in a job, the severity of legal and illegal drugs that induce disorders, and decisions about family. *Public matters* include the effectiveness of working relationships with clients, the frequency of community volunteerism, the new knowledge someone produced, and the degree of involvement in social policy (Rubin

& Babbie, 2017). With both private and public matters, performances of individuals can be classified continuously using metric numerical scales, such as "1 to 5," "1 to 10," or discretely as "excellent, good, average, or poor" (see Chapter 2 for continuous and discrete variables). While individuals can never casually predict the results of their performances or evaluate their degrees of effectiveness, one can offer explanations, predictions, and categorizations based on two types of statistical outcomes by applying the data summary technique referred to as "descriptive statistics" or the hypothesis test technique by mean of "inferential statistics" (see the following section).

TYPES OF STATISTICS

In quantitative research, there are two types or branches of statistics. Each type has its distinctive meanings, applications, and is mutually exclusive. One cannot try to learn one type and ignore the other type. Both types enable researchers, practitioners, and laypersons to understand the social world differently. The very basic type of statistics is called *descriptive statistics*. By itself, results produced from descriptive statistics are not to be generalized. The more generalizable and complex form of statistics is called *inferential statistics*. This form of statistics has basic computational descriptive statistics formula and added complex functions that must be carried out through various types of hypothesis tests. How does one distinguish the differences between them? Let us see in the following discussion (Digital E-Learning, 2018; Engel & Schutt, 2013; Science Direct, 2015;).

Descriptive Statistics

This type of statistics is best known as univariate analysis. Univariate means that the statistical analysis focuses on one variable at a time. For example, one can only state that in a research project, there are so many females and males who participated in the research project. There is no way to say that gender is or is not related to types of popular college degrees. Essentially, one cannot state that X is significantly related to Y in some merit fashions.

In turn, descriptive statistics are used to *organize* and show basic numerical and non-numerical values within a sample data set (Agresti, 2018; Barry et al., 2004). *A data set is a set of raw scores obtained from the research project.* The principle of descriptive statistics is to describe the data by reducing the amount of information in the data set through a process called *data summary* or *data reduction*. Descriptive statistics are important because if a research project includes 500 participants and 120 variables, the amount of data must be properly organized and summarize. In this case, it is difficult to visualize the entire data set by the naked eyes. For this reason, the researchers must organize and summarize the obtained data into an easily understandable format.

Typically, there are three ways to organize and summarize the sample data set. These include (1) frequencies, (2) measures of central tendency, and (3) measures of variability or dispersion. More detailed discussions about the meanings and presentations of their respective formula will be discussed in Chapters 3 and 4. Here is a quick summary of the three techniques:

- Frequencies (also known as frequency distributions) are used to organize the data set into raw count (frequency count), percentages, and graphs. Why are graphs a part of the frequencies? Because one cannot create a graph without the raw scores or their corresponding percentages.
- Measures of central tendency are used to identify the central locations for the data set by using the mean, median, and mode.
- Measures of variability are used to examine the deviation or dispersion of the scores from the mean by using range, quartile, mean deviation, variance, and standard deviation.

These three ways summarize the "typical" findings for each of the variables under investigation. For example, what is the typical detachment difficulty score for the parents and their child? What is the typical length of time for parents to be able to trust that their child can live independently at the university dormitory? And what is the typical age for first-time freshmen college students?

Inferential Statistics

This type of statistics is known by two names: (1) bivariate and (2) multivariate analysis. Bivariate means two variables (Agresti, 2018; Barry et al., 2004; Tokunaga, 2018). Multivariate means three or more variables, which is beyond the scope of this book. Chapters 7–11 are on bivariate analysis. Terms used commonly by researchers to report bivariate statistics include "relationship," "association," "means difference," "cause and effect," "prediction," and "factor." Of course, these terms are used in multivariate too. In summary, one can ALWAYS state that X is or is not significantly different from Y in some merit (scientific) fashion. The key purpose in inferential statistics is not to summarize the scores for the sample but to infer the findings from the sample to the population from which it was drawn. The inference concept is called a hypothesis test.

Assume that the participants discussed in the previous descriptive statistics example were parents whose children were first-time freshmen at a major university. Assume that the university was interested in knowing detachment difficulties among the 1,000 parents and their children. Recruiting one parent of each family (500) and their children (500) for a total of 1,000 participants to participate in the research project would be a good choice. Through this method, the university could calculate the mean and standard deviation of the 500 parents and the 500 students separately or lump them together into a single group on the detachment difficulty scores.

The parents and children of interest are called a *population*. The properties of mean and standard deviation (see Chapter 3) of the population are called *parameters*, as they represent the arithmetic average and the standardized unit of detachment difficulty for the incoming student population (Tokunaga, 2018). Similarly, suppose there is a huge metropolitan city with two million residents. The two million residents are the population. Often, however, in many situations, such as the metropolitan city with two million residents, it is impossible to recruit all adults or all children to participate in any research project. For this reason, a smaller sample or a subset of the population must be taken.

By taking a sample, a subset of the population, or the entire population, descriptive statistics are called sample statistics or sample data. In order to generalize findings from the sample statistics to the population where the sample was drawn, the term *inferential statistics* is used. Overall, inferential statistics serve two key purposes:

1. Use sample data to make an inference or draw a conclusion of the population, and
2. Use probability, based on confidence interval and margins of error (Chapter 5 and 6), to determine how confident one can be that the generalizations are correct.

In short, inferential statistics are best used with hypothesis testing. Tools used in inferential statistics are commonly referred to as *statistical tests* or *tests of statistics*. In health and human services, these tools enable professionals such as social work researchers and practitioners to use a relatively small number of observations to obtain generalized information about the entire population (Zeitlin & Auerbach, 2019). Overall, inferential statistics can help answer one or more of the following questions:

1. Is the sample representative of the population?
2. Is there a significant difference between or among the variables?
3. How related are the values of one variable to another?
4. How is one category associated with another category?
5. Which variable caused another variable to change?
6. How best to make a prediction about a situation?
7. How are the average scores different from the others?

Today, both descriptive and inferential statistics are widely used in evidence-based practices in health and human services—especially nursing, social work, sociology, and clinical psychology. Similarly, results from quantitative findings enable social researchers and practitioners to avoid biased views and perceptions about the social world.

EVIDENCE-BASED PRACTICE AND STATISTICS

Up to the early 1990s, the social work profession was largely based on humanitarian gestures of ideologies, values (including common sense and a sense of communal responsibility), and general skills, as well as programming logic and needs. Scientific knowledge was not much of relevance to social workers practicing effectiveness. However, today most employees—whether social workers, nurses, or clinical psychologists—need either new knowledge or to find existing literature to guide them in the development of intervention models that best fit unique practice situations and client conditions across settings. *The relevance of using knowledge to develop and improve programs reflects what is called evidence-based practice.* Rubin and Babbie (2014) state that evidence-based practice "*is a process in which practitioners make decisions in light of the best research evidence available*" (p. 27).

In this book, various ways are introduced for researchers and practitioners to incorporate both descriptive and inferential statistics in their evidence-based practice models.

ETHICAL ISSUES IN SOCIAL SCIENCE RESEARCH

In preparing to become a future employee or researcher, it must be emphasized that the work is not only a job but also a professional activity. Students, faculty, professional researchers, and community-based researchers around the world may unknowingly violate research ethics in pursuit of their goals. In the United States, to help everyone who is thinking about doing research not violate the Institutional Review Board's (IRB) guidelines, which are dictated by federal regulations and institutional policy, a brief discussion about the required contents regarding the protection of human subjects is provided. The principal investigator (PI) must always be concerned with the possibility that the reliability and validity of results may be affected if they are not careful.

Most college campuses and universities, county and state agencies, and school districts in the United States now have an IRB. Their duties are to review and approve research protocols to protect human subjects regarding risks and harms to physical, social, and psychological well-being. To ensure that the research project is ethically carried out and does not burden respondents, the reviewers may examine one or more of the following content areas: *informed consent, anonymity, confidentiality, sensitive information, reliability, and validity*.

Informed Consent

Either in research or practice, the informed consent is necessary. As the term indicates, prospective participants must first be informed of the research purpose. Second, individuals that are being recruited as research participants must consent to participation in the study. Informed consent can either be written or verbal. *In research, it is a process to get permission from the respondent before administering the questionnaires or getting the respondent to disclose their views and perceptions about the issue under investigation.* Informed consent is used to ensure that prospective participants understand the nature of the research and can knowledgeably and voluntarily decide whether to participate in the study. It protects both the participant and the investigator, who otherwise may face legal risks. The prospective participants or their representatives (i.e., parents of children) must be provided with enough time to consider whether to participate in a way that minimizes the possibility of real or perceived coercion or undue influence.

Anonymity

In research studies, *anonymity or anonymous means that before data collection, while collecting data, or after the research is completed, the research subjects must remain nameless or not identifiable.* Typically, this can require that no personally identifiable information such as names, telephone numbers, home addresses, social security numbers, or driver license numbers are allowed to appear anywhere in the questionnaires. One way to protect anonymity is to create a coding scheme or numerical scheme to represent each research subject.

Confidentiality

Maintaining and protecting the information collected, who provided the data, and aggregating results are the utmost important conditions in research. *Confidentiality is the condition(s) set forth by researchers to safe keep the identity of research subjects from being identified or discovered by others and the data provided by them are strictly protected.* Most research projects require the collection of a signed consent agreement from participants, and thus researchers are aware of the identity of their subjects. In such cases, maintaining confidentiality is a key measure to ensure the protection of private information.

The PI and their research associates must keep the collected information secure so that it is not easily visible or obtainable by another person, group, or entity. Safekeeping procedures may include such things as locking the collected information in a file cabinet; numbering the questionnaires instead of using identifiers such as names and addresses; if names and social security numbers are required by the project; shredding hard copies of the questionnaires as soon as the data are entered; erasing the data from the recording device; making sure that the Internet provider address of the respondent is not identifiable (if SurveyMonkey is used); and taking cultural competency issues into consideration. SurveyMonkey is an online development cloud-based company that provides free, customizable surveys, as well as a suite of paid back-end programs that include data analysis, sample selection, bias elimination, and data representation tools (Finley, 1999).

Sensitive Information

It is good practice, both in legal and ethical terms, never to collect more information than called for by the research purposes. Most often, collecting sensitive information, such as home address, name, age, sexual practices, phone numbers, history of arrests, drug and alcohol habits, and socially unacceptable behaviors should be avoided. Asking these questions, if irrelevant, may turn research subjects off and cause second thoughts about participating in the research project. Collecting unnecessary sensitive information also may bring harm to research subjects if the collected information is not properly protected and subsequently leaked to outsiders.

Reliability and Validity

When constructing questionnaires and collecting data, researchers must take into consideration the *reliability* and *validity* of the measurement. *The research methods—mainly the questionnaires and data collection procedures—are part of ethical responsibilities because even in a perfectly designed research project, the reliability coefficient (the result of the computation) does not ensure that the measurement tool (questionnaire) is valid (see Chapter 12 for types of reliability and validity).*

Will the questionnaires capture the intended research purposes? How well will the information obtained represent the population from which the sample was drawn? Can the information be trusted by social workers or other health and human services professionals at large? Can the results from the current sample be duplicated or replicated with another sample or population group? *These questions can be explained by reliability and validity. In brief, reliability is the consistency of the measuring instrument (questionnaire), and validity means it measures what it is intended to measure, and the findings accurately reflect the concept being measured*. For example, the significant difference between self-esteem and level of school truancy for high school students could be considered a reliable factor that commonly contributes to delinquent behavior.

Ethical issues in research projects are always embedded in research methodology. It is in the research methodology that researchers must clearly understand its research design, sampling, instrumentations, and the protection of human subjects. Without paying close attention to the research method used to plan and execute the research project, statistical results from the research study could become meaningless. Let us turn briefly to the relationship between research methods and statistics.

RELATIONSHIP BETWEEN RESEARCH METHODS AND STATISTICS

The relationship between research methods and statistics is as complex as the chicken and egg dilemma. Does one need to understand *research methodology* before being able to learn *statistics*, or is it the other way around? What types of research knowledge enable practitioners and researchers to make good decisions? Precise answers to these two questions are always debatable. *A conscious researcher may state that understanding research methodology is required to properly use statistics. Furthermore, statisticians could arguably state that research methodology enables one to collect good statistical data*. Good statistical data are what one needs in order to summarize the sample data and further test hypotheses.

Research Data, Hypothesis, and Statistics

The raw scores, numbers, words, or even the tables or figures collected for a research project are termed *data* or *research data* (*data set*). After data from one or more variables have been analyzed and interpretations have been given, it is known as *information* (Bachelor, 2019; Weinbach & Grinnell, 2006). With the data set, one can usually specify two or more hypotheses to be accomplished. Many define *hypothesis* **as an** "*educated guess, hunch, and supposition.*" In all, a hypothesis enables the researcher/practitioner to combine two or more variables into an algorithm for the event or phenomenon, with an intended explanation that the event or phenomenon is or is not statistically significant. *If it is significant, how confident the researchers trust that the event or the phenomenon is held true in the population is based on a specified confidence interval and margin of error used by the investigative team for the sample data set*. Together, descriptive and inferential statistics, mainly the part of the hypothesis test, forms the empirical evidence for a research study. Empirical evidence means something is based on random observation or experimentation.

The process used to collect the data set is termed *research methodology* (*research methods*). Take, for example, building a house. Research methods are the procedures used to sketch the house, the techniques used to examine the strength of the foundation and types of raw materials needed to build the house and create ground stability, the tools required for the construction, and the calculations to determine a price. *After the house is completed, it is the statistics that will explain "everything" about the house*. In short, statistics are the numerical and non-numerical values the builder uses to measure weight, height, length, and conditions of the house. *Together, research methodology and statistics form a scientific foundation and designs for the builder.*

In the previous example about parent-child detachment difficulties, the research methodology enables the university to collect proper data for the issue. Descriptive and inferential statistics enable the university not only to understand detachment difficulties for the incoming group of freshmen but also generalize its findings to first-time freshmen elsewhere—statewide, national, or international—as well as make predictions for future generations of college students. Either a one-time shot or a repeated measure study, researchers always follow a similar diagram called the "research cycle."

THE RESEARCH CYCLE

The scientific foundation is a cyclical and continuous process. In the field of health and human services, mainly social work, it is important to focus on a particular social, cultural, event, or behavioral issue that is impacting a type of service or the population at large (e.g., attention deficit and hyperactive disorder of children).

Most social work researchers use a research design like that in Figure 1.1. Normally, the researcher attempts to develop explanations for the factors observed and then makes predictions regarding how those factors will change if certain treatment modalities are provided or if behaviors do not change. Most importantly, *confirming facts or factors must be based on a scientific approach and replicable evidence*

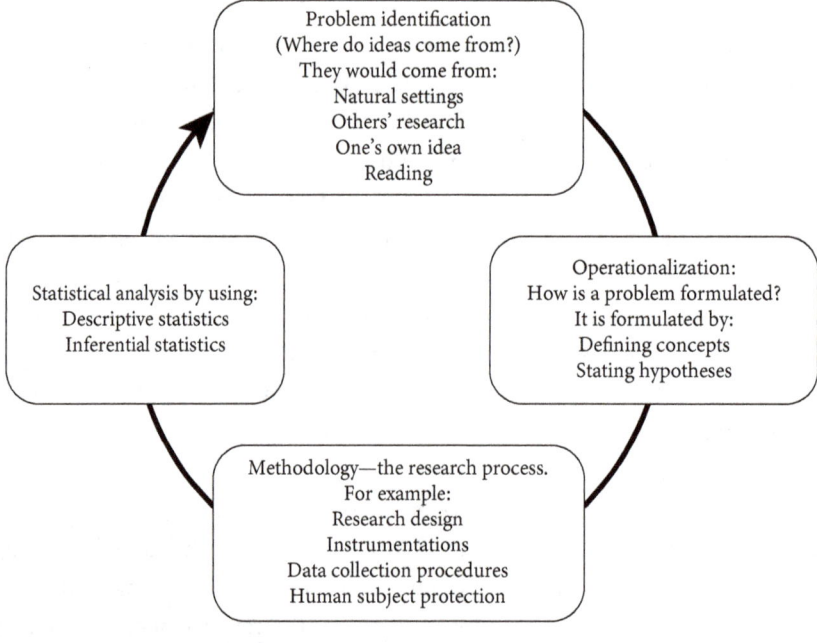

FIGURE 1.1 The Research Cycle

(Rubin & Babbie, 2014). This means that, in many social work studies, the findings may lead to additional questions or perhaps to the refinement of the researcher's thoughts about the issue—especially in the event that facts cannot be confirmed. For example, in a study of teenagers who run away from their homes, researchers find that most of those who run away come from diverse cultural backgrounds. As a result, the steps illustrated in Figure 1.1 can be repeated. In the subsequent research study, the researchers must at this time incorporate culturally specific variables into the new questionnaires.

Problem Identification

Problem identification is the first part of the research process used to diagram a research idea. In human societies and human conditions, there are endless numbers of research topics. One topic may be interwoven with several other topics. For example, factors that contribute to a stressful life could be related to separation and divorce, employment, terminal illness of a loved one, or delinquency of a child. The first part of the diagram in Figure 1.1 illustrates the thinking processes on how to identify research topics. Some people identify a topic from personal experiences, commonly referenced as *experiential reality*, such as being a social service worker at a county agency, hospital, community-based agency, or privately owned facility. Another way people identify a research topic is by way of reading, hearing, seeing, or being told about the issue. This type of problem identification is called *agreement reality*.

Operationalization

Operationalization is the abstract thinking process whereby vague concepts are organized into clear and precise statements, around which specific research procedures can be developed for empirical observation of the target issue. Translation of abstract thinking is often based on two defining criteria: (a) nominal or conceptual definition and (b) operational definition. *Nominal/conceptual definition is based on the definition of public sources such as a dictionary, online websites, books, and journal articles.* In the *operational definition, a specific set of indicators is used to determine the quantity or quality of an attribute of a variable.* As such, people tend to use social science theories or their own expertise to formulate the definition. *In short, nominal definition is based on public sources while operational definition is mostly based on expertise.*

Methodology

Methods are the preparation principles, data collection procedures, human subject protection guidelines, and test and retest reliability of the questionnaires that were developed and set up by the PI to complete a study and safeguard the study from errors commonly made in casual human inquiries. When a research project is being planned by a PI at a higher education institution or a public or private program, they must satisfy the conditions set forth by the IRB, which is dictated by federal regulations and institutional policy. Whether funded or not, the duties of the IRB board are to protect the rights, welfare, and privacy of human research subjects recruited to participate in research activities. The approval categories can be exempt, expedited, or full review. Regardless of the affiliated institution, at least one member of the IRB board must be federally certified for a minimum of 2 years.

Statistical Analysis

Statistical analysis refers to the use of either descriptive or inferential statistics or both. When one (a single) variable is analyzed, nothing but descriptive statistics are used or required. Depending on the levels of measurement (see Chapter 2), such as nominal data, not all descriptive statistics can be used for a single variable analysis. This is commonly known as a *univariate analysis. When two variables are analyzed—such as the relationship between them—the appropriate type of inferential statistics must be used beyond descriptive statistics* (see Appendix C). As stated earlier, Chapters 7–11 are focused on bivariate analysis. Chapter 11 is also focused on bivariate analysis, in addition to two or more values or categories. Bivariate analysis can be used for variables with the same or different levels of measurement. Every type of inferential statistics has its own statistical assumptions and requirements.

Statistical Package for the Social Sciences (SPSS)

As the world turned to the 21st century, technological software applications such as Excel, Qualtrics, SPSS, Statistical Software Suite (SAS), and Statgraphics have become powerful tools to easily compute statistics. In conjunction with the manual calculations, this book uses SPSS as the companion application. With clicks on various ribbons and easy to follow, this computer application is an anxiety-reducing program. Starting in Chapter 3, SPSS is used to replicate the practice questions so student learners can visibly validate that either by calculating statistical solutions with pen and pencil or with the use of technology, the same statistical outcome can be obtained. By doing so, student learners can significantly reduce their anxiety by learning statistics. Instructions on data entry and the functions of various SPSS ribbons are discussed at the end of Chapter 3 and in Appendix A.

SUMMARY

Chapter 1 provided the following background knowledge:

- The defense that statistics must be taken by bachelor's and master's social work students as a foundation course mandated by the CSWE—the accredited body of social work.
- Statistical concepts and how those concepts are relevant to social work.
- Introduces and differentiates the differences between descriptive and inferential statistics.
- Introduces evidence-based practice and how it is ethically correlated to research and statistics.
- Introduces the research cycle by diagraming the interconnections between problem identification, operationalization of the research concept, the research method, and statistical analysis to either organize/summarize and confirmed or disconfirmed the hypotheses.

Chapter 2 discusses the terms *variable, variable classifications, types of variables, types of data*, and *levels of measurement* that the author calls the "Statistics Bible."

Study Questions

Multiple Choice. To assist student learners, as well as practitioners, with grappling with statistics, the study questions that follow can be used. It is anticipated that after completing these study questions, one should be ready to embark on the descriptive and inferential statistics that are forthcoming.

1. In statistics, concepts are referred to as which of the following?
    a. Phrases people used to convey information.
    b. Feelings someone has toward research and statistics.
    c. Mental images that symbolize societal issues.
    d. All of the above.
    e. None of the above.

2. Which of the following statements is not a good reason to study statistics?
    a. To understand a relationship between/among the variables.
    b. To understand an association between/among the variables.
    c. To be able to make predictions about the variables.
    d. To be able to examine the effectiveness of one's practice.
    e. Only a and b.
    f. None of the above.

3. The main purpose of descriptive statistics is to
    a. test hypotheses.
    b. generalize findings to the population from which the sample was drawn.
    c. examine significant differences between/among the variables.
    d. organize and summarize numerical values within a data set.

4. The main purposes of inferential statistics are to
    a. test hypotheses.
    b. generalize findings to the population from which the sample was drawn.
    c. examine significant differences between/among the variables.
    d. organize and summarize values within a data set.
    e. all of the above
    f. only a, b, and c

5. When researchers discuss designing a research study and the data collection procedures that will be involved in the research project, the researchers have this discussion during which component of the research cycle?
    a. Problem identification
    b. Operationalization
    c. Methodology
    d. Statistical analysis

6. Suppose that your statistics instructor asked you to define *client retention* using two sources: *Wikipedia* and *Webster's Online Dictionary*. The mechanism that you used to define the concept is called
    a. online definition.
    b. electronic definition.
    c. nominal definition.
    d. operational definition.

7. In early decades, professions—mainly social services—based their practices largely on
    a. scientific knowledge.
    b. humanitarian gestures.
    c. medical models.
    d. sociological models.

8. In the modern day, when professionals such as social workers, nurses, and clinical psychologists make practice decisions in light of the best research evidence available, their decisions are called
    a. scientific merit.
    b. practice effectiveness.
    c. ethical decision.
    d. evidence based.

9. If a researcher is given $X = 8, 3, 4, 8, 9, 3, 2$, and 5, the scores represent
    a. data.
    b. information.
    c. some type of numbers.

10. Which of the following questions can be best quantified as quantitative study?
    a. What is your annual income?
    b. How long have you been in college?
    c. How is your relationship with your mother?
    d. All
    e. Only a and b

11. The type of statistical analysis that involves complex procedures and explanations most of the time is called
    a. descriptive statistics.
    b. inferential statistics.
    c. both

12. The type of statistical analysis in which findings are generalizable to the population from which the sample was drawn is called
    a. descriptive statistics.
    b. inferential statistics.
    c. both

13. Consider the following statement: "*Of individuals who decided to work as health and human services workers, 75% are committed to helping those who are unable to help themselves and to promote the health and wellness for others.*" The statement itself is called

    a. data.
    b. information.
    c. both
    d. none of the above

14. When a statistics instructor states, "*I am conducting a research study to look at the relationship between child sexual abuse and pornographic materials.*" The instructor's study purpose can best be described as a

    a. child sexual abuse study.
    b. research hypothesis.
    c. an operational definition.
    d. all of the above

Answers to Study Questions

QUESTION	ANSWER	QUESTION	ANSWER
1	c	8	d
2	f	9	a
3	d	10	d
4	f	11	b
5	c	12	b
6	c	13	b
7	b	14	b

CHAPTER 2

Variables, Variable Classifications, and Levels of Measurement

OVERVIEW

Before descriptive and inferential statistics can be conducted, there are several important issues that must be understood. This chapter discusses those issues that are the main structures for collecting quantifiable data—most importantly, variable, variable classification, types of variables, and levels of measurement. Important terminology used in data gathering and preparing data for descriptive and inferential statistics are also discussed. These are the terms used by statistics students, social and behavioral scientists, private practitioners, and those involved in social services settings, develop research questionnaires, organizing data, and conducting statistical analyses.

In today's high-tech era, it is crucial for the PI to recognize that statistics applications will do what it is asked whether the data are correctly collected or entered. The utmost important question is, "Does the result really indicate what happens in real human situations?" Or, "Does the data really represent the values of the variables under investigation?" Often in social science research, mainly social work and clinical psychology, a research project will examine behaviors, personality traits, conducts, conditions, and events encountered by ordinary people and clients. For example, it would be incorrect to state that the average *gender* for the research study was 2.25 for females and 7.75 for males. Similarly, if not careful, a researcher could report that the average *race* for Asians is 0.25 and 1.75 for American Indians. What's wrong with these two scenarios? It will be discussed later that unless in an advanced statistics course, one should never calculate the arithmetic average for nominal variables, such as gender and race.

In statistics, unless one clearly understands the term "variable," "variable classification," "dependent and independent variable, including moderator, mediator, and confounding variable" and "levels of measurement," seeing is not believing. The sections that follow explain the meaning of these concepts and how to avoid making mistakes.

WHAT IS A VARIABLE?

The best way to understand variable is to think of a symbol that can be used to store the datum (singular for data). *One symbol can have many values (numbers), and many symbols can contain lots of values. Values are the precoded and not precoded answers to close-ended or quantitative questions.* It is the values collected that will be manipulated to produce information (i.e., knowledge base and empirical knowledge). The sole purpose of assigning symbols is to label and store data in the data bank. Because statistics is another branch of mathematics, x, y, and z are common symbols. Of course, there are endless ways of creating symbols. For example, x (x = Age) can be used to represent the ages of first-time freshmen at a college campus. Each of the symbols created becomes known as a "variable." Overall, a research project can contain few variables, or it can have a hundred or more variables. In this case, the identification of each variable can have $x_1, x_2, x_3,..., x_n$ (n is the numbers of respondents) and $y_1, y_2, y_3,..., y_n$.

The way a variable is constructed is what allows the researcher to *quantify, measure,* or *categorize* the objectives of the research focus. Some of the constructed variables may contain numerical meanings, while other variables may contain non-numerical meanings. *Numerical meanings mean that the numerical score responded to by the research subjects on a research question does carry important metrical meaning. Non-numerical meanings mean that the numerical score responded to by the research subjects in a research question does not carry real metrical meaning or is not needed.* For example, when asking a research subject "How old are you?" The research subject will respond to the question with an infinite number such as 23, 45, or 19. When adding, multiplying, dividing, or subtracting a person's age from the other, the difference has real metrical meaning. In contrast, when asking, *"What is your nationality?"* Even with a precoded answer like 1= African American, 2 = Hmong, and 3= Latino, the finite numbers 1, 2, and 3 do not carry real meaning. In fact, the codes 1, 2, and 3 are not even needed. Why? Because when adding, subtracting, multiplying, or dividing 1, 2, and 3, the results do not carry any real metrical meaning.

More specifically, the reason some variables are said to have numerical meanings has to do with the summation of their values. In this case, the Greek capital letter *sigma* (Σ) is used. In the previous chapter, if the university wanted to know the total age for the entire 500 incoming freshmen, the university can designate x for age. To sum up the total age, they could simply write: Σx = #. The number symbol (#) is where the university would insert the age of the research subjects. The Σx symbol is read as *the sum of all the ages in the x set*. Suppose that the first three freshmen gave their ages as 19, 18, 19. To get the total age for the set, the university simply writes Σx = 19 + 18 + 19 = 56.

And the reasons to state that some variables do not carry numerical meanings also have to do with not being able to use the sigma sign. Suppose that the second question the university asked the entire 500 incoming freshmen for their gender (y) is written as the following:

What is your nationality? Please check 1 if you are African American, 2 if you are Hmong, and 3 if you are Latino.

1. African American   _____
2. Hmong   _____
3. Latino   _____

Now assume that the first two students stated that they were African American, and the third student indicated they are Latino. In this situation, the university cannot write $\Sigma y = \#$. Mathematically, it is impossible, $\Sigma y \neq 1 + 1 + 3 \neq 5$. More logically, adding two African Americans to a Latino does not equal anything (*African American* + African American + *Latino* $\neq$ 5). In this particular case, unless one is a fool, the person will say that adding 1 + 1 + 3 equates to 5. *Because of this issue, all "Yes" and "No" answer variables are considered to have non-numerical meanings. There is no way to add or multiply a Yes to a No and state that there is a result.*

In summary, the first example can be said to have *values or metric meanings.* In the second example, one must state that the variable has *categories or value categories.* This simply translates to mean the variable has *non-numerical meanings.* Category 1 is designated as "African American", category 2 as "Hmong", and category 3 as "Latino." Unless one has taken an advanced statistics class, Likert scales like "1" for "*Not happy at all,*" "2" for "*Somewhat happy,* "3" for "*Happy,*" "4" for "*Very happy,*" and "5" for "*Extremely happy*" are all considered as having non-numerical meanings. More importantly, the researcher can alter the numbers 1, 2, 3, 4, and 5 that were assigned from "*Not happy at all*" to "*Extremely happy*" any which way they want. The reason is that the researchers must be able to manipulate these rank-ordered variables. Table 2.1 provides a visual display for the age and gender variables discussed earlier.

TABLE 2.1 Age and Nationality of Research Subjects

Participant No.	Age	Nationality
1	19	African
2	18	African
3	19	Latino

Whether variables have numerical or non-numerical meanings, there are powerful statistical functions in descriptive and inferential statistics that enable one to make a concise and clear scientific report about the situation under investigation. These statistical functions begin in Chapter 3. In addition to being able to clearly understand the concept of numerical and non-numerical meanings, *variable classification* is another guideline that should help to avoid making mistakes in statistical computations and report findings.

VARIABLE CLASSIFICATION

In quantitative research, mainly research that uses mathematical functions, a variable can be continuous or discrete. *Continuous variables can take on two real values between them, while discrete variables take a finite value.* This explanation may be short and difficult to understand, but a few examples will clarify the confusion. *For continuous variables*, take a family of five as an example. Assume that the age of the youngest person in the family is 3 and the oldest is 35. The variable is continuous since a family member's age could take on any value between 3 and 35. Similarly, if one wants to examine the relationship among family members by using a scale from 0 to 5, the family's relationship in this case is also continuous. Why? Because each family member's score will fall between 0 and 5 (assuming everyone answered the researcher's questions).

In this sample family, there are many discrete/finite variables. Just to list a few examples of discrete variables: their gender (each family member can list only one category), type of smartphone owned by each member, and each member's mode of transportation. One could easily argue that sometimes people can claim more than one gender or own multiple smartphones or multiple cars. Well, in the case of gender, the person was born with one associated gender. In the case of smartphones, the question asked for the brand name of the smartphone, not how many phones someone possessed. Hence, it can easily be said that all *categorical variables with finite numbers or names are considered discrete.* With either the continuous or discrete variables, one or more of the variables can be identified by the researcher as the dependent or independent variable.

TYPES OF VARIABLES

In social and behavioral science research, especially in the methodology section, it is of utmost importance to differentiate between the *types of variable* and other variables that are associated with either one of them. There are two types—dependent and independent. *The dependent variable is what is being studied or measured. It is the topic of interest. The independent variable is what the researcher intends to change, or it can change on its own.* It is the variable(s) being manipulated with the hope that the manipulations (i.e., intervention, treatment program) have effects on the topic of interest or the subject under investigation ((Barry et al., 2004; Hays, 1994; Rubin & Babbie, 2014).

The independent variable is also called the *predictor variable.* An important distinction of the independent variable is the time order of the variable. To qualify as an independent variable, the factor must have happened before the outcome of the dependent variable. *Typically, the independent variable is the one being controlled or manipulated by the researchers in hopes of making an effect or changing the dependent variable.* In social services, types of intervention or treatment modalities, such as behavior modification and narrative therapy, are best described as independent variables. Why? Because it is the intention of the social workers to manipulate the intervention and hope that it affects or changes the client's behaviors, attitudes, personality traits, or events.

The dependent variable, also called the outcome or criterion variable, is the variable that can be affected by other variables. A school social worker or school psychologist may say that school truancy is affected by stress levels in the families of the students when higher stress levels are associated with higher rates of school truancy. The variable "school truancy" is the dependent variable because the number of days of truancy is affected by, or depends on, the level of family stress. Mindfulness can also be considered a dependent variable. The mental state of a person is dependent on many factors. The factors could include things like faith and spiritual beliefs, self-care, food and nutrition, and frequent family visitations. In social science, examples of dependent variables are those that occur often in society, such as mental health or mental illness, domestic violence, homelessness, delinquent behavior of children, and racial discrimination. *Reasons for picking which variables in a study project are the dependent and which are the independent variables are of utmost importance because the selected variables are the ones that will be used to examine the relationship, association, cause and effects, and make predictions. It is based on the results of the selections that one can say whether there is or there is not a significant difference between the variables.* Say, for example, child abuse is found to be significantly correlated to parental behaviors; then the risk of child abuse can be reduced by increasing parenting skills. *In this scenario, child abuse is what the researchers intended to measure (dependent variable) and the knowledge on parenting skills is what the researchers intended to change or manipulate (independent variable).*

When conducting hypothesis testing, there are three other variables that are directly related to the dependent and independent variables. There are three other variables that are beyond the scope of this book. They are (1) mediator, (2) moderator, and (3) confounding.

The mediator variable is used to explain the relationship between the predictor and criterion variable. A mediator variable explains why or how there is a relationship between the variables. For example, why higher hourly wage is strongly correlated with the years one spent in college (assume the person graduated). If years one spent in college is used as the independent variable, it is this variable that can be manipulated to cause increases to a higher hourly wage. When someone completes the doctorate degree, presumed to be between 9 to 10 years of college education, the variable "years one spent in college" can go away.

The moderator variable is used to examine the strength of the relationship between the predictor and criterion variable. Essentially, it is the amount of strength between the variables. It is usually referred to as the "interaction effects" in a statistical model, such as logistic regression.

Confounding variables are known by two other names: "confounders" or "confounding factor." These types of variables are often used in research projects in which the researchers attempt to examine cause and effect between the predictor and criterion variables. Two statistical conditions are required: (1) the variables must be correlated. In fact, it requires a strong correlation. And (2) the variables must be causally correlated. This essentially requires that the variables under investigation must be causally related to the dependent variable.

To obtain data for the dependent and independent variables, understanding types of data is necessary. As stated earlier, *data are numbers and words collected from the respondents. Client logs, memos, diaries, and published tables and figures are all considered data*. There are two types of data: (1) quantitative and (2) qualitative. Quantitative data is the focus of this book and must be produced by the levels of measurement (end of chapter). Qualitative data must be learned from a qualitative research class.

TWO TYPES OF DATA

Social science research is very different from medical science research. *In medical science, there are specific instruments used to measure and detect viruses and diseases. In social science, data are dependent on numbers and words collected.* As a result, when collecting data for social science research, the main goal is to recruit or draw enough samples so the collected data can be generalized from the sample to the population from which it was drawn. *Because of this, good knowledge about the respondents from which the sample will be drawn is strongly correlated to the development of the questionnaires.* Essentially, better research data allow researchers to understand more clearly the population from which the sample was drawn.

Quantitative Data

Aron et al. (2011) state that quantitative data, or numeric variables, are things, objects, characteristics, attitudes, behaviors, or personality traits collected from an observation that can be counted or represented as an *amount* or a *category*. Quantitative data analysis usually involves responses from a set of individuals who participate in a study or scores from a program evaluation. Such data may also be used to do content analysis, such as examining the frequency of medical noncompliance for a behavioral health facility.

Essentially, quantitative researchers use numbers to represent characteristics, events, attitudes, personality traits, and so on. Examples of quantitative data are the age of the participants, the amount of money given to charities the previous year, racial identification of a group of people, or the level of social support currently received by a group of individuals (if coded low, medium, and high). Often, the questionnaires for a quantitative research study are precoded prior to data collection. For example, in the case of determining the binary gender of the respondent, the researcher may precode the questionnaire with 1 = *female* and 2 = *male*. *Note that the equal sign (=) is used in statistics to represent the words equals to, stands for, or represents.* In this example, "1" stands for the word female and "2" for the word male. Sometimes, the question is asked using an open-ended format. *If the respondents answer the question using a number, the question is still quantitative.* For example, *"How old are you?"* or *"What is your household size?"* Both are open-ended, but the responses to the questions will always be in numeric form.

For quantitative data, the way that the dependent or independent variables are structured automatically determines whether they fall into one of four levels of measurement, discussed next. The term *automatic* is used here because the values of the variables do not take shape and form beyond these four scales. Of course, the values can be manipulated, but even manipulations do not produce fifth- or sixth-level data. In short, regardless of what one does to the data, the results of the manipulation are still quantitatively confined within the four levels.

Qualitative Data

It has already been mentioned in Chapter 1 that qualitative data are words or codes representing a category or a class of the sample. Qualitative research is another branch of statistics highlighted in Chapter 12.

In short, qualitative researchers often conduct in-depth interviews of small samples to obtain quality information rather than counting or quantifying the numerical data (Creswell, 2009; Grinnell, 2000). In addition, qualitative analysis (in the scientific application) normally cannot be generalized to the population parameters. For example, social science researchers want to understand how teen mothers nurture their newborns. In this scenario, the researchers may conduct interviews, or observe a sample of teens and older mothers from a variety of perspectives, and then provide narratives about best practices with these mothers. Among the interviewing questions, one of them could be asked, "How do you take care of your baby in the morning?" If the research study includes both teens and older mothers, then the researchers can also quantify qualitatively the differences between the two groups. However, findings from this observation cannot be applied to teens and older mothers in general. Why? Because words can change meanings and interpretations.

LEVELS OF MEASUREMENT

The author of this book called levels of measurement the "Statistics Bible." It is the levels of measurement that determine whether one's research report is or is not correct. In this modern era, with clicks of ribbons and the selections of various statistical functions, computer applications will compute any result. Since they are in their own little rooms and no one is watching over them, some researchers will simply report what is in front of their computer monitor. Right or wrong, they think nobody knows. However, it is the statistical rules and assumptions that "good" researchers must ethically abide by. These are the researchers who clearly conceptualize the research instruments.

When constructing quantitative research questionnaires (instruments), it is imperative that the researcher think not only about the questions to be asked but also about the expected nature of responses to the questions. Preferable in ascending order (lowest to highest), a variable has one of four different *levels of measurement*: nominal, ordinal, interval, and ratio (Aron et al., 2011; Geher & Hall, 2014; Lee et al., 2016). *The values (answers) coded to each question dictate the correct type of statistics*. At each level, different terms are used interchangeably to describe each measurement or scale. For example, at the lowest level, *nominal, nominal data, nominal level of measurement, and nominal scale* are used throughout the book.

Nominal Variable (Nominal Data)

The nominal variable is the simplest and lowest measurement. At this level, there is no way to quantify one response (value) with another. Data at this level simply classifies the values of the variable into discrete and separate categories based on some defined characteristic or "name" of the variable. *The categories or names are not numerically rank ordered*.

In some situations, categories can be divided into subcategories. For example, to make a nominal measurement of ethnic background for Asian American clients at a local social service program, classifying the service recipients as members of Cambodian, Chinese, Hmong, Japanese, Thai, and Vietnamese ethnic groups is helpful. *Yes and No types of values are all nominal data.*

Sample nominal data questions are as follows:

What is your nationality? ___ African/Black ___ Asian ___ Latino/Hispanic ___ White ___ Other

Have you ever attended a conference on human relations organized by social workers?

1. Yes, I have
2. No, I have not
3. Decline to state

In the first question, the categories are name tags of five categorical values of the variable "nationality." Unless the racial categories are compared/contrasted with some other features, such as physical appearances (i.e., skin color), there is no possible way to rank order the values of the categories. The second question, measuring the variable of conference attendance, has three categorical values, which are nominally measured (yes/no/decline to state). Note that "*yes*" is neither numerically higher nor lower than "*no*" or "*decline to state.*" Rather, yes is simply different from the other two categories.

Ordinal Variable (Ordinal Data)

When the research questions (the questionnaires) go beyond categorizing the variable using nominal data and seek to rank order cases or values of the variable in terms of the degree given to any characteristic, the questions are focusing on the ordinal level of measurement. The measurement process is slightly different for ordinal measurement compared to nominal measurement.

Specifically, when a variable is measured on an ordinal level, differences in the amount of the measured characteristic are rank ordered, and either numbers or symbols are assigned according to that category, unmeasurable amount, or quality. A rank-ordered characteristic does not indicate the magnitude of differences. For example, there is no way to measure the magnitude between "*not happy at all*" and "*extremely happy.*" Typically, ordinal is used to *broadly* measure consumers' and clients' satisfaction with products and services. Ordinal is more precise than nominal but less precise than the interval and ratio levels of measurement to be discussed next.

Sample ordinal data questions are as follows:

How satisfied are you with your current job as a social worker?

1. Not satisfied
2. Somewhat satisfied
3. Satisfied
4. Very satisfied

How likely is it that someday you might become a foreign officer concentrating solely on global child literacy?

1. Not likely at all
2. Somewhat likely
3. Likely
4. Very likely

Again, the values revealed by the first question, *"Not satisfied," "Somewhat satisfied," "Satisfied,"* and *"Very satisfied,"* indicate the rank order from smallest (not satisfied) to highest (very satisfied), which nominal-level variables do not have. However, *notice that the distance, the quantity, the weight, and the time between the attributes (or unit of the variable) cannot be measured.* There is no way to tell how far the distance or the amount is between *"Not satisfied"* and *"Very satisfied."* Also, note that the wording of the responses can come in any order, for example, possibly beginning with the highest order (very satisfied) and ending with the lowest order (not satisfied) or vice versa. *It is important to note that the numbers assigned to each of the responses are only being designated as such so that statistical analysis can be performed. Beyond that, the numbers (one to four) for each of the questions have absolutely no meaning.*

Interval Variable (Interval Data)

The values assigned to interval and ratio variables are remarkably different from nominal and ordinal variables. Specifically, at the interval level, the differences between two continuous values, such as temperature at 8 a.m. and 11 a.m. on a specific day, the weight of person A and person B at the same time, and the household size of 500 families, are all termed intervals. *The interval level of measurement reveals the ordering of values, does not have a zero point, and indicates the exact distance, amount, weight, and time between them (equal interval or "unit").* This indicates that the distance between the first and second values is the same as the distance between the second and the third values and so on.

Take the household size as an example. A family must have one member for the household to exist and the total household size could be as large as 15 members. Since each household must have at least one member, there cannot be a zero.

Four sample interval data questions are as follows:

On a scale from 1 to 10, how happy are you?

   1 2 3 4 5 6 7 8 9 10

What is the monthly salary for a newly hired MSW degree social worker for county X?

   _____ amount/month

On average, how long does it take a person to complete a four-year college degree?

   _____/years

What are the typical sleeping hours for newborn babies per day?

   _____/hours

In the first question, the variable to be measured is the level of happiness for a respondent. The scale was precoded from 1 to 10. There is no zero. In the second question, imagine that county X's current monthly salary for a newly graduated individual with a master's degree in social work is $5,000. Presumably, as the wage increases for all master's degree social workers in county X, the new social worker will receive some salary adjustment over a continuum time line. For example, the increases could be something like $1.38 per hour per year for the next 5 years. Overall, all individuals with a master's degree pay rate will fall under some type of scale instead of getting no pay at all (no zero dollars/hour). In the third example, the amount of time it takes any college student to complete the baccalaureate degree could be any length of years but cannot be zero years. For the final question, typically (common sense or scientifically measured), newborn babies sleep so many hours per day. An argument may be that when the child is sick, the child will not sleep. Well, in a day (24 hours), it is improbable that a newborn will not sleep for at least an hour (again, no zero hours).

Ratio Variable (Ratio Data)

The highest, most precise, and most informative measurement scale is the ratio variable. This level of measurement has all the properties of nominal ("names/categories"), ordinal ("rank order"), interval levels ("equal distance") plus a property other scales do not have: the zero point that reflects a possible absence of the characteristics measured. Thus, when variables are measured on a ratio scale, statements can be made not only about the equality of the differences between any two points (i.e., number of siblings, number of family interactions per month, number of times a person has been hospitalized) on the scale but also about the proportional amounts of the characteristics that two objects possess (i.e., amount of liquor consumption per week, money spent on college textbooks per term).

Sample interval data questions are as follows:

How many siblings do you have? _____/# of brothers/sisters

What was your annual household income last calendar year? _____

How many times have you been a consumer of mental health services? _____

How much money have you donated to charities the previous year? _____/amount per year

In the first question, the responses can vary from 0, 1, 2, 3, 4, or more. Likewise, the zero amount in the second question means that the respondent did not earn any money or did not report any income in the previous year. Similarly, the third question focuses on individuals who have and never have been a consumer of mental health services.

When collecting data, except the background of the respondents, it is advisable to use interval and ratio variables wherever possible. At the minimum, ordinal variables are strongly encouraged. Why? *Because inferential statistics produced from interval and ratio variables are more powerful.* In some situations, for example, the means test (t-tests, Chapter 9), interval- and ratio-level data are required for the dependent variable. Furthermore, in cases like the economic well-being of a group or a community, to make a precise measurement about the group or the community, ratio-level data are needed. This way, the research outcome can be used to compare with the Federal Bureau of Statistics to show whether the group or the community is below, at, or above the poverty line.

SUMMARY

This chapter discussed the meaning of variable, variable classifications, types of variables, types of data, and the four levels of measurement for the variable. Each of the key concepts can be summarized as follows:

- Variable. It is the variables constructed for which the researchers can quantify, measure, or categorize the objectives of the research focus. Some of the constructed variables may contain numerical meanings, while other variables may contain non-numerical meanings. Numerical meanings mean that the numerical score responded to by the research subjects on a research question does carry important metrical meaning. Non-numerical meanings mean that the numerical score responded to by the research subjects in a research question does not carry real metrical meaning or is not needed.
- Variable classifications. A variable can be continuous or discrete. Continuous variables can take on two real values between them while discrete variables take a finite value.
- Types of variables. There are two types of variables. One is the dependent variable. It is what is being studied or measured. The independent variable is what the researcher intends to change, or it can change on its own.
- When conducting hypothesis tests, three other variables are important to take note of. These variables include mediator, moderator, and confounder. The mediator variable is used to explain the relationship between the predictor and criterion variable. A mediator variable explains why or how there is a relationship between the variables. The moderator variable is used to examine the strength of the relationship between the predictor and criterion variable. Essentially, it is the amount of strength between the variables. It is usually referred to as the "interaction effects" in a statistical model, such as logistic regression. Confounding variables are known by two other names: "confounders" or "confounding factor." These types of variables are often used in research projects in which the researchers attempt to examine cause and effect between the predictor and criterion variables.
- Types of data include quantitative and qualitative. Quantitative data, or numeric variables, are things, objects, characteristics, attitudes, behaviors, or personality traits collected from an observation that can be counted or represented as an amount. Quantitative data analysis usually involves responses from a set of individuals who participate in a study or scores from a program evaluation. Qualitative data are words or codes representing a category or a class of the sample. Qualitative researchers often conduct in-depth interviews of small samples to obtain quality information rather than counting or quantifying the numerical data. In addition, qualitative analysis (in scientific application) normally cannot be generalized to the population parameters.

- Quantitative data can be represented by four levels. The four levels are nominal, ordinal, interval, and ratio. Nominal data classify the values of the variable into discrete and separate categories based on some defined characteristic or "name" of the variable. The categories or names are not numerically rank ordered. When a variable is measured on an ordinal level, differences in the amount of the measured characteristic are rank ordered, and either numbers or symbols are assigned according to that category, unmeasurable amount, or quality. A rank-ordered characteristic does not indicate the magnitude of differences. The interval level of measurement reveals the ordering of values, does not have a zero point, and indicates the exact distance, amount, weight, and time between them (equal interval or "unit"). The highest, most precise, and most informative measurement scale is the ratio variable. This level of measurement has all the properties of nominal ("names/categories"), ordinal ("rank order"), and interval levels ("equal distance") plus a property other scales do not have: the zero point that reflects a possible absence of the characteristics measured.

The next chapter will discuss the meaning of frequency distributions, which is a branch of descriptive statistics.

Study Questions

Multiple Choice. The following study questions are helpful for understanding the statistics terms discussed in this chapter.

1. In statistics, a variable is
   a. used to discuss descriptive and inferential statistics.
   b. a research topic in which someone decided to conduct the research study.
   c. anything the researcher can quantify, measure, or categorize about research subjects.
   d. all of the above.

2. Which of the following questions will produce data with numerical meaning?
   a. How are you this morning?
   b. Why did you choose social work as a major?
   c. How old is your mother?
   d. Where did you go last summer?

3. The variable "type of most popular military service served by veterans in the last 10 years" is best classified as a/an
   a. discrete variable.
   b. continuous variable.
   c. dependent variable.
   d. independent variable.

4. The variable "average sleeping hours per client in past 3 weeks" is best *classified* as a/an

    a. discrete variable.
    b. continuous variable.
    c. dependent variable.
    d. independent variable.

5. The variable "hourly wage of a newly graduated MSW employee" is best *classified* as a/an

    a. discrete variable.
    b. continuous variable.
    c. dependent variable.
    d. independent variable.

6. Assume that Professor X and student Y decided to investigate perfectionism on a group of students at an elite university. The variable "perfectionism" is best called a/an

    a. discrete variable.
    b. continuous variable.
    c. dependent variable.
    d. independent variable.

7. In Question 6, suppose that Professor X predicted that financial burdens might be a stress factor for this elite university. As a result, Professor X wants to advocate for tuition reduction to see if college stress can be reduced. The variable "financial burdens" in this case is called a/an

    a. discrete variable.
    b. continuous variable.
    c. dependent variable.
    d. independent variable.

8. In Question 6, if Professor X writes, "Forty-five percent of the student respondents reported that financial burdens significantly affected their ability to concentrate on classes," the professor's statement is based on

    a. qualitative data.
    b. quantitative data.
    c. information given by the student participants.
    d. all of the above.

9. In Question 6, if Professor X requested that student Y ask 100 students throughout the campus about the city in which each of the students currently resides. The professor's request is based on

    a. a nominal level of measurement.
    b. an ordinal level of measurement.
    c. an interval level of measurement.
    d. a ratio level of measurement.

10. In Question 6, Professor X's questionnaire also included the number of times students have traveled outside their country of birth. Responses generated from this question are best called

    a. nominal data.
    b. ordinal data.
    c. interval data.
    d. ratio data.

11. In Question 6, Professor X's questionnaire also included the student respondents' household size. Responses generated from this question are best called

    a. nominal data.
    b. ordinal data.
    c. interval data.
    d. ratio data.

12. In Question 6, one of Professor X's questions asked the students to rate their self-perceptions about the course using the scale not happy at all, somewhat happy, happy, and very happy. The student participants' responses can best be called

    a. nominal data.
    b. ordinal data.
    c. interval data.
    d. ratio data.

13. Similarly, assume that every student in Professor X's class walked at least 1,000 steps per day. Professor X wanted to know the number of steps each of the student participants walked per day. The responses generated from this question are best known as

    a. nominal data.
    b. ordinal data.
    c. interval data.
    d. ratio data.

14. In Question 6, before each student participant agrees to participate in the research project, student Y must explain the research objectives and make sure that the prospective students understand the nature of the study and voluntarily participate in the research project. This part of the research process is called

    a. anonymity.
    b. confidentiality.
    c. informed consent.
    d. reliability.
    e. validity.

15. In Question 6, before each student participant agrees to participate in the research project, student Y must explain the research objectives and make sure that the prospective students understand that information would be kept in a locked file cabinet. This part of the research process is called

    a. anonymity.
    b. confidentiality.
    c. informed consent.
    d. reliability.
    e. validity.

Answers to Study Questions

QUESTION	ANSWER	QUESTION	ANSWER
1	c	9	a
2	c	10	d
3	a	11	c
4	b	12	b
5	b	13	c
6	c	14	c
7	d	15	b
8	b		

CHAPTER 3

Descriptive Statistics
Frequency Distributions

OVERVIEW

It was discussed in Chapter 1 that the first business in gathering information about the sample is describing its distribution or the population parameters. The starting purpose of any statistical analysis is to organize the collected data clearly and precisely so that readers can easily understand data summaries. The chapter also introduces the *SPSS, the featured software application in this book*. In today's high-tech era, data are rarely organized by hand. Software programs, such as SPSS, Excel, SAS, and Qualtrics, do the job more efficiently and accurately.

The processes involved in research design, questionnaire construction, data collection procedures, and preparing data for analyses are complex and should be taken in a research methods course. As stated in Chapter 2, after the variables are operationally structured, the first order of business is to organize and summarize the variables. *There are two relatively simple tools that researchers use to organize and summarize the data set: frequency distributions and graphs*. The American Psychological Association (APA) refers to frequency counts or frequencies as *tables* and graphs as *figures*.

Usually, when people are going to complete a project of some sort, they draw or sketch a diagram for the concept (perception). The drawing becomes a picture of the concept (SAS, n. d.). This chapter is about drawing pictures of the values for each variable in the research study. *The pictures, namely tables and graphs, drawn for the categories or values of the variables are known as distributions*.

FREQUENCY DISTRIBUTIONS

Frequencies

Table 3.1 shows a hypothetical situation where a questionnaire with five variables is administered to a group of 15 students taking statistics. The variables include age, gender, current class standing, anxiety about taking statistics, and the degrees of self-care used by the students. Recall from

Chapter 2, one knows that gender is a nominal variable, age is interval, current class status and level of anxiety are ordinal, and the degree of self-care is ratio.

Let's take a closer examination of the gender and anxiety variables. The first student (ID 01) is a male (1 = *Female*, 2 = *Male*) with an anxiety score of 5. The anxiety variable has the following values: 1 = no anxiety at all, 2 = little anxiety, 3 = some anxiety, 4 = high anxiety, and 5 = extremely high anxiety. First, notice that the table is helpful only when the sample size (n) is small. Although there are just 15 hypothetical student participants, Table 3.1 is already long. If 1,500 or 150,000 college students were represented, the table would consist of several pages. How does one turn the data in Table 3.1 into information? *Just a reminder: data are the raw scores collected and information is the knowledge produced.* Notice that the scores in the table do not come in any specific order. Why? Because they were the scores provided by the participants.

TABLE 3.1 **Sample Research Data**

ID	Gender	Age	Class	Anxiety	Self-Care
01	2	23	4	5	4
02	1	19	3	4	0
03	1	22	1	4	3
04	2	20	2	3	1
05	1	28	4	1	3
06	2	31	4	5	2
07	1	29	3	1	0
08	2	26	4	2	0
09	2	21	1	3	2
10	1	24	3	4	1
11	2	20	4	5	3
12	1	34	3	2	2
13	2	23	4	3	1
14	1	26	4	2	1
15	2	23	4	4	0

Once the original scores are organized, say for the first variable of gender and either manually or by technology, the gender table will look somewhat like Table 3.2. When looking at any frequency table, the starting procedure is at the very first column. The table almost always lists the name of the first category (i.e., female). If the variable is ordinal or higher, it will show the lowest value first. It is best to start with the lowest value and end with the highest value (see Table 3.2 on anxiety). For nominal variables, which category is listed first is up to the researchers. The second column counts the total values for each of the category or scale values for a variable. The third column calculates the percentages for each of the values (see Table 3.4). The fourth column calculates the percentages by taking into consideration missing scores. The fifth and final column adds the percentages in one row to the next. *This entire process is called frequency distribution.* Beyond organizing the scores into columns by hand, the featured application SPSS will organize the scores into frequency count, percent, valid percent, and cumulative percent (see Table 3.5 shown by SPSS). Graphs can be simultaneously created by hand or completed by a computer application such as SPSS.

At times, a table can be several pages long, but the basic tenet is making it easier for the naked eye, so counting the categories or values for each of the variables is best. In fact, constructing a table is the more viable option. Table 3.2 provides the fundamental tenet in organizing the sample variables of gender and anxiety.

TABLE 3.2 Frequency for Sample Data on Gender and Anxiety Variables

Gender	Frequency Count *(f)*	Anxiety Level	Frequency Count *(f)*
Female	7	No anxiety at all	2
Male	8	Little anxiety	3
		Some anxiety	3
		High anxiety	4
		Extremely high anxiety	3
Total (n)	15		15

Although the appearance of Table 3.2 already looks pretty good, the information display is too broad. *It has not taken into account the individual representation of the gender categories and anxiety levels.* One still needs to know: what proportion of the sample size do 7 females out of the total 15 students represent? This question must be answered with both the *frequency count (f)* and *percentage (%)*. The APA requires that the term *frequency count* is designated with the lowercase *f*, and it is to be *italicized*.

Frequency Count and Percentage

The simple algorithm for a frequency count is listing the number of times a category or value occurs. Recall that "category" is used for discrete variables, while "value" is used for continuous variables (see Chapter 2). In mathematics, *a percentage is the ratio of some numbers that represent a fraction of 100 denoted by the % symbol*. Please note that this book is not about percentage changed; therefore, everything discussed for the descriptive or inferential statistics is within 100%. Table 3.3 displays the percentage formula for variables with and without missing scores.

TABLE 3.3 Formula for Percentage and Valid Percentage Calculations

Percentage Formula	Valid Percent Formula
Percentage (%) = $\sum \frac{f}{n}(100\%)$	Percentage (valid %) = $\sum \frac{f}{\text{valid cases}}(100\%)$
Σ = Greek sigma used to represent the sum of a value (note that category cannot be added)	Valid cases = Number of cases that present a real number without missing scores
f = Actual frequency count	Note: When there are no missing scores, the percent and valid percent columns show the same percentages.
n = Number of all cases, including the cases with missing scores	

To calculate the percentages for the female respondents for Table 3.2, simply take

$$\text{Percentage for female respondents} = \frac{7}{15}(100\%) = 46.7\%$$

To calculate the percentages for the students that said they have no anxiety at all, simply take

$$\text{Percentage for no anxiety at all} = \frac{2}{15}(100\%) = 13.3\%$$

By repeating the same process for all five values, the entire result for the variable "anxiety" can be used to construct a frequency table that looks just like Table 3.4.

TABLE 3.4 Frequency Count for the Variable Anxiety

Anxiety Level	Frequency Count (f)	Percent
No anxiety at all	2	13.3
Little anxiety	3	20.0
Some anxiety	3	20.0
High anxiety	4	26.7
Extremely high anxiety	3	20.0
Total	15	100.0

Just note that in case there are missing scores, the denominator for each of the variables will be different. These are the simple and individually calculated percentages for the categories or values in a variable. After the categories or the values of a variable are calculated, one can then use the following graphical criteria to construct a proper graph for the information.

Graphs

Graphs are helpful in summarizing data, especially in visualizing the categories or values of the variables and in making a large group of scores easy to understand. *The APA refers to graphs, charts, and diagrams in a manuscript as figures.* In contrast to tables, figures simply illustrate condensed data—conveying only essential facts. This reduction in the amount and type of data presented tends to make the information easier to read and understand; however, the risk is that if used excessively, valuable written information may be overlooked.

The four figures often used are *bar charts, pie charts, histograms*, and *frequency polygons* (better known as *line graphs* or *line* charts). Other types of graphs such as area, boxplot, high-low, and population pyramid must be used with care. Even though there are suggestions regarding which type of graph is the best fit to illustrate a measurement, the fact is that there is no single correct way to graph data. Common suggestions are discussed below.

Bar Graphs (Bar Charts)

Bar charts or bar graphs are best used to depict frequency counts or percentages associated with nominal variables. It makes sense to use an individual bar to represent an individual category. As discussed in Chapter 2, nominal variables have finite values; therefore, variables that use bar graphs reflect the fact that there is no continuity among the categories on the scale.

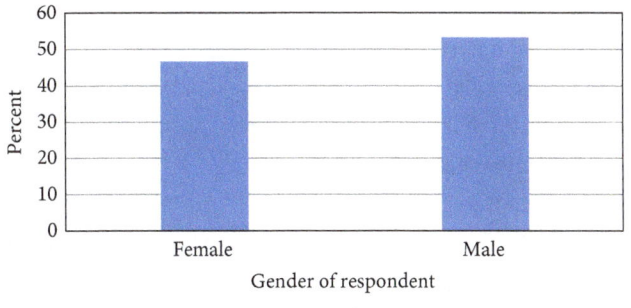

FIGURE 3.1   Bar Graph for Gender From Table 3.1

Pie Graphs (Pie Charts)

Pie graphs are better known as the crossover type of graphs (Rubin, 2013). *This means that they can be used with all four levels of measurement.* However, be cautious that variables that have numerous categories or values, such as race, age, and the number of times clients involved in self-destructive behaviors in the past 2 years, may not be suitable for a pie graph. When the figure of a pie is broken into many pieces, it is difficult to see how the pieces represent the situation. An example is the racial background of students at a college campus. At any college campus, the racial background could have as many as 20 or more categories. By graphing the 20 categories on a pie graph, they will become too small to read. When there are more than five categories or values, consider other forms of graphs such as bar graphs instead of pie graphs. *If it is possible, combine the categories so to shrink the pieces of the pie.* Figure 3.2 illustrates a good (left) and not a very good (right) pie graph.

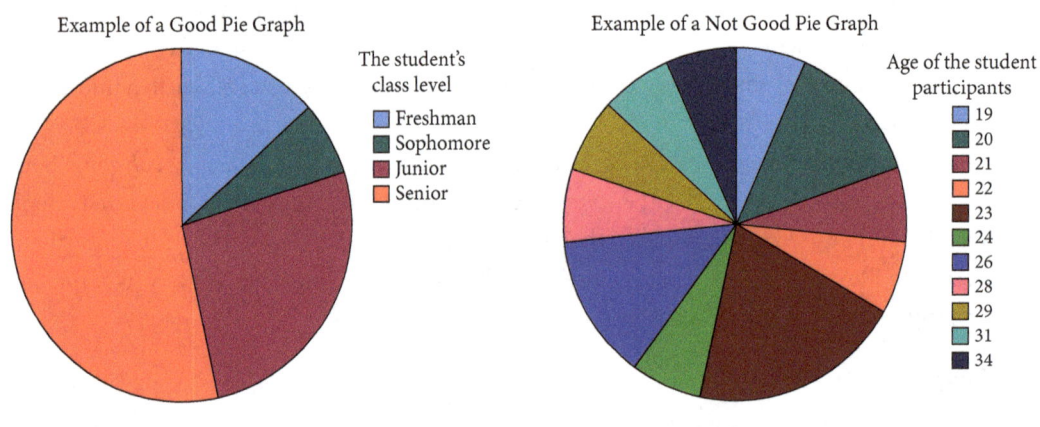

FIGURE 3.2 Sample of Good and Not so Good Pie Graphs

Histograms

Histograms (see Figure 3.3) are best suited for use with interval- or ratio-level data. *The graph displays continuous bars of different heights that group numbers into ranges.* The height of each bar shows how many numbers fall into each range. The difference between a bar graph and a histogram is that the bars of a histogram touch one another and the bars in a bar graph do not. Figure 3.3 illustrates the histogram. *Please note that the bars in Figure 3.3 are supposed to touch one another, but apparently, SPSS left visible spaces among the bars.*

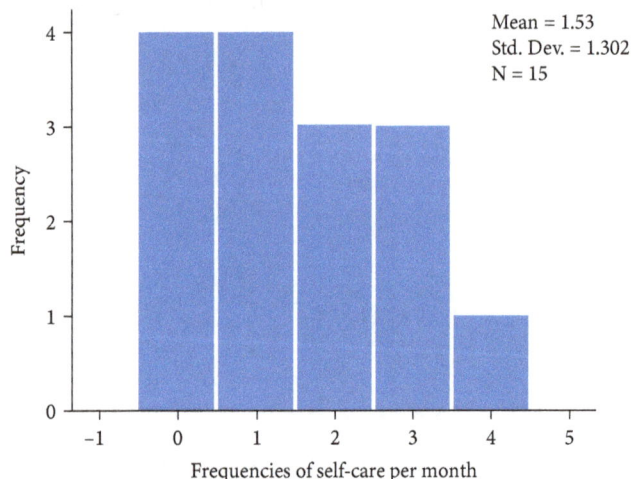

FIGURE 3.3 Histogram Graph

Frequency Polygons (Line Graphs or Line Charts)

Like the histogram, a frequency polygon (Figure 3.4) assumes the distribution of interval- or ratio-level scores. Frequency polygons are used to display the shape of the data and the trends that a particular data set follows. Not always but it is usually drawn with the help of a histogram on two or more variables. Of course, a frequency polygon can be drawn with just one continuous variable. However, it is the recommendation of this book that when drawing a graph for one continuous variable, a histogram is a better choice. The frequency polygon is also known as the line graph or line chart. Figure 3.4 displays a frequency polygon for the variables age and anxiety level from Table 3.2.

In real research projects, there are hundreds, thousands, or even millions of categories and values. In such situations, it is extremely tedious to complete the entire data summary by frequency count, percent, and graph. To make the task relatively economical, simple, and fast, statistical software applications are the most convenient ways. How can one use the SPSS to complete the tasks? First, let's understand the capability of SPSS.

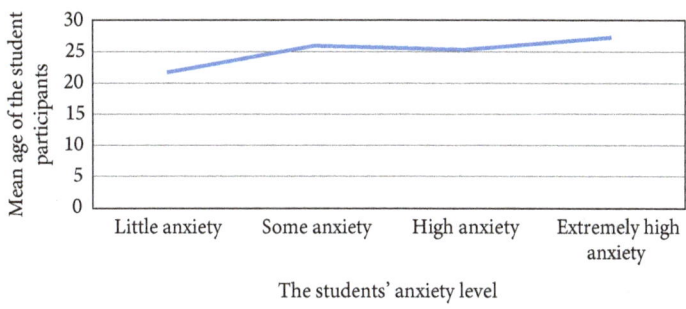

FIGURE 3.4 Frequency Polygon on Age and Anxiety Level

INTRODUCTION AND DATA ENTRY USING SPSS

Overview

The term Statistical Package for the Social Sciences (SPSS) is featured throughout the book. SPSS is a popular statistical software own by the International Business Machines (IBM). As stated by IBM, SPSS is a powerful software program. Its graphic environment is powerful. The descriptive menus (ribbon) have simple dialog boxes useful for most facets of statistical computation. Once the data entry is completed, most other tasks are accomplished simply by pointing and clicking the mouse. This book is organized using the instructions provided by SPSS 27 (SPSS, 2020).

In basic statistical computations, especially activities that are relevant to the contents of this book, two types of files are introduced: (1) a *data or system file* and (2) an *output file*. The *data file is where variable* names are created, the title of a variable is created, the values of the variable are entered, the correct levels of measurement for the variables are selected, and data are entered into the system. *Data file simply refers to the common concept for data entry. The output file is where information ready for analyses has been computed and stored.* In addition, the output file contains outcome information based on descriptive and inferential statistics and information that is ready to be printed. *Simply put, the output file is the result of the statistical computations.*

Data Entry Using SPSS

Once SPSS is started, either a blank screen or a question mark appears asking which file is to be opened. If the user is unsure, click to return to a blank screen. The blank screen is where the user can create a personal data file or open other files on the computer (IBM SPSS, 2020). *To create a new data file, simply follow these steps or use Appendix A:*

- As a reminder, each variable in the questionnaires must be given a code name or be defined. For example, if a research study uses 50 questions, then 50 variable names or code names must be given. To define a name for each of the variables, look at the bottom left of the screen (see Figure 3.5). There, two keywords are visible. These two keywords are Data View and Variable View. Data View is where the raw scores must be entered and stored. However, before data can be entered, various tasks must be created under Variable View. *Variable View is where several tasks must be completed—namely, Name, Type, Label, Value, and Measure must be created.*

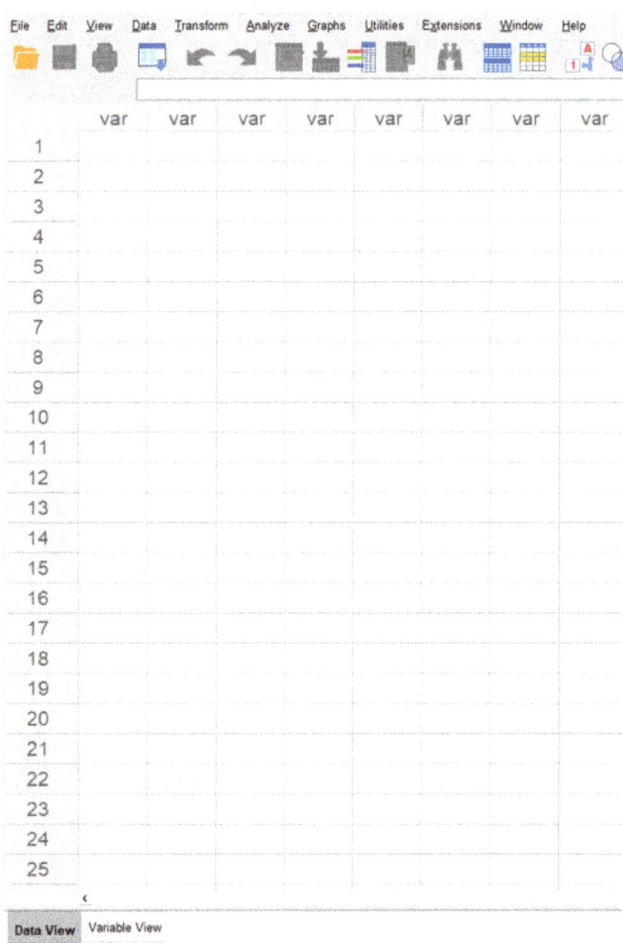

FIGURE 3.5   Variable View Blank Screen

- *"Name" is the code name given to the variable.* SPSS prefers that each name is eight characters or less, and the name does not have to make sense. While creating a code name for the variable, do not use these special characters: Period (.), semicolon (;), question mark(?), front slash (/), backslash (\), underscore (_), space bar, and dollar sign ($). These special characters are reserved for internal usages. In brief, when the term *"Variable name contains an illegal character"* pops up after pressing the "Enter" key, give a different name to the variable.

- *"Type" is where to select whether the variable is numeric, string, or other symbols such as the dollar ($) sign.* It is also the location to change the width and decimals for the variable. For example, gender will not have a decimal, but school grade point average (GPA) must use decimals. Typically, *Numeric is the preferred mode for data entry*. But in some cases, such as the date of data collection, other types may have to be used.

- *"Label" is the title of the variable.* When the research project uses numerous variables, it is best practice to type the title as clear as possible. It is strongly recommended that the title should not be longer than two lines. Also, it is NOT recommended that the title be entered exactly as how the questions were phrased.

- *"Values" are the responses/answers precoded for the variable.* If the question has precoded answers such as 1 for *female* and 2 for *male* or 1 for *no anxiety at all* to 5 *extremely high anxiety*, then the precoded categories or values must be entered. Open-ended questions such as "*How old are you?*" without precoded answers can be left as "None."

- *"Measure" is the scale used for each of the questions.* Nominal and ordinal scales must be individually checked or SPSS will treat the variable as an unknown scale. Scale is used for interval and ratio variables.

With the aforementioned instructions, one can easily create an SPSS data file for Table 3.1. *To create a data file for Table 3.1, do the following*:

- Once SPSS is opened, click *Variable View* (bottom left screen).

- Put the cursor on column 1 row 1 and type *"Gender."* Since Table 3.1 is in alphanumeric form, move the cursor to the *Decimal* column. Click on the right-hand corner on that square, click the downward arrow (↓) to change 2 to 0.

- Move the cursor to the *Label* column. Type "*Gender of the student respondents.*"

- Once you are finished with the title of the variable, move the cursor to the *Values* columns. As stated above, *Values* are the precoded answers/responses to a question. Click the right-hand corner on that bubble. A new mini window that looks like this will pop up.

Image 3.1

- Put the cursor on *Value*, then type "1." Move the cursor to *Label*, then type "*Female.*" Press Enter. Note that when 1 = "*Female*" is entered onto the mini window, the cursor immediately moves back to the *Value* rectangle. Now, type "2." Move the cursor to Label and type "*Male.*" Press Enter. Click *OK*. Note that only the word "*Female*" is visible.

- The next three columns are other options. Select them based on the research criteria. On *Missing*, many researchers enter 999 for the missing scores. On *Align*, choose how you want the scores to appear (whether you want them to appear on the left, right, or center of the SPSS screen).

- Move the cursor to the *Measure* column. Click on the right-hand corner. Select *Nominal*.

- Move the cursor to column 1 row 2. Repeat the same process for the variables age, class, anxiety, and self-care. On values for the "*Age*" variable, leave it as *None*, and on *Measure*, select *Scale*. For the variable "*Class*," use 1 = Freshman, 2 = Sophomore, 3 = Junior, 4 = Senior. On the "Anxiety" variable, list 1 = No anxiety at all, 2 = Little anxiety, 3 = Some anxiety, 4 = High anxiety, and 5 = Extremely high anxiety. In *the Measure* column for the anxiety variable, select *Ordinal*. For the "*Self-Care*" variable, repeat the same process as you entered for the variable "*Age.*" Leave *Value* as *None* and select *Scale* for *Measure*.

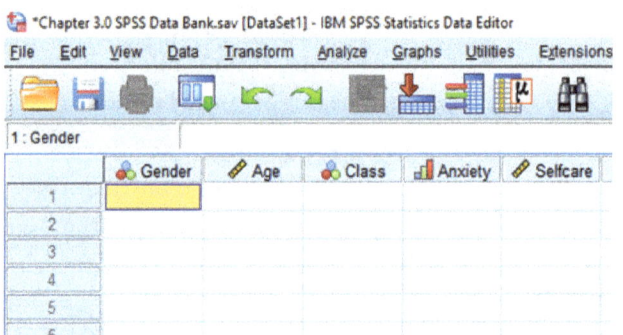

- After the *Variable View* for the five variables is constructed, click *Data View*. Your window now should look like this:

- Note that "*Gender*" now appears with three balloons of different colors. The colors of the balloons indicate that they are in different categories. The "*Age*" and "*Self-Care*" variables show a ruler, which indicates interval-level data. The variables "*Class*" and "*Anxiety*" show bars of different colors (from low to high) to indicate rank order (ordinal data).

- Now enter the scores in Table 3.1 in their respective variables. After the data entry is completed, the data spreadsheet will look like this:

- The *Data File* is now created. All kinds of descriptive and inferential statistics can be computed from this data file.

Practice Example

To get the first practical experience with the SPSS file that you have just created, take the following steps. For practical purposes, let's create a frequency table for the anxiety variable.

- Click the *Analyze* ribbon in the middle of the top menu. Move the cursor down to *Descriptive Statistics*, select *Frequencies*. A mini window will pop up. To change the variable *Label* to *Name* as it appears in the following image, click the right mouse. Another mini window will pop up; select the first bubble in the list.
- Select "*Anxiety*." Hit the forward arrow (→) in the middle of the screen. The variable "*Anxiety*" will move to the functional mini window. Click *OK*. Momentarily, the Output file will display the completed frequency count, as shown in Table 3.5.

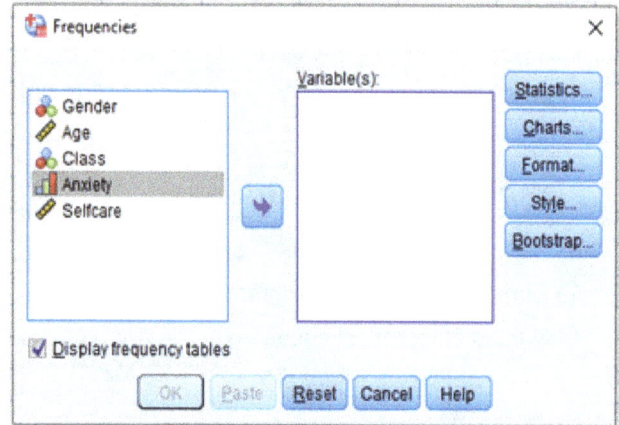

TABLE 3.5 **The Students' Anxiety Level**

		Frequency	Percent	Valid Percent	Cumulative Percent
Valid	No anxiety at all	2	13.3	13.3	13.3
	Little anxiety	3	20.0	20.0	33.3
	Some anxiety	3	20.0	20.0	53.3
	High anxiety	4	26.7	26.7	80.0
	Extremely high anxiety	3	20.0	20.0	100.0
	Total	15	100.0	100.0	

As stated earlier, when there are no missing scores, the Percent and Valid Percent show similar percentages. When there are missing scores, the *Valid Percent* column, will always be higher than the *Percent* column. Cumulative Percent is the addition of the percentages from one row to the next.

Now, let's try to create a bar graph for the variable gender. To get the same bar graph as in Figure 3.1, take the following steps:

- Click *Graphs*, move the cursor down to *Legacy Dialogs*, and select *Bar*. A mini window will pop up. On the Bar Graph, select Simple. Click *Define* at the bottom of the mini window.

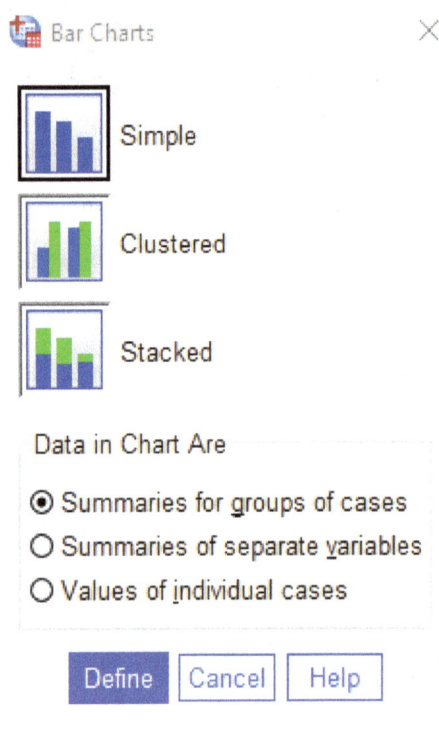

Image 3.5

- On the new mini window, highlight *Gender*. Move it to *Category Axis*. Hit *OK*. Momentarily, the same graph as shown in Figure 3.1 will appear. To design any part of the graph, double-click the graph, and various design functions will pop up. Once you finish constructing the graph, X it out. All the new designs will be displayed on the original graph.

SUMMARY

This chapter introduced basic statistical functions, mainly frequencies. Generally, frequencies or frequency distributions refer to the following:

- Raw scores (frequency count), percents, valid percents, cumulative percents, and graphs are counted.
- Graphs are part of frequencies because they cannot be created without either the raw scores or the percentages.
- The four commonly used graphs are bar, pie, histogram, and frequency polygon (line graph/line chart). It is strongly recommended to use nominal variables for a bar graph. A pie graph is known as the crossover type of graph, which means that it can be used for all four levels of measurement. However, the users must be mindful of the pieces of the pie. When the pie is divided into too many pieces, it is difficult for the naked eye to tell the difference between the pieces. When there is only one interval/ratio variable, it is recommended to use histograms, and when there are two or more interval/ratio variables, use a frequency polygon. The type of graph for ordinal level data is up to the preference of the researcher.
- This chapter also introduced data entry using SPSS. SPSS knowledge from this chapter is sufficient for researchers to complete simple, as well as complex, data entry.

Study Questions

Multiple Choice. Use the following study questions to test your knowledge of frequency distributions.

1. Which of the following groups of statistics are not part of the frequency distributions?
    a. Raw score, percentage, variable, graph
    b. Raw score, percentage, cumulative percentage, graph

c. Raw score, percentage, cumulative percentage, valid percent
   d. Percentage, cumulative percentage, graph
2. Frequency distributions are a part of which branch of statistics?
   a. Qualitative
   b. Descriptive
   c. Inferential
   d. All of the above
3. The difference between a histogram graph and a bar graph is
   a. the bars of a histogram graph do not touch each other.
   b. the bars of a bar graph always touch each other.
   c. the bars of a histogram graph always touch each other.
   d. any of the above as long as the researcher knows what they are doing.
4. The proper level of measurement for a bar graph must be
   a. nominal.
   b. ordinal.
   c. interval.
   d. ratio.
5. The histogram graph and frequency polygon graph can be used for interval- and ratio-level data with which of the following common practice?
   a. Histograms cannot be used to display the values of two or more variables.
   b. Frequency polygons must be used to display the values of ordinal and ratio data.
   c. Frequently, histograms must be used with the values of two or more variables.
   d. Frequency polygons are best with the values of two or more variables.
6. The type of graph that is best known as the crossover graph is a
   a. bar.
   b. frequency polygon.
   c. histogram.
   d. pie.
7. Suppose that you want to graph the variable "city of residency" of college students at a particular campus. City of residency is classified as "rural" and "urban." The most appropriate type or types of graph(s) for this situation is/are
   a. bar or pie.
   b. histogram or frequency polygon.
   c. all of the above.
   d. none of the above.

8. Suppose that you want to graph the variables "self-esteem" and "level of happiness" of high school students at a particular high school. The most appropriate type of graph for this situation is a

   a. bar.
   b. frequency polygon.
   c. histogram.
   d. pie.

9. Suppose that a farmer wants to graph the prices of corn, rice, tomatoes, and beans at a specific farm over the past 10 years for presentation to high school students who might consider becoming farmers after graduation. The simplest graph for this situation is a

   a. bar.
   b. frequency polygon.
   c. histogram.
   d. pie.

10. Suppose that the same farmer wants to graph the longevity of beans from first planting to harvesting time. The simplest graph is a

    a. bar.
    b. frequency polygon.
    c. histogram.
    d. pie.

11. Suppose that 50 homeless individuals were recruited from a local municipal center to participate in a research project about mental health issues of homeless persons. At the end of the data collection process, only 21 of the 50 respondents answered the question about his or her gender. The denominator for the valid percentage calculation is

    a. 50.
    b. 21.
    c. unable to be determine.

12. In Question 11, suppose that 9 of the 21 respondents indicated they were male. What is the total percentage of the male respondents?

    a. 42.86%
    b. 18%
    c. 42%
    d. Any of the above answers is correct

13. In a computer application such as SPSS, the frequency polygon is better known as

    a. bar graph.
    b. pie graph.
    c. line graph.
    d. any of the above answers.

14. The term "Name" in SPSS is used for which of the following purposes?

    a. Discrete variables
    b. Continuous variables
    c. Name of a graph
    d. Code name of the variable

Answers to Study Questions

QUESTION	ANSWER	QUESTION	ANSWER
1	a	8	b
2	b	9	b
3	c	10	c
4	a	11	b
5	d	12	a
6	d	13	c
7	a	14	d

CHAPTER 4

Descriptive Statistics
Measures of Central Tendency and Variability

OVERVIEW

This is one of two chapters in which the main contents in descriptive statistics are discussed. Chapter 3 presented statistical tools useful for summarizing data using simple frequencies and graphs. This chapter introduces some ways to organize and summarize data using procedures that are more complex, thus providing researchers with the core foundation necessary for understanding descriptive statistics (Lee et al., 2016). As discussed in Chapter 2, the kinds of data and their corresponding levels of measurement are of utmost importance in helping researchers to select the correct statistical calculations. Beyond types of data and levels of measurement, statistics discussed in this chapter are *keys to understanding the center and the dispersion of the values* in a data set. Terms to be covered include *measures of central tendency or central locations and measures of variability or dispersion*. Each term involves several distinctive types of statistical calculations.

The term *measures of central tendency* has different meanings across professions; however, statisticians generally use it to refer to the *mean, median,* and *mode* of the distribution set the research data collected for a research project. *Except for the mode in advanced statistics courses where nominal and ordinal data can be recoded or simplified into different levels of measurement, in simple statistics courses, the values of the variable for the measures of central tendency must be interval or ratio* (see "Mode" section).

The term *measures of variability* is used to understand the dispersion or data spread of the values of the variable around the sample mean (to be discussed later in the chapter).

When analyzing data beyond the simplest forms of statistics, such as counting the absolute frequencies, calculating its respective percentage and valid percentage, and building charts/graphs, the next step is usually examining the measures of central tendency.

MEASURES OF CENTRAL TENDENCY

Generally, after data have been examined for frequency distributions (percentages and graphs), measures of central tendency determine how values for a given variable are clustered and identify the key central locations in the distribution set (Frost, n.d., Lee et al., 2016). For example, the "average" time it takes someone to complete a task is 32 hours.

More specifically, *when dealing with data that are at the interval and ratio levels of measurement, the words "average," "middle," and "most frequently/most often" can be explained by the terms mean, median, and mode* (Weinbach & Grinnell, 2015). Each term has a distinct meaning and application. Do note that unless one is knowledgeable in statistics, measures of central tendency for nominal and ordinal data do not have much meaning. For example, it would be incorrect to report the average racial background of the employees at a nonprofit organization or the average college degree of the social workers at a social service agency.

The Mean

The mean (often denoted by $\bar{x}$; pronounced x bar), better known as the *sample mean* or *simple statistic*, is the arithmetic average or the numerical center of an evenly distributed variable (Hays, 1994; Lee et al., 2016; Monette et al., 2005). Do not be surprised by the words "an evenly distributed variable." *Unless several variables with the same values (scale) are added together, the sample mean must be calculated for one variable at a time.* Furthermore, statisticians state that, *if scores are measured at the interval and ratio levels and normally distributed, the mean ($\bar{x}$) is most often used and reported along with the standard deviation (SD). This is a statistical assumption and an APA condition*. In Chapter 5, the discussion is expanded regarding the informative attributes of the mean when reported with the standard deviation and another statistical configuration, the *confidence interval*. For the moment, just know that confidence interval enables researchers to set the margins of error for the hypothesis test.

To compute the mean ($\bar{x}$), all the scores in the distribution set (Σx) for that particular variable are summed and then divided by the total number of subjects (n) who participated in the research study. Mathematically, the mean is calculated by

$$\bar{x} = \frac{x_1 + x_2 + x_3 \ldots x_n}{n}$$

Therefore, the mean ($\bar{x}$) is calculated by

$$\bar{x} = \frac{\sum x}{n}$$

This formula is also used when calculating the population mean (μ). N is used for the population size.

$$\mu = \frac{\sum x}{N}$$

Now, let's calculate the mean for the "Age" variable in Table 3.1.

$$\bar{x} = \frac{23+19+22+20+28+31+29+26+21+24+20+34+23+26+23}{15} = 24.6$$

The result of the calculation indicates that the average age for the sample is 24.6 years. *Calculating the mean ($\bar{x}$) is simple, yet it contributes to data interpretation in many ways, particularly when the data set is randomly drawn from the population and when it is used with the standard deviation.* The randomization of the population is beyond the scope of this book. The importance of reporting the sample mean ($\bar{x}$) with SD is discussed later in the chapter, as well as in Chapter 5.

Trimmed Mean

For games such as gymnastics in the Olympics and springboard water jump, the lowest two scores and the highest two scores are dropped. It is the same concept as the trimmed mean. The trimmed mean is an averaging method that eliminates a partial percentage (x%) of the largest and smallest values (often in a large data set) before computing the sample mean (Trochim, 2020; Witte, 1993). *This is usually done in cases like age and income where there are extremely low and high scores. It is also helpful for data sets that are extremely skewed and unstable.*

For example, in a self-esteem scale, the scores include 1, 4, 5, 3, 5, 8, 4, 5, and 9 (n = 9). Typically, 20% (1/5) is trimmed from the data set. To calculate the trimmed mean from this hypothetical data set, follow these steps:

1. Multiply the self-selected proportion (assume that 20% is used) by the sample size (0.20 × 9 = 1.80). Round off the multiplication to 2. The result indicates that the two lowest and highest numbers will be removed before the mean is computed.
2. Arrange the scores into *an array*: 1, 3, 4, 4, 5, 5, 5, 8, 9. Remove first two (1, 3) and last two (8, 9) numbers from the distribution set.
3. Compute the trimmed mean the same way as computing the sample mean by

$$\bar{x} = \frac{4+4+5+5+5}{5} = 4.6$$

Without the trimmed mean, the sample mean would have been

$$\bar{x} = \frac{1+3+4+4+5+5+5+8+9}{9} = 4.89$$

As shown by this example, trimming the mean can reduce the effects of outlier bias in a sample by 0.29 (4.89 − 4.6 = 0.29).

In this sample situation, in case it is applied to a group of students with severe anxiety, the result helps the campus counselors to reduce their biased perceptions of students by roughly 6.3% (.29/4.6 x 100%).

The Median

The *median* is another measure of central tendency for data gathered using an interval or ratio scale that can be formed into an array. *An array is an ordering of every raw score value that occurred from the lowest or smallest to the highest or largest. The median is also the second quartile, or the 50th percentile, which divides the scores into two equal proportions or halves* (Aron et al., 2011; King et al., 2011). *A quartile represents the 25th, 50th, and 75th percentile of an array.* Practitioners, especially school counselors and school social workers, often use the quartile range to identify students who are at risk of certain behaviors or to identify students who may need additional remedial education. *The median can be identified by following these two statistical rules*:

- *First, arrange the scores in descending or ascending order (from highest to lowest or lowest to highest).*
- *Next, if the number of scores (n) is odd, the median is the middle score. If the number of scores is even, then average the two middle scores.*
- *Because of this statistical rule, regardless of sample size, there will always be just one median for all calculations.*

Use "*Age*" in Table 3.1 as an example. x_{age} = 23, 19, 22, 20, 28, 31, 29, 26, 21, 24, 20, 34, 23, 26, 23 (n = 15).

By arranging the scores into an array, x_{age} = 19, 20, 20, 21, 22, 23, 23, 23, 24, 26, 26, 28, 29, 31, 34. Notice that the 15 scores cannot be divided into two equal halves. No matter what is tried, seven scores (19, 20, 20, 21, 22, 23, 23) or eight scores (19, 20, 20, 21, 22, 23, 23, 23) will be on one side and seven scores (24, 26, 26, 28, 29, 31, 34) or eight scores (23, 24, 26, 26, 28, 29, 31, 34) will be on the other side. By following the statistical rules provided, notice that the data set is an odd array. Because it is an odd array, select the middle score of 23 as the median (seven scores to the left and seven scores to the right of it).

Similarly, suppose that the same age variable was collected from 16 students (n = 16) and the last student was 25 years old. The new age scores now look like this, $x_{age(new)}$ 19, 20, 20, 21, 22, 23, 23, 23, 24, 25, 26, 26, 28, 29, 31, 34. The subage$_{(new)}$ is designated as the new group of participants. This time, no matter what one does, there will be eight numbers on the left and another eight numbers on the right. Because it is an even array (n = 16), average the two middle scores to obtain the median, which is 23.5 (23 + 24/2 = 23.5). *This is one of the reasons why the median tends to be called the 50th percentile for the distribution set, knowing that half of the scores will be above it and the other half will be below it.*

The Mode

The term associated with the simplest type of central tendency is the mode. *It is the most frequently occurring score in a distribution set.* Because it does not lend itself to mathematical manipulation, it has limited value as a statistics tool (Aron et al., 2011; King et al., 2011). *The mode is the best measure of central tendency for nominal variables.* Reason? The mode only takes into account the scores that occurred most frequently in the distribution set.

By using the age distribution in Table 3.1, the mode can be calculated by redisplaying the values of the variable as

$$x_{age} = 19, 20, 20, 21, 22, \mathbf{23, 23, 23}, 24, 26, 26, 28, 29, 31, 34.$$

Because the age 23 occurs three times (more than any other score in the data set), the mode is 23. Please note that a data set may have no mode or multiple modes.

EFFECT OF THE MEAN ON OUTLIERS

A statistical outlier is a value that is much smaller or larger than most of the scores. The outlier can be a recording error or an actual value. *In actual values, outliers tend to affect variables like income, home price, and age.* If the value is so extreme that it affects the arithmetic mean or another statistic, then special steps must be taken to account for the unusual value. An example is the housing price in a metropolitan area. For some of the houses, mainly in poor neighborhoods, the prices are extremely low while house prices in better neighborhood areas or downtown are extremely high, thereby causing the mean to be skewed. If the value is simply an error, it can be corrected or handled as a missing value. *If an actual value is like that described in the next example, then the median would be a better measure for the central tendency.*

Suppose that a team of medical social workers is interested in the financial status of their outpatient clients to see if the hospital can demand the same copayment when someone comes to the hospital. Assume that the federal poverty line for the year is $68,000. In turn, clients who visit the outpatient clinic who meet the federal poverty guideline shall not pay a copayment. The medical social workers then randomly selected 11 records from a master list of all patients that had visited the hospital for the past 12 months. After the data collection was completed, the research team arranged the scores into an array that looks like this: 35,000, 49,000, 58,000, 67,000, 68,000, 75,000, 79,000, 89,000, 98,000 and 150,000. The arithmetic mean is 768,000/10 = 76,800. The median is 71,500, and the mode is 35,000.

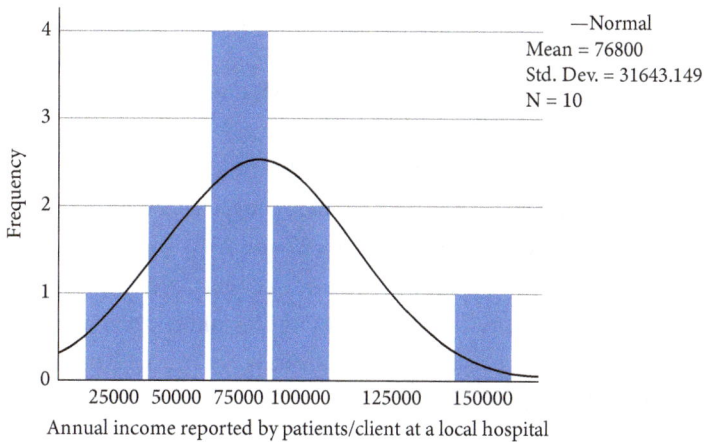

FIGURE 4.1 Annual Income Reported by Patients/Clients at a Local Hospital

In this outlier situation, the median provides a better description of the patients' income distribution than the mean, which is severely affected by one data point, the 150,000. *In a situation like this, if the team of medical social workers still wants to report the mean, then they must report it with and without the outlier.* By using the median as a decision-making process, all outpatient clients, including the family that reported $150,000 per year, will be required to make a copayment when they come to the clinic.

By using the histogram graph as an illustration for outliers, Figure 4.1 shows a big gap between the $98,000 and the $150,000.

MEASURES OF VARIATION

This is the final main content on descriptive statistics. Other main content discussed thus far were frequency distributions and measures of central tendency. Although frequency distributions and measures of central tendency are helpful when summarizing research findings, the information presented is too broad. Thus, this last part focuses on data spread or dispersion. *Data spread essentially refers to how a normally distributed score deviates from $\bar{x}$.* The key question is, "How are scores clustered around the mean?" *Data spread is called variability or dispersion* (King et al., 2011). According to King and colleagues, *variability is a measure of the variation or difference among observations in a distribution*. Most statistics books use the term *dispersion* to describe the spread of a data set for a research variable. Use of the term *variability* or *dispersion* is one's personal preference. *Common measures of variation are the range, quartile and interquartile range, mean deviation, variance, and standard deviation.*

The Range

The simplest way to measure variation is the range. It is simply a measure of the difference between the highest and the lowest values in the distribution, and it is calculated as follows:

Range = Maximum value (score) − minimum value (score)

Suppose that 10 clients ($n = 10$) are randomly selected from a social services program and their ages recorded as 23, 24, 20, 24, 21, 26, 28, 27, 25, and 28 (10 values). In computing the range, take 28 (the highest age) minus 20 (the lowest age), which equals 8. This result simply indicates that there are eight intervals for the values of the variable. The first interval is between ages 20 and 21. The second interval is between 21 and 22. The last interval is between ages 27 and 28.

Range clarifies the sample drawn from the population. For example, in a research study that examines income, age, years of employment, family size, or minutes and hours one does physical fitness per week, the range enables researchers to estimate the probability of the least (smallest) and most (highest) values the population may encompass.

Quartile and Interquartile Range

The measures of central tendency are used to find the numerical center locations for the distribution set by using the mean, median, and mode. Another way to describe data is as finding *positions* for the distribution set. *Positions enable researchers to the point at which a given percentage of the data falls below, or above, that point.* Because the median is already known as the middle point or 50th percentile in a distribution set, all that is left to find is the point below it and the point above it. The point below it is the 25th percentile (also known as first quartile (Q_1)), and the point above it is the 75th percentile (also known as third quartile (Q_3)). Finding the quartile (Q) and interquartile range (IQR) are quite simple. Let us continue with the hypothetical age range discussed above: 23, 24, 20, 24, 21, 26, 28, 27, 25, and 28. Next, follow the same rules for finding the median for the distribution set as follows:

1. Arrange the numerical scores into an array and then find the median. You must remember whether the numerical scores are even or odd numbers.
2. The median for the distribution set becomes the 50th percentile (Q_2).
3. The median for the lower distribution is the first quartile or the 25th percentile (Q_1).
4. The median for the upper distribution is the third quartile or the 75th percentile (Q_3).
5. By subtracting Q_3 from Q_1, the result becomes known as the interquartile range (IQR). Interquartile range is the distance between the first and third quartile or the center half of the data set.

By using these five steps, the quartile and interquartile range for the age distribution can be calculated as follows:

Step 1: 20, 21, 23, 24, **24, 25**, 26, 27, 28, 28

$$\text{Median: } \frac{24+25}{2} = 24.5 \text{ (This is the 50th percentile or } Q_2\text{)}$$

Step 2: Finding the lower quartile (Q_1)

20, **21, 23**, 24

$$\text{Median: } \frac{21+23}{2} = 22 \text{ (This is where the 25th percentile falls under)}$$

Step 3: Finding the upper quartile (Q_3)

26, **27, 28**, 28

$$\frac{27+28}{2} = 27.5 \text{ (This is where the 75th percentile falls under)}$$

Step 4: Finding the interquartile range

$$Q_3 - Q_1 = 27.5 - 22 = 5.5 \text{ (This is the IQR)}$$

By counting from the lowest score to the middle score, there is a 5.5 age gap. Similarly, by counting from the highest score down to the middle score, there is also a 5.5 age gap. Please note that there may be a small contradiction between manual and computer computation. When it comes to quartile and interquartile range, computer applications such as SPSS will round off the result to match with the raw data.

Properties of the Mean and Mean Deviation (MD)

To find how a data set clusters about the mean, especially when a score falls above or below the mean, the interest is in the difference between the score and the mean and how far the score deviates from the mean. *The result is called the properties of the mean and mean deviation (MD).* Some statistics books do not distinguish the slight difference between the two terms. Essentially, *they are used to measure distance between each x from the $\bar{x}$.*

The properties of mean are calculated by

$$\text{Properties of mean} = (x - \bar{x})$$

Whereas the formula for MD is calculated by:

$$MD = \sum \frac{|(x - \bar{x})|}{n}$$

Properties of the mean and mean deviation indicate almost the same thing. *The minor difference between them is that, in the mean deviation, the sum of the absolute value is divided by the sample size (n), whereas in the properties of the mean, the goal is to find the difference between the pluses and minuses.* Properties of mean and MD are discussed and illustrated in Table 4.1.

The "*Self-Care*" variable in Table 3.1 shows the number of times students performed self-care per month. The scores clustered between 0 and 4, and the reported $\bar{x}$ is 1.53. If $\bar{x}$ is subtracted from every x in the distribution set, the total of all values with the negative sign is −8.24. Similarly, by adding all the positive values together, the total is +8.29. This finding shows that the sum of the properties of the mean is .05 (almost zero). *This calculation confirms what Witte (1993) stated: "The sum of the deviations of all observation scores from the mean is balanced at the center point on the number line, which is equal to or very near to zero"* (p. 63).

TABLE 4.1 Calculate Self-Care Scores From Table 3.1

ID	Self-Care	Properties of the mean	MD
01	4	4 − 1.53 = +2.47	$\sum \left\| \frac{(x - \bar{x})}{n} \right\|$ = Sum of MD from all scores in the distribution set divided by the sample size (n)

56 STATISTICS FOR SOCIAL WORK WITH SPSS

02	0	0 − 1.53 = −1.53	$MD = \dfrac{8.29 + 8.24}{15} = 1.1$ (by ignoring +/− sign)
03	3	3 − 1.53 = +1.47	
04	1	1 − 1.53 = −0.53	*Note that 1.53 is the sample mean calculated for the degrees of self-care.*
05	3	3 − 1.53 = +1.47	
06	2	2 − 1.53 = +0.47	
07	0	0 − 1.53 = −1.53	
08	0	0 − 1.53 = −1.53	
09	2	2 − 1.53 = +0.47	
10	1	1 − 1.53 = −0.53	
11	3	3 − 1.53 = +1.47	
12	2	2 − 1.53 = +0.47	
13	1	1 − 1.53 = −0.53	
14	1	1 − 1.53 = −0.53	
15	0	0 − 1.53 = −1.53	
		Sum of positive (+) = 8.29	
		Sum of negative (−) = 8.24	
		Difference = +0.05	

Beyond the properties of the mean, the mean deviation enables researchers to clearly understand the average distance between the mean and the overall scores in the distribution set. The mean deviation is a measure of dispersion, which is equaled to the mean of the absolute values of the deviation scores. An absolute value is one in which the algebraic sign of the variable is disregarded (Witte, 1993). For the fourth column in Table 4.1, by ignoring the positive and negative signs for the difference between x and $\bar{x}$, by adding the two values together, and by dividing the result by the sample size (n) the precise variation among the scores is indicated. *The result of the mean deviation shows that on average, every score across the batch has a 1.1-unit difference either above or below $\bar{x}$—assuming that $\bar{x}$ is centered on 0 under the number line.* Figure 4.2 shows when the result of the mean deviation is laid on the number line.

Students often have difficulty understanding the slight difference between the properties of mean and mean deviation. To make it simpler, look at two other characteristics of the measures of variability: the variance (SS^2) and standard deviation (SD).

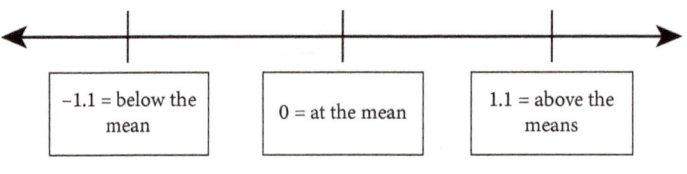

FIGURE 4.2 The Property of Mean Deviation

The Variance (SS^2)

Once the mean deviation (MD) is calculated, the distance between the mean and each number in the set and the distance with every other number in the set still must be accurately measured. This is when the variance (SS^2) becomes a part of the computation. *In calculating the mean deviation, ignoring the pluses and minuses, and then calculating the distance between $\bar{x}$ and all other x in the set is simply not mathematically accurate.* The SS^2 and the SD resolved this inaccuracy. *Essentially, they are the more precise statistics.*

The SS^2, also known as the sum of the squared deviations from the $\bar{x}$, provides an understanding of the spread of scores about the sample mean ($\bar{x}$) (Leon-Guerrero & Frankfort-Nachmias, 2012; Rubin, 2013). This provides a more precise measure than the range and the MD. A function of the variance is to help eliminate all the pluses and minuses so that the data set can be used to make a more accurate estimation of the population from which the sample was drawn. Variance is also helpful in many other statistical functions, such as correlating variables and comparing means.

Variance (SS^2) is obtained by first squaring the difference between the deviation scores (x – $\bar{x}$) for each score (*x*) and the sample mean ($\bar{x}$) and then dividing the total summation by the sample size minus 1 (see Table 4.2). One of the main goals of research is to obtain an unbiased estimate of the population from which the sample was drawn. For this reason, statisticians suggest that the sum of squares be divided by *n* – 1 (unbiased sample) instead of just *n* (biased sample). This is often referred to as definition variance.

To calculate the variance, complete this step:

$$SS^2 = \frac{\sum (x - \bar{x})^2}{n-1}; n - 1 \text{ is for unbiased calculation.}$$

Note that the formula for the variance is the same as the mean deviation. The only difference is that the numerator must be squared, and the denominator is *n–1*. For this reason, simply transfer the difference of each of the scores on the mean deviation column to the variance column and then square all the differences (see Table 4.2). *After all the values are squared, add them together, and then divide the total variances by n–1.* Often, students forget the sigma sign (Σ), so they get confused as to why the sum of the squared must be added together.

TABLE 4.2 Calculating the Variance (SS^2) for the Self-Care Variable

ID	Self-Care	Mean Deviation	Variance (SS^2)
01	4	4 − 1.53 = +2.47	$(2.47)^2 = 6.10$
02	0	0 − 1.53 = −1.53	$(−1.53)^2 = 2.34$
03	3	3 − 1.53 = +1.47	$(1.47)^2 = 2.16$
04	1	1 − 1.53 = −0.53	$(−.53)^2 = 0.28$
05	3	3 − 1.53 = +1.47	$(1.47)^2 = 2.16$
06	2	2 − 1.53 = +0.47	$(0.47)^2 = 0.22$
07	0	0 − 1.53 = −1.53	$(−1.53)^2 = 2.34$
08	0	0 − 1.53 = −1.53	$(−1.53)^2 = 2.34$
09	2	2 − 1.53 = +0.47	$(0.47)^2 = 0.22$
10	1	1 − 1.53 = −0.53	$(−.53)^2 = 0.28$
11	3	3 − 1.53 = +1.47	$(1.47)^2 = 2.16$
12	2	2 − 1.53 = +0.47	$(0.47)^2 = 0.22$
13	1	1 − 1.53 = −0.53	$(−0.53)^2 = 0.28$
14	1	1 − 1.53 = −0.53	$(−0.53)^2 = 0.28$
15	0	0 − 1.53 = −1.53	$(−1.53)^2 = 2.34$
			23.72
			$SS^2 = \dfrac{23.72}{15-1} = 1.69$

The Standard Deviation (SD)

Anyone who teaches statistics will always state that in a randomly selected sample, the SD is the most used and useful measure of variability, especially when reporting it along with $\bar{x}$. It was stated earlier in the chapter that when data are normally distributed, the sample mean ($\bar{x}$) becomes the most used and most powerful measure of central tendency. As to variability, the standard deviation (SD) is the most informative measure of variability.

The standard deviation is integral to two other statistical analyses: (a) *It is related to the normal distribution (see Chapter 5), which is the most important probability distribution in statistics; and (b) it plays a vital role in many common applications of inferential statistics* (Aron et al., 2011; King et al., 2011). For a simple explanation, if the data are collected from a randomized sample, then once the standard deviation is computed, it becomes the standardized unit (precision unit) of measurement that is representative of the population from which the sample was drawn.

The formula for the sample standard deviation (SD) is quite simple. All that is needed is taking the square root of the variance (SS^2). Mathematically, the standard deviation (SD) is calculated by

$$SD = \sqrt{\frac{\sum(x - \bar{x})^2}{n - 1}}$$

Because calculating SD is the same as calculating SS^2, to find SD for the result calculated for Table 4.2, simply take the square root of the variance.

$$SD = \sqrt{1.69} = 1.3$$

Assuming that the data set in Table 3.1 is drawn from a randomized major campus about the degrees of self-care for students who study statistics in social work, the computed 1.3 becomes the standardized unit of measurement for the self-care variable. This means that unless something new is done (i.e., adding/subtracting scores) to the degrees of self-care for college students, the difference among the values of the variable is set at 1.3. This result essentially says that if the 15 hypothetical self-care scores come from a randomized sample, then the average self-care score for the population from which the sample was drawn will cluster around 1.3 above or below the mean of 1.53.

The Coefficient of Variation (CV)

In reading research reports, the authors typically do not display the data set other than reporting the mean and standard deviation as required by APA. One way to interpret the relative magnitude of SD is to divide it by $\bar{x}$.

$$CV = \frac{SD}{\bar{x}} (100\%)$$

This is called the coefficient of variation (CV). For example, if the annual average income for bachelor-level social workers at a specific locale is $57,280 and the standard deviation is $3,917, the coefficient of variation is computed by

$$CV = \frac{3,917}{57,280} (100\%) = 6.84\%.$$

The result indicates that variability for the variable is approximately 6.84%. Even knowing nothing about the data set, the coefficient of variation helps us see that even a lower standard deviation does not mean less variability. Montcalm and Royse (2002) state that the coefficient of variation plays three important roles:

1. The coefficient of variation is derived from the ratio of the standard deviation to the nonzero mean, and the absolute value is taken for the mean to ensure it is always positive. Recall that to obtain the standard deviation, the variance is squared inside the square root. The sum of squares essentially eliminates negatives.
2. It helps researchers understand the relative variability of a variable when only the sample mean and its corresponding standard deviation are present.
3. It helps researchers to compare variability between or among variables in the data set—for example, the relative variability among college students on college stress, study hours per week, and their energy level.

USING SPSS TO CALCULATE MEASURES OF CENTRAL TENDENCY AND VARIABILITY

Chapter 3 introduced the SPSS application and how to use it to complete data entry, as well as computing the frequency distributions and graphs. This section instructs how to use SPSS to compute measures of central tendency and measures of variability. As in most "typical" research studies, the instructions given in this section are all one needs to complete the data analysis and do the report.

As explained in Chapter 3, once a data file has been created, the first step is to examine the frequency distributions of the variables. For further assistance on data entry, see Chapter 3 or Appendix A. *If the data set contains only a nominal and ordinal level of measurement and the user does not want to generalize the findings, then the display and discussion of frequency tables is enough. If the user has interval- or ratio-level scale data, then going beyond frequency tables is important.* For this reason, two of the variables from Table 3.1 are applicable for the measures of central tendency and variability. The two variables are *"Age"* and *"Self-Care."*

What this means is that the researchers are mindful that beyond frequency tables and graphs, more meaningful information is to be reported. More meaningful information includes measures like the range of the score, the arithmetic average, the deviation of each of the scores from the mean, and the standardized unit of measurement. Note that the variables *"Age"* and *"Self-Care"* showed a ruler in front of them and even after clicking the *"Value Labels"* (see this symbol on Figure 4.3), the numerical scores remain unchanged. This is showing that the values of the variables are in the interval- or ratio-scale data. *When clicking Value Labels, only nominal and ordinal variables will switch between numeric and string.*

To compute measures of central tendency and measures of variability for the variables *"Age"* and *"Self-Care,"* follow these steps:

- Pull down the *Analyze* ribbon, move the cursor down to *Descriptive Statistics*. It is preferred that the researcher select *Frequencies* rather than *Descriptives*. It is in Frequencies that users can select all descriptive statistics. If the users select *Descriptives*, then the *Quartile* will not be available.
- Notice that after selecting the label *Frequencies*, small windows will pop up. The window on the left lists all variables from Table 3.1. The one on the right is currently blank.

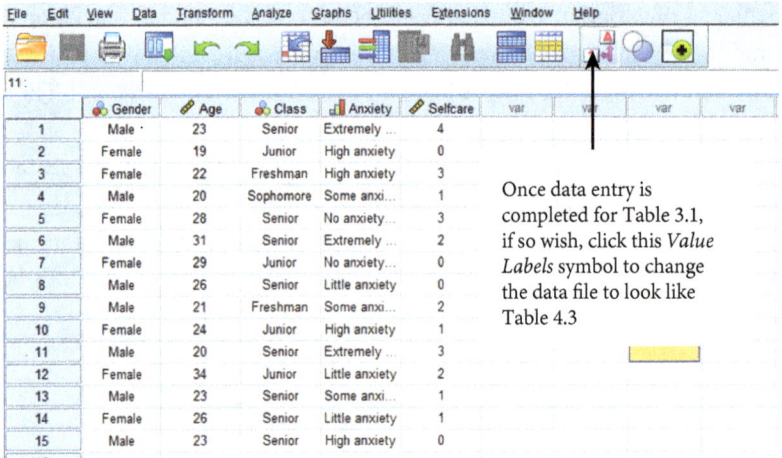

FIGURE 4.3 SPSS Data Created From Table 3.2

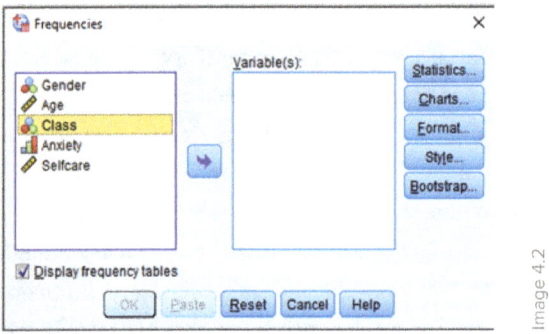

- To get the variable list as displayed on *Data View* while completing the data entry, hit the right side of the mouse. Another subwindow pops up. Select the first circle labeled "*Display variable names.*"
- Use the cursor, select "*Age*," then click the forward arrow in the middle between the two windows. The variable "*Age*" automatically moves into the window on the right. Move the cursor to "*Self-Care*," click the forward arrow key to move the variable to the functional desktop window. You now see this figure.

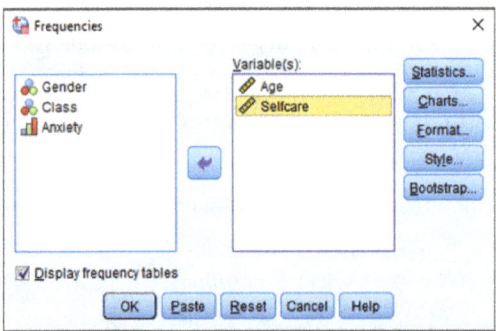

- To get the desired descriptive statistics, click *Statistics* (top-right corner of the screen), then select whatever you want for the study. *As discussed earlier, due to APA conditions, Mean and Standard Deviation must be selected*. All that is left is for the researchers to select other options for the research study. Please note that if Quartile is selected as below, DO NOT select Percentile(s). Recall that as discussed in Chapter 3, frequency counts include tables and graphs. *Either one of them used percentages to construct the table and graph*. Because of this condition, there is no need to use percent to construct another percent.

- Assume that *Variance, Median, Mode*, and *Quartile* are also selected.
- After satisfying with the statistical selections, click *Continue*.
- Upon clicking *Continue*, the term *OK* on the bottom left of the mini window is **darkened**. It now indicates that SPSS is ready to execute (compute) the selections.
- Click *OK*. Momentarily, the results for the descriptive statistics (i.e., measures of central tendency and variability) are displayed in a single table that looks like Table 4.3.

TABLE 4.3 Measures of Central Tendency and Variability

		Age of the student participants	Frequencies of self-care per month
Mean		24.60	1.53
Median		23.00	1.00
Std. Deviation		4.356	1.302
Variance		18.971	1.695
Percentiles	25	21.00	.00
	50	23.00	1.00
	75	28.00	3.00

The SPSS results shown in Table 4.3 are the same as those manually calculated earlier in the chapter. The quartile now shows the 25th, 50th, and 75th percentile for the variable age and degrees of self-care for the sample participants. The 50th percentile is the cutoff point. With that in mind, the researchers now know that the cutoff for age was 23 and for self-care was 1 on a scale from 0 to 5.

Either manually computed or using SPSS, the average age for the hypothetical respondents in Table 3.1 is the same at the mean age of 24.6 years with both the median and mode at 23. Similarly, the manual and SPSS computations for the variable frequencies of self-care per month averaged 1.53 with a standard deviation of 1.3 times per month. This demonstrates that if the statistical calculations are done correctly, both manual and computer applications can produce the same research outcomes.

Practice Example

The juvenile justice system and child protective services (CPS) are interested in knowing the likelihood that adolescents ages 10 to16 who received poor or little guidance about delinquent behaviors from parents or caretakers may commit a crime. As a result, both institutions decided to complete a major study on the issue. Among the various variables developed for the research project, one of the questions instructed, "On a scale from 0 to 10, please rate yourself on the likelihood that you may commit a minor crime in the next 2 years."

To get a representative sample, 30 students were randomly selected from a pool of 4,500 students from a large, unified school district that constituted diverse student populations. The student respondents provided the following responses: 0, 7, 9, 3, 5, 8, 6, 10, 4, 8, 2, 1, 5, 3, 8, 4, 3, 7, 8, 1, 0, 0, 6, 7, 2, 1, 1, 6, 7, and 10.

Tasks to Be Completed:

1. Manually and using SPSS, complete the measures of central tendency for the variable under investigation.
2. Manually and using SPSS, complete the measures of variability, mainly the variance and standard deviation for the variable under investigation
3. Suppose that the juvenile justice system and CPS set a mean benchmark unit of 2.5–4.5 as low risk, 4.6–6.60 as moderate risk, and 6.70 or higher as high risk. Would you say the students from this school district are low risk, minimal risk, or high risk for committing minor crimes?

Answer to Practice Example

1. Measures of central tendency:

$$\Sigma x = 142; n = 30$$

- Mean $(\bar{x}) = \dfrac{142}{30} = 4.73$

- Median. By arranging the scores into an array x = 0, 0,0, 1,1, 1, 1, 2, 2, 3, 3, 3, 4, 4, **5, 5**, 6, 6, 6, 7, 7, 7, 7, 8, 8, 8, 8, 9, 10, 10. This is an even array, therefore, must average the two middle scores. As a result, the median is = $\dfrac{5+5}{2} = 5$ (this is a new 5)

- Mode. There are four 1s, four 7s, and four 8s. Therefore, the mode is 1, 7, and 8, or call it multiple modes
- SPSS. After the data entry is completed. Pull down the *Analyze* ribbon. Select *Descriptive Statistics*. Move the cursor to *Frequencies*. Select it. Move the variable to the functional mini window. Click *Statistics* on the top-right corner. Highlight Mean, Median, and Mode. Click *Continue* and then hit *OK*. Momentarily, the following table will pop up.

Statistics

Likelihood that adolescents may commit a minor crime in the next 2 years

N	Valid	30
	Missing	0
Mean		4.73
Median		5.00
Mode		1[a]

Multiple modes exist. The smallest value is shown

2. Measures of variability:
   - Mean Deviation (MD) and Variance (S^2)

ID	Risk	MD	Variance
01	0	0 − 4.73 = −4.73	$(-4.73)^2 = 22.373$
02	7	7 − 4.73 = 2.27	$(2.27)^2 = 5.153$
03	9	9 − 4.73 = 4.27	$(4.27)^2 = 18.233$
04	3	3 − 4.73 = −1.73	$(-1.73)^2 = 2.993$
05	5	5 − 4.73 = 0.27	$(0.27)^2 = .073$
06	8	8 − 4.73 = 3.27	$(3.27)^2 = 10.693$
07	6	6 − 4.73 = 1.27	$(1.27)^2 = 1.613$
08	10	10 − 4.73 = 5.27	$(5.27)^2 = 27.773$
09	4	4 − 4.73 = −.73	$(-.73)^2 = .533$
10	8	8 − 4.73 = 3.27	$(3.27)^2 = 10.693$
11	2	2 − 4.73 = −2.73	$(-2.73)^2 = 7.453$
12	1	1 − 4.73 = −3.73	$(-3.73)^2 = 13.913$

13	5	5 − 4.73 = 0.27	$(0.27)^2 = .073$
14	3	3 − 4.73 = −1.73	$(-1.73)^2 = 2.993$
15	8	8 − 4.73 = 3.27	$(3.27)^2 = 10.693$
16	4	4 − 4.73 = −.73	$(-.73)^2 = .533$
17	3	3 − 4.73 = −1.73	$(-1.73)^2 = 2.993$
18	7	7 − 4.73 = 2.27	$(2.27)^2 = 5.153$
19	8	8 − 4.73 = 3.27	$(3.27)^2 = 10.693$
20	1	1 − 4.73 = −3.73	$(-3.73)^2 = 13.913$
21	0	0 − 4.73 = −4.73	$(-4.73)^2 = 22.373$
22	0	0 − 4.73 = −4.73	$(-4.73)^2 = 22.373$
23	6	6 − 4.73 = 1.27	$(1.27)^2 = 1.613$
24	7	7 − 4.73 = 2.27	$(2.27)^2 = 5.153$
25	2	2 − 4.73 = −2.73	$(-2.73)^2 = 7.453$
26	1	1 − 4.73 = −3.73	$(-3.73)^2 = 13.913$
27	1	1 − 4.73 = −3.73	$(-3.73)^2 = 13.913$
28	6	6 − 4.73 = 1.27	$(1.27)^2 = 1.613$
29	7	7 − 4.73 = 2.27	$(2.27)^2 = 5.153$
30	10	10 − 4.73 = 5.27	$(5.27)^2 = 27.773$

$$\text{Variance } (S^2) = \frac{289.87}{29} = 9.995$$

Note: SPSS used three decimals for variance and standard deviation.

- Standard Deviation (SD) = $\sqrt{9.995} = 3.161$
- SPSS computations. Repeat the same procedures as answers to part one above. On Statistics, highlight *Std. deviation* and *Variance*. Click *OK*. Momentarily, the following table will pop up.

Statistics		
Likelihood that adolescents may commit a minor crime in the next 2 years		
N	Valid	30
	Missing	0
Std. Deviation		3.162
Variance		9.995

3. The sample mean for the school district is 4.73 with a standard deviation of 3.161. The students are at moderate risk, but one could also state that the risk is low because of very high variability. *The coefficient of variation is too high (66.83%).*

   ○ Coefficient of variation (CV) = $\dfrac{3.161}{4.73}$ (100%) = 66.83%

SUMMARY

Chapter 4 discussed measures of central tendency and measures of variability. Measures of central tendency and measures of variability require interval- or ratio-level data or advanced statistics knowledge. They are the last content on descriptive statistics. Table 4.4 below provides a diagram of how best to distinguish the differences between the two. In summary:

- When dealing with a single variable that has interval or ratio levels of measurement, measures of central tendency must be used. Statistics for measures of central tendency include mean, median, and mode. These statistics are used to find the central locations for the distribution set.
- Measures of variability or dispersion are the last statistics for descriptive statistics. Variability or dispersion is about the data spread. Common measures of variation are the range, quartile and interquartile range, mean deviation, variance, and standard deviation.
- The APA states that when the data set is normally distributed, the mean ($\bar{x}$) or simple statistics are the most often used and must be reported along with the standard deviation (SD). Why? Because SD is the most informative measure of variability.
- The coefficient of variation is discussed as well. It helps researchers understand the relative variability of a variable when only the sample mean and its corresponding standard deviation are present.

TABLE 4.4 Summary of Descriptive Statistics

Purpose	Statistic	Descriptive Statistics
Distributions	Frequency count	Percent, valid percent, cumulative percent, graphs
Central locations for the distribution	Measures of central tendency (required interval/ratio data)	Mean, median, mode
Distance and data scatter	Measures of variability (required interval/ratio data)	Range, quartile, mean deviation, variance, standard deviation

Figure Credit

Fig. 4.3: Copyright © by Microsoft.

Study Questions

Multiple Choice. The following study questions can be used to enhance one's statistics knowledge in regard to measures of central tendency and measures of variability.

1. If a researcher wants to find the most appropriate central location for the ages of five million people, the *one most* suitable statistical configuration to be reported is

    a. mean.
    b. median.
    c. mode.
    d. all of the above.

2. In Question 1, suppose that the researcher wants to report only those 85 years and older. The proper measure of central tendency to be reported is

    a. mean.
    b. median.
    c. mode.
    d. all of the above.

3. In Question 1, suppose that the researcher wants to discuss the ages that occur most frequently in the distribution set. The most appropriate measure of central tendency to be reported is

    a. mean.
    b. median.
    c. mode.
    d. all of the above.

4. In Question 1, suppose that the researcher wants to estimate the middle percentile for the distribution set. What is the most appropriate frequency they should report?

    a. Percentage
    b. Valid percentage
    c. Cumulative percentage
    d. All of the above

5. Assume that the monthly salary for 10 bachelor-level social workers is listed as $3,400, $3,100, $2,900, $3,700, $4,500, $2,800, $3,000, $4,100, $5,100, and $12,000. The most appropriate measure of central tendency to be reported is

    a. mean.
    b. median.
    c. mode.
    d. all of the above.

6. What is the level of measurement for the variable "monthly salary" for Question 5?

    a. Nominal
    b. Ordinal
    c. Interval
    d. Ratio

7. In Question 5, the median salary for the distribution set is

    a. $3,400.
    b. $3,650.
    c. $3,550.
    d. $3,700.

8. In Question 5, the salary standard deviation for the distribution set is

    a. $2,700.07.
    b. $2,750.08.
    c. $2,754.09.
    d. $2,754.07.
    e. all of the above.

9. In statistical analysis, the term "*array*" applies to which of the following?

    a. Making sure that the data set is clearly typewritten
    b. Arranging the distributive scores vertically or horizontally
    c. Arranging the distributive scores from low to high or vice versa
    d. Arranging the distributive scores in an odd or even set

10. Variability or dispersion refers to which of the following statement(s)?
    a. Finding the central locations for the distribution set
    b. The frequency distributions for the data set
    c. The range of the distribution set
    d. All of the above
    e. None of the above

11. Which of the following sets of statistical terms do not belong to "measures of variability"?
    a. Mean, median, variance
    b. Range, quartile, variance
    c. Mean deviation, variance, standard deviation
    d. None of the above

12. In descriptive statistics, especially when the data set is normally distributed at the interval or ratio level, which of the following measures of central tendency do researchers use often?
    a. Mean
    b. Median
    c. Mode
    d. All of the above

13. In descriptive statistics, especially when the data set is normally distributed at the interval or ratio level, which of the following measures of variability do researchers use often?
    a. Range
    b. Mean deviation
    c. Variance
    d. Standard deviation

14. In statistical analysis, which of the following sets of measures of central tendency and measures of variability are most vital in inferential statistics?
    a. Mean and variance
    b. Median and standard deviation
    c. Mode and variance
    d. Mean and standard deviation

15. Which of the following statistical terms explains the relative magnitude between or among the variables?
    a. The variance
    b. The trimmed mean
    c. The standard deviation
    d. The coefficient of variation

16. Calculate the sum of squares for Question 5.

Answers to Study Questions

QUESTION	ANSWER	QUESTION	ANSWER
1	b	9	c
2	d	10	e
3	c	11	a
4	c	12	a
5	b	13	d
6	c	14	d
7	c	15	d
8	d	16	7,584,888.89

CHAPTER 5

Normal Distribution and Z Score

OVERVIEW

Major statistical concepts were discussed in Chapters 1 and 2, followed by key descriptive statistics in Chapters 3 and 4. Those key descriptive statistics were frequency distributions, measures of central tendency, and measures of variability. Measures of central tendency and variability were used to explain the central locations and dispersions for the distribution set, respectively. *Before getting into the business of inferential statistics, one still needs to understand the shape of the distribution* (Chapter 5) *and make speculations about the population from which the sample is drawn* (Chapter 6). More importantly, when plotting an interval or ratio variable along the x-axis, depending on the scores for the variable, the data distribution will be scattered and form distinctive shapes. *In statistics, the shapes are called normal curves.* The normal curve is one of many possible models of probability distributions credited to Abraham de Moivre approximately 1733. Regardless of the distributions, the shapes of the curves show similar properties (see "Properties of the Normal Curve" section).

The four main properties for the normal curve are summarized as (see Figures 5.1, 5.2 [a & b], and 5.4):

- All normal curves share a bell-shaped curve, with most of the area falling in the middle.
- All normal curves are bilaterally symmetric, which means that the left side mirrors the right side. Just as in human beings' brains, *a "typical" person will need the left and right sides of the brain to balance the body so they can walk straight.*
- *Regardless of the size and length of the shape, the tail never touches the x-axis.* In the number line (the horizontal line), the left side contains the negative values and the right side contains the positive values. In normally distributed attributes, the bell-shaped curve comes very close to the x-axis but never touches it. Thus, in drawing a normal curve, one must think of an infinite bell shape.

- However, there are situations where the normal curve may not be perfect. In some situations, the data set may positively skew to the left as in Figure 5.2(a) or negatively skewed to the right as in Figure 5.2(b). Scores distributed heavily to the right side are positively *skewed* (Figure 5.2[a]) and scores clustered heavily to the left side are *negatively skewed* (Figure 5.2[b]). Notice that in Figure 5.2(b), the mode was hypothetically placed at the very left end, the median (middle) in the center, and the mean (average) to the right of the bell-shaped curve.

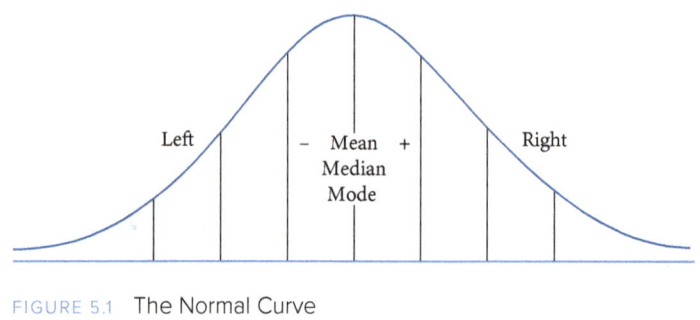

FIGURE 5.1 The Normal Curve

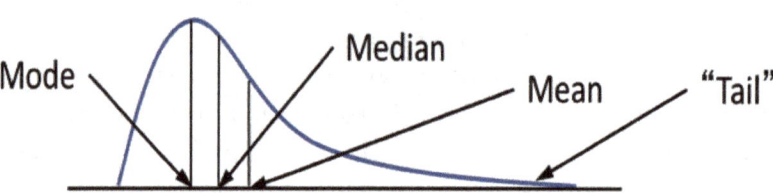

FIGURE 5.2(A) Positively Skewed

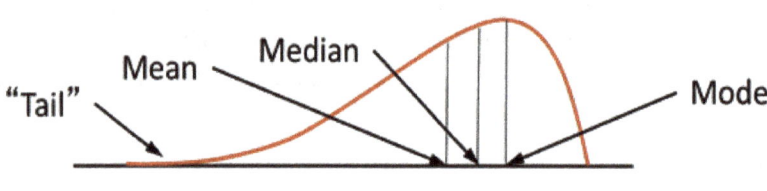

FIGURE 5.2(B) Negatively Skewed

These properties enable researchers to better understand the relationship between the abscissa (x-axis) and the ordinate (y-axis), particularly $\bar{x}$ and SD. More importantly, when conducting a hypothesis test, how is $\bar{x}$ related to SD?. Witte (1993) states that when the property of $\bar{x}$ and the correspondence x cluster closely together, then *the sum of the deviations of all observation scores from the mean is balanced at the center point on the number line, which is equal to or very near to zero.* This is the reason why the mean, median, and mode were placed at the center of Figure 5.1 above zero. It was stated in Chapter 4 that when data are normally distributed, the mean and standard deviation become the most used and reported. *Since they are the most used and reported, when drawing a curve, they are used to define a normal curve.*

In this case, the mean, median, and mode are all equal. The shape of such a distribution is referred to as a *normal distribution* or *normal curve.*

Students often wonder how it is that Figure 5.2 (a & b) even happens in real human situations. The answer is simple. Think of Figure 5.1 as for an "*ideal*" situation. In "*real*" human situations, in fact, Figure 5.2 (a & b) happens more frequently. More concrete answers will be given in Chapter 6. *The gaps between the "ideal normal curve" and the "real normal curve" are the reasons researchers conduct hypotheses tests.* For now, just think about this in most human conditions: the probability is that the mean will not be equal to the median and the median will not be equal to the mode. The explanation for this is that participants in a research project are not likely to provide researchers with the same numerical responses. For example, when asked about factors attributed to their personal good health, respondents will likely give different answers. Even a simple question like, "*On a scale from 1 to 5, how do you rate your self-care?*" Some respondents may state that it is a 1, while others will reply with a 2, 3, 4, or 5.

BACKGROUND OF THE NORMAL CURVE

The concepts of normal distribution and the z score are critically important to help us understand inferential statistics. *This concept is the antecedent to understanding probability and hypothesis testing.* Getting lost in the realm of normal distribution, probability, and hypothesis testing essentially derails one's ability to properly compute any inferential statistics and report its respective findings.

The main distribution statistic is referred to as a normal curve or normal distribution (Welkowitz et al. 2012; Witte, 1993). The normal curve is illustrated by a bell-shaped curve: an equal but opposite shape on each side of a curve drawn on a paper folded down the middle. According to Witte (1993), Abraham de Moivre (1667–1754)—a French mathematician—developed the concept of normal distribution and based it on his observations of games of chance and then created the equation to determine the probability of certain outcomes. King and colleagues (2011) discussed the concept of probability as the number of possible successes divided by the total number of possible outcomes. Probability can range from 0 (no chance of success) to 100 (certainty of success), and the sum of probabilities for all possible outcomes must be equal to 100% (see Chapter 6).

In his observations, de Moivre stated that normally distributed interval or ratio variables must contain relatively few extreme outliers to no outliers. In this situation, most values tend to cluster near the mean and few values cluster far from the mean. *Witte (1993) explained de Moivre's concept of a normal distribution as not an empirical distribution but rather a theoretical or ideal model distribution.* This means that a normal distribution does not come from an actual research project but from a mathematical equation.

PROPERTIES OF THE NORMAL CURVE

As stated in the "Overview" section and illustrated in Figure 5.1, a normal curve is obtained from a mathematical equation based on its symmetrical bell-shaped curve. The degree of peakness (the highest peak of the distribution) in the bell-shaped curve of the standard normal distribution is known as *kurtosis*. The values of any variable that are normally distributed with a high kurtosis always show that a higher proportion of the cases are distributed in the very center of the distribution (Agresti, 2018; Freeman et al., 1978; Lee et al., 2016). *Furthermore, it is known that a normal distribution that displays a kurtosis shape is a direct result of the size of the standard deviation.* Why? In a large sample, when SD is small, there is less variability; in turn, SDs are clustered very closely to each other. In this situation, the pieces of the bell-shaped curve will be squeezed very closely together and the degree of peakness will be higher as shown in Figure 5.3.

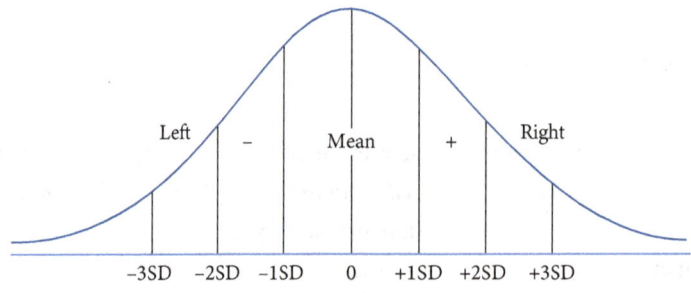

FIGURE 5.3   Normal Distribution With a High Peak or Kurtosis

Freeman et al. (1978) and Mogull (2004) explained symmetry as *the single highest point (the peak) of the curve in the data set where the ideal measures of central tendency (the median, the mode, and the mean) are all equal to one another. The peak of the curve is what makes the normal curve unimodal.* The area under the normal curve is divided into two equal halves (50/50) as shown in Figure 5.4. *The left half (below 0) is labeled as negative, and the right half is labeled as positive. As a result, the positive and negative signs are used to indicate position (tail) for the normal curve.* This is in contrast to other mathematical functions where the result of a negative sign is always smaller or less than the result of a positive calculation. In short, positive and negative signs in statistical results are used to indicate positions or directions in the normal curve.

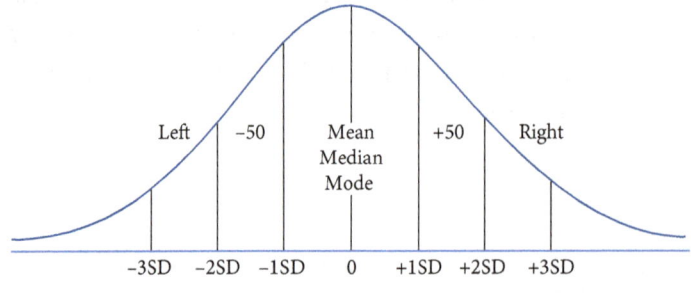

FIGURE 5.4   Normal Curve With SD

76   STATISTICS FOR SOCIAL WORK WITH SPSS

Notice that there are three standardized units (SD) to the left (negative) of the mean ($\bar{x}$) and three standardized units to the right (positive) of the mean. The remainder to the left or right side of the normal curve can be considered the fourth standard deviation, but statisticians rarely label them as such. From the peakness of the normal curve, each unit becomes smaller as they are laid along the x-axis. *Keep in mind that these ideal standardized units will never change. Only in real situations will researchers use these ideal standardized units to calculate the results for their own research project based on the values of the data set obtained and the confidence interval set forth by the researchers.* Confidence interval is discussed in the next section. How are the values in terms of percentages calculated?

AREAS UNDER THE NORMAL CURVE

First initiated by de Moivre, he divided the normal curve into six equal units. Montcalm and Royse (2002) stated that this is sometimes known as the "*1/6 rule*." This is a bit confusing. Above all, it is stated that the normal curve is divided into four units to the left and four units to the right. Why is it not called the "1/8 rule?" In Chapter 6, it will be discussed that the very end of the two-tailed units is reserved for hypothesis testing.

Early mathematicians, including deMoivre, started with the notion that nearly all scores of a normally distributed variable will fall within three standard deviations (3SD) above (right side) or below (left side) the mean ($\bar{x}$). Together, they reflect the variation that exists within virtually all values of a normally distributed interval- or ratio-scale variable. Each unit corresponds to 1 SD (±1 SD). *The more variations among the values in the data set, the farther the standard deviation moves away from the mean, causing the normal curve to become flatter.* When variations among the values are less in the data set, the curve will be narrower, and the peak of the distribution will be higher (Coolidge, 2013; King et al., 2011). *In short, flatter normal curves constitute a longer distance, and narrower curves constitute a shorter distance.* In social services situations, sometimes social workers prefer a longer distance (longer time line) between the service provided to clients and their relapse. Sometimes, the social workers prefer a shorter distance between the service provided and their relapse of the situation.

Figure 5.4 shows the mathematical distribution of the normal curve with 3 units of SD to the left (−3SD) and 3 units of SD to the right (+3SD) of $\bar{x}$. Table 5.1 provides the summary of the standardization units. Let us look more closely at these units.

To the right, the notations for the 3 *SD* are +1*SD*, +2*SD*, and +3*SD*. Similarly, to the left, the notations are −1*SD*, −2*SD*, and −3*SD*. Statisticians, such as Hays (1994) and Nowaczyk (1988), use complex tables to display values of areas under a normal curve. This book uses simple steps as presented by King et al. (2011) and Welkowitz et al. (2012). That is, tracking the *percentile rank to the left with a minus* and *percentile rank to the right with a plus in front of the calculated z score*. The z score is discussed later in the chapter.

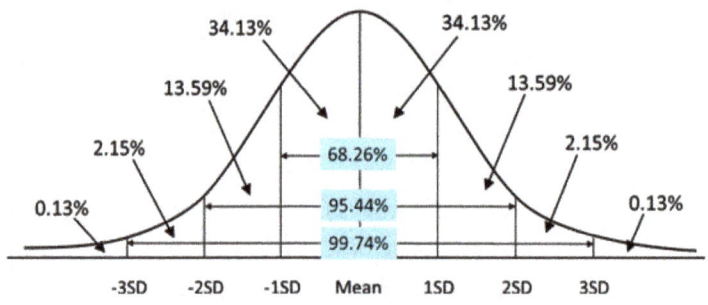

FIGURE 5.5 Normal Curve With Correspondence Percentages

TABLE 5.1 Distance Between the Sample Mean ($\bar{x}$) and SD

Distance From the Mean and Standard Deviation	Left Side Only of the Curve Between Mean and SD (−SD)	Right Side Only of the Curve Between Mean and SD (+SD)	Both Sides Under the Areas of the Normal Curve
1 SD	34.13%	34.13%	68.26%
2 SD	13.59%	13.59%	27.17%
3 SD	2.15%	2.15%	4.30%
Total areas under the normal curve	49.87%	49.87%	99.74%

Because of the symmetrical shape (see Figure 5.4 and Table 5.1), the distance between $\bar{x}$ and 1 SD always corresponds to 34.13% to the left and 34.13% to the right of the mean for a total of 68.26% (34.13% × 2 = 68.26%). The distance between 1 *SD* and 2 *SD* is 13.59% or 27.18 (as shown in Table 5.1) for both sides under the areas of the normal curve (13.59 × 2 = 27.18). Because of this, anything that falls 2 *SD* to the left or right of the mean is equal to 47.72% (34.13 +13.59 = 47.72). And the distance between 2 *SD* and 3 *SD* corresponds to 2.15% to the left and 2.15% to the right of the mean for a total of 4.30% (2.15 + 2.15 = 4.30). Therefore, the distance between the mean and 3 *SD* is equal to 49.87% (34.13 + 13.59 + 2.15) to either side of the curve for a total of 99.74% (49.87 × 2 = 99.74). *The total summation of ±3 SD is called the confidence interval (CI).* The regions in the remaining areas of 0.26% (100 − 99.74 = 0.26) for one-sided tests or 0.13% (0.26/2 = 0.13) for two-sided tests are called *rejection or extreme regions and are typically reserved for hypothesis testing.* In Chapter 6, the meaning of one-sided and two-sided tests is explained.

Note that 99.74% is based on a mathematical equation formulated by de Moivre for games of chance. In actual research studies, a researcher may adjust the confidence interval (CI) to accommodate other percentages, such as 97% or 99.99% (see Chapter 6).

What are the confidence intervals? Whether one is a statistician or a layperson, everybody understands that regardless of the societal situation, there is no way to know how the situation affects the truth about the population. If everybody knows the reasons for child maltreatment, the causes for mental illness, or the secrets to longevity, then there is no need to conduct research. But since the truth (i.e, scientific evidence) to various societal conditions or situations are unknown, research must be conducted. *When research is needed, then the confidence interval is also needed.*

Confidence intervals enable researchers to calculate the standard error (SE) of a sampling distribution and estimate with a certain degree of confidence the closeness of the true population to the sample mean. Calculating SE is discussed in Chapter 6. According to Coolidge (2013, p. 238), the confidence interval is based on three elements:

1. A value of a parameter around which the confidence interval will be built.
2. The standard error (SE) of the measure.
3. The desired width of the confidence interval (i.e., the 95% confidence interval or the 99% confidence interval).

The primary statistical tool used to estimate the population based on the normal curve is called the z score. *The z score is commonly referred to as the standard score because, once computed, the value of the z score is comparable to the SD unit.* Recall, it was stated in Chapter 4 that once the SD is calculated, it becomes the standardized unit of measurement for the situation under investigation.

UNDERSTANDING THE Z SCORE

As discussed, mathematicians created a standardized, unimodal, *symmetrical, bell-shaped curve with an $\bar{x}$ of 0 and an SD of 1*. A mathematical equation called the *standard score*, or *the z score*, is used to transform the original scores to standardize scores. Every score in a normally distributed population has a corresponding z score that reflects how many SD it falls above or below $\bar{x}$ (Hays, 1994; Nowaczyk, 1988; Rubin, 2013). *The solution from the z score enables researchers to rank the value of any interval or ratio variable and serves two major purposes: (a) because the mean is zero, a given score is above (right or a positive sign) or below (left or a minus sign) the mean, and (b) because an SD is 1, the numerical size of a standard score indicates the number of standard deviations above or below the mean.* These two purposes have a great deal of meaning. Let's see why.

Because the z score is based on mathematical probability, the solution can be converted to a percentile. *The main question is how a raw score can be transformed to a z score and then be converted to a percentile.* While the calculation for the z score is simple and straightforward (see Table 5.2), its interpretation is powerful. Table 5.2 and the statistical rules laid down in the table are the simplest way to calculate the z score and then convert the result of the z score to a percentile for interpretation. *The rule also helps to find the original score* (x) *when other values are known.*

TABLE 5.2 Calculating the Z Score and Converting to a Percentile

The formula for calculating the z score and statistical rule for percentile conversion:

$$z = \left(\frac{x - \bar{x}}{SD}\right).$$

z = Standard z score. *Once calculated, the value of the z score is comparable to the value of the standard deviation*
x = Score of a particular case
$\bar{x}$ = Sample mean
SD = Sample standard deviation
Statistical rules for the conversion of the z score into percentile rank:

- Always round the calculated score to two decimal places.
- When finding the critical values for the calculated z score, move downward on the first column of the *Percentage Area under the normal curve between the mean and z, typically called the* **Standard Normal Curve table** (see Table 5.3) with the letter z to locate the first two digits, and then move across to locate the third digit.
- If the calculated z score is positive (+), add 50% to the percentile obtained from the Standard Normal Curve table, typically called the Critical Values ($z_{critical}$)
- If the calculated z score is negative (–), subtract the percentile obtained from the Critical Values of the Standard Normal Curve ($z_{critical}$) from 50%.
- Please note that once calculated, the result for the z score is comparable to the standard deviation (standardized unit of measurement for the situation under investigation).

Practice Example 1

Suppose that the county court mandated that families whose children have been removed because of the ruling of a county court judge and want to reunite with their children within 3 months must be 90% compliant on conditions set forth by CPS. Those with 84%–89% compliance must wait 4 to 6 months, and those with less than 84% compliance must wait longer than 6 months. CPS is using a comprehensive tool to measure the degrees of compliance.

Furthermore, CPS posted on its county court website that the average parental compliance in the past 2 years was 88% ($\bar{x} = 88$) per month with an SD of 4.75. Now, suppose that a child was removed from their parents' home. After 6 weeks, the county social service worker reported that based on the county assessment tool, the child's parents scored 86% ($x = 86$). Using the information available through the county court website and the assessment score reported by the county social worker, how likely will it be possible for this couple to get their child back home within the 3-month period?

As displayed in Table 5.2, to compute the z score for the scenario, it is quite simple.

$\bar{x} = 88$

$x = 86$

$SD = 4.75$

$z = \left(\dfrac{86-88}{4.75}\right) = -0.42$ (Note that this is a negative z score and is comparable to 0.42 standard deviations below the mean.)

How can this calculated z score be converted to a percentile so that it can be used to interpret the rule set forth by the county courthouse? As stated in the conversion rule in Table 5.2, the result shows three things:

1. As discussed in the confidence interval section, this calculated z score is comparable to a 0.42 SD ($SD = 0.42$).
2. Not only is it comparable to a 0.42 SD, but it is also below the mean (the negative sign).
3. The fourth part of the conversion rule in Table 5.2 reflects this calculated z score.

The next step is figuring out how the calculated value (−0.42) corresponds to the area of the standard normal curve. Now, turn to Table 5.3 *Percentage Area Under the Normal Curve Between the Mean and z*, to look for the *Critical Values* ($z_{critical}$).

To find the percentage of parents that scored 86% in the last 6 weeks while complying with the county court, do the following: (1) go to the first column with the letter z, scan down to the row labeled 0.4 (the first two digits in the calculated z score); (2) put a mark on that spot; (3) then move across that row until locating the value 0.02 (the third digit in the calculated z score); and (4) move across the row labeled 0.4, while simultaneously moving down from the decimal 0.02, notice that the two values meet at 16.28. *As a result, the critical value obtained by the couple that their child was removed from the home by CPS is 16.28% inside the areas of the normal curve.* This proportion will be used to arrive at the final solution when combined with the statistical rule in Table 5.2. *Notice that in the calculation, a minus sign is placed in front of the calculated z score for the parents that scored 88% in the past 6 weeks.*

Now, use the statistical rules in Table 5.2 to explain the final percentile, which will inform the parents of whether retrieval of their child from CPS may occur sooner rather than later. To reiterate the statistical rules in Table 5.2, when the calculated z score is negative (−), subtract the percentile obtained from the normal curve table from 50%.

Applying this statistical rule to the couple that scored 88% ($x = 88$) during the last 6 weeks, their final percentile is

$$z_{final} = \dfrac{\begin{array}{r} 50.00 \\ -\ 16.28 \\ \hline 33.72 \end{array}}{}$$

This means that the couple is ranked at 33.72%. By comparing this couple's percentile rank to the county court rule, they ranked too low. Therefore, they must wait 6 months or longer before the court even considers their case. Applying this situation to the population in general, especially evidence-based practice, there is little chance that parents in a similar situation will see their children any time soon. Figure 5.6 shows the area under the normal curve indicating the chance the couple will get their child back within 3 months. They ranked 0.42 standard deviation below the mean (SD = −0.42).

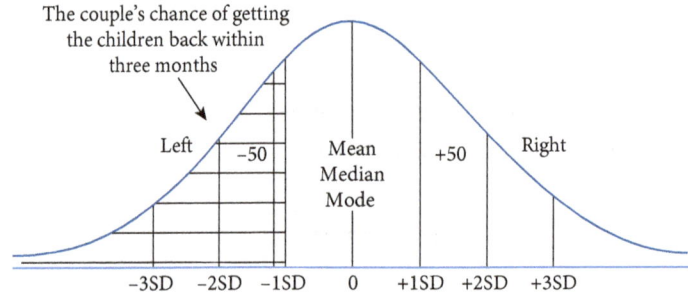

FIGURE 5.6 Likelihood the Couple Will Get Their Child Back Within 3 Months

TABLE 5.3 Percentage Area Under the Normal Curve Between the Mean and Z

z	0.00	0.01	0.02	0.03	0.04	0.05	0.06	0.07	0.08	0.09
0.0	00.00	00.40	00.80	01.20	01.60	01.99	02.39	02.79	03.19	03.59
0.1	03.98	04.38	04.78	05.17	05.57	05.96	06.36	06.75	07.14	07.53
0.2	07.93	08.32	08.71	09.10	09.48	09.87	10.26	10.64	11.03	11.41
0.3	11.79	12.17	12.55	12.93	13.31	13.68	14.06	14.43	14.80	15.17
0.4	15.54	15.91	16.28	16.64	17.00	17.36	17.72	18.08	18.44	18.79
0.5	19.15	19.50	19.85	20.19	20.54	20.88	21.23	21.57	21.90	22.24
0.6	22.57	22.91	23.24	23.57	23.89	24.22	24.54	24.86	25.17	25.49
0.7	25.80	26.11	26.42	26.73	27.04	27.34	27.64	27.94	28.23	28.52
0.8	28.81	29.10	29.39	29.67	29.95	30.23	30.51	30.78	31.06	31.33
0.9	31.59	31.86	32.12	32.38	32.64	32.89	33.15	33.40	33.65	33.89

1.0	34.13	34.38	34.61	34.85	35.08	35.31	35.54	35.77	35.99	36.21
1.1	36.43	36.65	36.86	37.08	37.29	37.49	37.70	37.90	38.10	38.30
1.2	38.49	38.69	38.88	39.07	39.25	39.44	39.62	39.80	39.97	40.15
1.3	40.32	40.49	40.66	40.82	40.99	41.15	41.31	41.47	41.62	41.77
1.4	41.92	42.07	42.22	42.36	42.51	42.65	42.79	42.92	43.06	43.19
1.5	43.32	43.45	43.57	43.70	43.82	43.94	44.06	44.18	44.29	44.41
1.6	44.52	44.63	44.74	44.84	44.95	45.05	45.15	45.25	45.35	45.45
1.7	45.54	45.64	45.73	45.82	45.91	45.99	46.08	46.16	46.25	46.33
1.8	46.41	46.49	46.56	46.64	46.71	46.78	46.86	46.93	46.99	47.06
1.9	47.13	47.19	47.26	47.32	47.38	47.44	47.50	47.56	47.61	47.67
2.0	47.72	47.78	47.83	47.88	47.93	47.98	48.03	48.08	48.12	48.17
2.1	48.21	48.26	48.30	48.34	48.38	48.42	48.46	48.50	48.54	48.57
2.2	48.61	48.64	48.68	48.71	48.75	48.78	48.81	48.84	48.87	48.90
2.3	48.93	48.96	48.98	49.01	49.04	49.06	49.09	49.11	49.13	49.16
2.4	49.18	49.20	49.22	49.25	49.27	49.29	49.31	49.32	49.34	49.36
2.5	49.38	49.40	49.41	49.43	49.45	49.46	49.48	49.49	49.51	49.52
2.6	49.53	49.55	49.56	49.57	49.59	49.60	49.61	49.62	49.63	49.64
2.7	49.65	49.66	49.67	49.68	49.69	49.70	49.71	49.72	49.73	49.74
2.8	49.74	49.75	49.76	49.77	49.77	49.78	49.79	49.79	49.80	49.81
2.9	49.81	49.82	49.82	49.83	49.84	49.84	49.85	49.85	49.86	49.86
3.0	49.87									
3.5	49.98									
4.0	49.997									
5.0	49.99997									

Reprinted from Welkowitz, J., Cohen, B. H., & Lea, B. R. (2012). Introductory statistics for the behavioral sciences (7th ed.). John Wiley & Sons.

Practice Example 2

In Table 3.1, on a scale from 0 to 5, it was shown that the first student respondent reported their self-care level at a 4. In Chapter 4, it was calculated that the average self-care for the entire student respondents was 1.53 with an SD of 1.3 (see Table 4.1 and standard deviation calculation). This practice example has two parts. First, manually calculate the degree of self-care for this student. Second, use SPSS to duplicate the same calculation for the standard normal curve.

TABLE 5.4 **Calculating the Z Score for the First College Student**

$$\bar{x}_{selfcare} = 1.53$$

$$SD_{selfcare} = 1.30$$

$$x_4 = 4$$

$$z_4 = \left(\frac{4-1.53}{1.30}\right) = 1.90$$

$$z_{critical} = 47.13$$

$$z_{final} = \frac{+\ 50.00}{\ \ \ \ 47.13} \over 97.13$$

As shown in Table 5.4, the level of self-care for the first student respondent was at the 97th percentile. The result essentially indicates that a raw score of 4 on a scale from 0 to 5 can be converted to an extremely high percentile.

To use SPSS to compute the final percentile for the same variable, simply follow these steps:

a. Turn on SPSS. Create a new file or simply put the new variables next to the SPSS data file that you had created for Table 3.1

b. On *Variable View (bottom left corner)*, create three new variables. To be less confused, for the first variable enter "x." Give the label "*Score of the respondent*." Create the second variable. Name it "*Mean.*" Give a label. Create a third variable. This time, name it "SD" for standard deviation. *On the Decimals column, change it to four decimals*.

c. Click *Data View* to return to the data file sheet. *Enter 4 for x, 1.53 for Mean, and 1.3 for SD*. What you are doing here is plugging in the same scores as displayed in Table 5.4 into SPSS.

d. On the top drop-down ribbons, click *Transform*. Select *Compute Variable*. The mini window as shown in Figure 5.7 will pop up. On *Target Variable*, enter a name such as "Probability." On the third mini window, click *CDF and noncentral CDF*. A new mini window will pop up. Scroll down and select *CDF. Normal*. Click the upward arrow. Note that as soon as the upward arrow is clicked, there is an instruction on *CDF. Normal* is shown. The first word inside the parenthesis is quant. *Quant is for the x value*. The second word is the *mean* and the third word is the *standard* deviation. *Type in 4, Mean, and SD* as instructed in "c." Make sure there are no typos. In case there is a typo, such as no space, SPSS will not let the computation continue.

e. Click *OK* and *OK* again. X out the output. Scroll to the last column on the variable list. The value 0.9713 is shown. To convert it into percentile, simply move two decimal places or multiply the result by 100%. It is now confirmed that either doing it by hand or using technology, the same outcome of 97.13% is obtained.

f. *Do take note that at times, there may be small discrepancies between manual and SPSS calculations. The reason is that not all standardized normal curve tables enter exactly the same percentiles into their programs. If that is to happen, as instructed on "c" earlier, simply change the mean ($\bar{x}$) to zero and standard deviation (SD) to 1.*

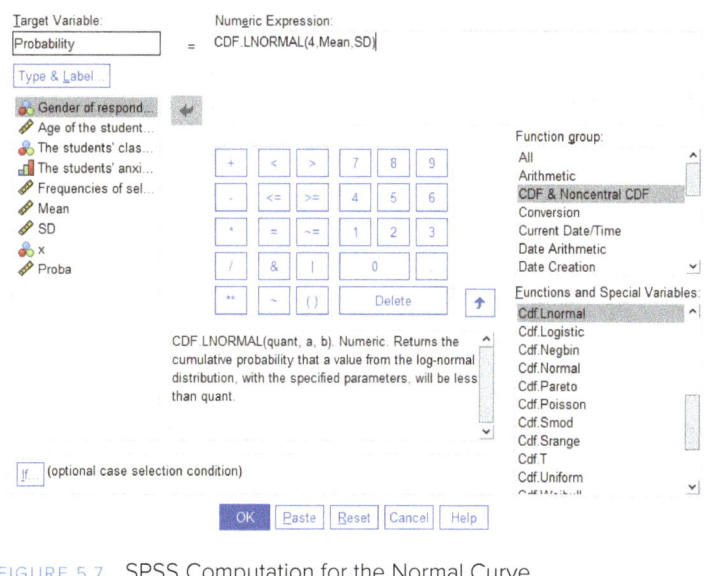

FIGURE 5.7   SPSS Computation for the Normal Curve

ADDITIONAL NOTE ABOUT THE Z SCORE

The algebraic equation for the z score can be used for a variety of purposes: discovering whether a health and human services worker may need additional training for such purposes as evaluating the effectiveness of job performance, improving rank performance on an examination, or estimating living conditions of a population parameter. As long as two or three values (scores) in the z score equation are given, the unknown value can be recovered algebraically. Researchers frequently use the z score equation/formula to determine the value of the score (X) when the final percentile or p value (see Chapter 6) and its corresponding SD are known. The z score can be helpful in such circumstances.

In peer-review journal articles, most often only the sample mean ($\bar{x}$), its corresponding standard deviation (SD), and the confidence interval (*p value*) are stated. It's very rare that the authors provide the data set. Now, let's continue with Practice Example 2. *Assume that the raw score (x) was not provided.*

How does one know that research participant #1 in fact rated their self-care at four times per month? First, let's complete the algebraic function. To get x in the z score, solve it algebraically (Table 5.5).

TABLE 5.5 Solve the Z Score Formula to Get x

$z = \left(\dfrac{x - \bar{x}}{SD} \right)$ To solve for x, first, multiply *SD* to both sides

$(SD)(z) = x - \bar{x}$ *SD* is canceled on the right side. Only this part of the equation is left. Now add $\bar{x}$ to both sides. The $\bar{x}$ on the right side is canceled. All that is left is this formula:

$(SD)(z) + \bar{x} = x$. To make it easier for the naked eye, reverse the display of the formula.

$$x = (SD)(z) + \bar{x}$$

By recalling the values in Table 5.4:

$$SD = 1.30,$$
$$z = 1.90,$$
$$\bar{x} = 1.53$$

Now solve for x:

$$x = (1.30)(1.90) + 1.53$$
$$x = 4.00$$

Based on the result of the calculation, it is confirmed that the first subject in Table 3.1 in fact rated their self-care at a 4.

Practice Example 3

In the first practice example, suppose that after hearing CPS and the juvenile court state that the couple must wait for 6 months or longer before the court will even consider their family reunification, the couple wants to know if they can seriously work on the court mandate and that CPS and the court will reconsider their case in the following month. Their main question is, "If we work extremely hard on the court mandate, how many percentage points must we accumulate?"

Suppose the responses from CPS and the juvenile court were unanimous in not reconsidering the case unless the couple met the top 90% threshold set up by the county court and social services division. After hearing this, the couple decides to consult with a statistician.

After the couple met and presented the result in Practice Example 1 to a local researcher, the researcher summarized their scores and posed this question (x = ?).

x = ? (These are the percentages needed for the juvenile court to reconsider the case.)

SD = 4.75

$\bar{x} = 88$

Confidence interval (CI) = 90%

This time, to solve for x, critical thinking is required. The z score conversion rule stated in Table 5.2 must be factored into the equation. The rule states that depending on the calculated z score, if it is positive, add 50% to the critical value, and in case it is negative, subtract the critical value from 50%. For this particular case, the county court set 90% as top compliance (see Practice Example 1). First, notice that this is above the mean. By following the z score conversion formula, subtract 50% from 90%, which is equal to 40%. Now, go to the body of Table 5.3 to find the z score for the equation. The z score that is closest to 40% is 1.28. Review Table 5.2 on how to find this z score. The percentage required by CPS and the county court can now be easily calculated.

$$x = (SD)(z) + \bar{x}$$

$$x = (4.75)(1.28) + 88$$

$$x = 94.08$$

Therefore, parents who want to be ranked by the juvenile court at the top 90% when it comes to compliance with court orders must earn 94% or higher on the assessment score. Now, notice that the standard division set forth by CPS and the county court is not even near the +2 SD (z = 1.28). This is also equated to +1.28 SD (see Figure 5.8).

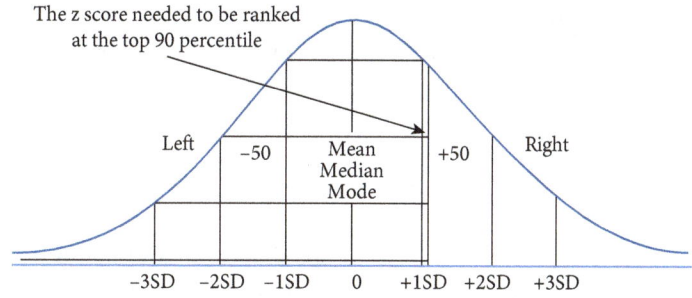

FIGURE 5.8 CPS Case With a 90% Confidence Interval

SUMMARY

This chapter discusses the meaning of normal distribution and the z score and its usefulness in evidence-based social work and other health and human services professions. The normal curve was constructed by Abraham de Moivre using a mathematical equation that has four main properties:

- All normal curves share a bell-shaped curve, with most of the area falling in the middle.
- All normal curves are bilaterally symmetric, which means that the left side mirrors the right side. Just as in human beings' brains, *a "typical" person will need the left and right sides of the brain to balance the body so they can walk straight.*
- *Regardless of the size and length of the shape, the tail never touches the x-axis.* In the number line (the horizontal line), the left side contains the negative values and the right side contains the positive values. In normally distributed attributes, the bell-shaped curve comes very close to the x-axis but never touches it. Thus, in drawing a normal curve, one must think of an infinite bell shape.
- There are situations where the normal curve may not be perfect. In some situations, the data set may positively skew to the left or negatively skew to the right.

Dr. de Moivre started with the notion that nearly all scores of a normally distributed variable will fall within three standard deviation (3SD) above (right side) or below (left side) the mean ($\bar{x}$). Together, they reflect the variation that exists within virtually all values of a normally distributed interval- or ratio-scale variable. A mathematical equation called the standard score, or the z score, is used to convert the original scores to new scores. Every score in a normally distributed population has a corresponding z score that reflects how many standard deviations it falls above or below the mean (Hays, 1994). The solution from the z score enables researchers to rank the value of any interval or ratio variable and serves two major purposes: (a) because the mean is zero, a given score is above (right) or below (left) the mean; and (b) because a standard deviation is 1, the numerical size of a standard score indicates the number of standard deviations above or below the mean.

Chapter 6 further discusses how researchers use the normal curve to conduct hypothesis tests.

Study Questions

Multiple Choice. The following study questions in this chapter should enable learners and users to understand the meaning of normal distribution and z score.

1. In a normal distribution, if all things are equal, the measures of central tendency are centered on a particular location inside the bell-shaped curve. Where is this particular location? It is centered at
    a. −1.0.
    b. +1.0.
    c. −3.0.
    d. +3.0.
    e. 0.00

2. In a normal distribution, when the scores are distributed heavily to the left-hand side of the bell-shaped curve, the distribution is known as

   a. positively skewed.
   b. negatively skewed.
   c. peakness.
   d. normal curve.

3. Normal distribution and the z score were founded by which of the following individual(s)?

   a. Witte
   b. Freeman, Pisani, and Purves
   c. King, Rosopa, and Minium
   d. De Moivre
   e. All of the above

4. The degree of peakness of a normally distributive curve in the bell-shaped curve is known as

   a. normal distribution.
   b. negative skewed.
   c. positive skewed.
   d. kurtosis.
   e. all of the above.

5. The areas inside the bell-shaped curve that constitute either ±3.0 SD or 99.74% are best known as

   a. normal distributions.
   b. peakness.
   c. confidence intervals.
   d. z scores.

6. When someone states that their annual income is two standard deviations above the mean, how much of the person's income is above average?

   a. Unknown
   b. 34.13%
   c. 47.72%
   d. 49.77%

7. In the hypothesis test, the confidence interval enables researchers to calculate which of the following?

   a. Sample standard deviation.
   b. Coefficient of variation for the sampling distribution and the population.
   c. Standard error of a sampling distribution and the true population.
   d. Estimated sample mean and population mean.
   e. All of the above.

8. The area at the extreme tail of the bell-shaped curve is known as
    a. confidence interval.
    b. peakness.
    c. kurtosis.
    d. none of the above.

9. If someone is given a z score of +1.89, what would you say about the standard deviation (SD) for the distribution set? Would you say
    a. it was 1.89 SD?
    b. it was 18.9 SD?
    c. it was 1.89 SD above the mean?
    d. it was 1.89 SD below the mean?

10. Which of the following statement(s) is/are correct about converting the z score into percentile rank?
    a. Always round the calculated z into three decimals.
    b. When the calculated z is positive, add 50% to the critical value.
    c. When the calculated z is negative, subtract the critical value from 50%.
    d. All
    e. Only b and c

The remaining questions are based on this statement: Ms. Avatar and Mr. Moonshine Star took an examination to compete for the upcoming hiring of various positions in the county Department of Social Services (DSS). There were 591 applicants who took the same test. After the examination, the county reported that based on the 99% confidence interval, the average score for the test takers was 89% with a standard deviation of 5.25%. Assume that Ms. Avatar scored 94% and Mr. Moonshine Star scored 88% on the test. You, as a member of the administrators who will conduct the interviews and hire the new workers, decide to use normal distribution and the z score to help with the decision-making process.

11. Prior to calculating the z score, Mr. Moonshine Star's score would fall
    a. above the mean.
    b. at the mean.
    c. below the mean.

12. By using the z score as a decision-making process, what would you say about Ms. Avatar's overall percentile rank among the 591 test takers? Would you say she ranked at
    a. 94%?
    b. 95%?
    c. 32.89%?
    d. 82.89%?

13. By using the z score as a decision-making process, what would you say about Mr. Moonshine Star's overall percentile rank among the 591 test takers? Would you say he ranked at

    a. 88%?
    b. 19%?
    c. 7.53%?
    d. 42.47%?

14. If the county administrators state that those whose scores ranked at the third standard deviation will be put on the waitlist, who is eligible to be on the waitlist?

    a. Both Ms. Avatar and Mr. Moonshine Star
    b. Ms. Avatar alone
    c. Mr. Moonshine Star alone

15. By using the upper limit for the standard deviation, what type of score does Ms. Avatar receive from the county exam?

    a. 94
    b. 95
    c. 96
    d. 97

16. By using the upper limit for the standard deviation, what type of score does Mr. Moonshine Star receive from the county exam?

    a. 88
    b. 89
    c. 90
    d. 91

Answers to Study Questions

QUESTION	ANSWER	QUESTION	ANSWER
1	e	9	c
2	a	10	e
3	d	11	c
4	d	12	d
5	c	13	d
6	c	14	b
7	c	15	a
8	d	16	c

CHAPTER 6

Probability and Hypothesis Testing

OVERVIEW

In the last three chapters, statistics such as frequency distributions, measures of central tendency, measures of variability, and normal distribution were discussed. These statistics only involve calculating the values of one variable at a time. Usually, these are not all the statistical analyses needed to describe the distributions of a sample or a population. The researchers still need to draw inferences. In most research studies, the goal is to generalize to the population from which the sample was drawn. *Generalization suggests findings from a particular research study represent causal effect or relationship and apply to the population beyond the study conditions* (Rubin & Babbie, 2014). Essentially, it is a broad statement or thought process that researchers use to apply to situations or population groups.

The concept of generalization from the sample to the population from which it was drawn is called inference. *Inference requires researchers to assess their degree of confidence in the data analysis after they have concluded that the real relationship between the dependent variables* (DVs) *and independent* (IVs) *from a sample is representative of the population.*

To assess their degree of confidence in the relationship between or among variables, researchers must follow several important statistical guidelines. These guidelines, such as population and sample, probability and sampling distribution, hypothesis and hypothesis testing, and confidence interval (CI) estimation, are discussed in this chapter (Nowaczyk, 1988; Lee et al., 12016).

POPULATION AND SAMPLE

Population

The term *population* refers to the real or hypothetical group of people, personal attributes, organisms, or events intended for study (Lee et al., 2016). If the goal is to count the number of wild plants that grow near someone's front porch during the summer months, then wild plants become the targeted population. Wild plants were selected as an example, but it is unlikely that there is any way to make a precise count of all wild plants near anyone's front porch. In short, population is used to describe all potential observations that can be included in the study. Because this book does not aim to discuss organisms, the focus is on populations related to health and human services.

Examples of populations in health and human services typically include the total number of workers in a particular county, types and quality of patient care at a local hospital, number of homeless individuals in a particular region, number of active child protective cases, and annual poverty rates. *A distribution of all the raw scores or complete group of observations is called a population distribution.* Descriptive summaries of measurements, such as the proportion of homeless individuals at a locale in a particular year, are *parameters*—sometimes referred to as the *population parameters*. Parameter was discussed earlier in Chapter 1.

Sample

In most situations, the population is large, or it is difficult to get a full list of the entire group/community or organization. If a population parameter is large, it may be impractical or impossible to observe the behaviors or personal attributes of everyone in the population. Therefore, a subset of the population must be either conveniently or randomly drawn as research respondents. The subset of the population is characterized as a *sample* (Lee et al., 2016). *The sample population is commonly referred to as a group or condition.* Statisticians suggest that randomized sampling provides the best technique to generalize findings to the population from which it was drawn. *The concept that directly links drawing samples from the population is called probability.*

PROBABILITY AND SAMPLING: DISTRIBUTION OF THE MEAN

Probability

As briefly discussed in Chapter 5, probability is a mathematical equation that shows the proportion or fraction of times that a particular outcome will occur. A probability can range from no chance of the event occurring (0% or 0) to an event that is absolutely occurring (100% or 1.0). *The term "probability sample" refers to sampling approaches in which each member of the population or condition has an equal chance of being selected for inclusion in the sample* (Rubin & Babbie, 2017; Zeitlin & Auerbach, 2019). The most common sampling strategy is *simple random sampling*, for which a name, an identifier, or a score from a list that contains the true or an estimated population is drawn. The reason that researchers use simple random sampling is to lessen the role of bias, which thereby increases the likelihood that a sample will be representative of the study population or condition (Rubin & Babbie, 2014). The probability theory is depicted as follows:

$$\text{Probability of an event} = \frac{\text{Number of ways the event can occur}}{\text{Total number of outcomes possible}} (100\%)$$

For example, a researcher wants to study the psychological impacts it has on the families who lost loved ones to COVID-19. Assume that the state provides a list to the researcher with the names of 10,000 individuals that have died from the virus. In this case, if the researcher wants to contact the survivors of the families to recruit them as potential research subjects, they could randomly draw 1,000 names from the list by

$$\text{Probability of COVID}-19 \text{ family members as research subjects} = \frac{1,000}{10,000} (100\%) = 10\%.$$

Thus, 10% of the individuals who were victims of COVID-19 will be contacted by the researcher to recruit them as prospective research participants. *Please note that the researcher could also keep drawing and recruiting prospective participants from the list until 10% of the list have agreed to participate in the research project.*

Sampling Distribution of the Means

As discussed in Chapter 1, in inferential statistics, the goal is to move from a known sample distribution to a potentially observable, yet unknown, population distribution. The move is used to protect the subjects from being identifiable by any means of a public inquiry. *To help move from the known to the unknown, a theoretical concept known as sampling distribution of the mean proves useful. Sampling distribution of the mean is a social construct that takes into consideration the size of a sample as well as the sampling error it theoretically may contain* (King et al., 2011; Freeman et al., 1978). According to Freeman and colleagues (1978), the data distribution reveals how closely related the mean, median, mode, quartile, mean deviation, and standard deviation are to each other and the population sample.

The sampling distribution of the mean is the advanced version of the z score. It is the probability distribution of means for all possible random samples of a given size from the same population or condition. In simple vocabulary, the distribution of the mean of all possible random samples will form a normal curve.

In inferential statistics, one of the major theoretical principles of probability that helps researchers understand the distribution of the sample mean is the *central limit theorem*. Essentially, *this theorem states that as the size (n) of the sample becomes sufficiently large, the sampling distribution of the mean will become normal regardless of how the characteristics are distributed within the population* (Engel & Schutt, 2013; Witte, 1993). More specifically, King et al. (2011) stated, "The random sampling distribution of the mean tends to move toward a normal distribution irrespective of the shape of the population of observation sampled; the approximation to the normal distribution improves as sample size increases" (p. 176).

For example, the mental health issues of 3,000 junior high and high school students in a school district were examined. After completing the data collection, 500 students from the pool of 3,000 were randomly sampled to examine their stress level while being confined to study at home. The observation, as expected, revealed a normal distribution of the stress level for the 500 sampled students, as well as for all of the junior high and high school students in the nation. Thus, the sampling distribution of the mean for a large sample has the following properties:

- The distribution was normal.
- The mean of the distribution was equal to the population mean ($\bar{x} = \mu$).
- The standard deviation (SD) of the distribution of the sample means is called the standard error of the mean (SD_E) and is computed using formula 6.0:

Formula 6.0 calculating the standard error of the mean can be completed by

$$\text{Standard error of the mean } (SD_E) = \sqrt{\sum \frac{(x-\bar{x})^2}{n-1}} / n.$$

The standard error of the mean (SD_E), also called *standard error (SE)*, is used to indicate how different the population mean is likely to be from a sample mean (Zeitlin & Auerback, 2019). Essentially, in a repeated study, it is the amount of difference or the variation in the samples within a single population.

Some other statistics books used a simplified formula. Note that the first part of the formula is the variance; therefore, to make it easier, simply take the square root of the variance (SS^2) and divide it by *n* as follows:

$$SD_E = \sqrt{\frac{SS^2}{n}}$$

Zeitlin and Auerbach (2019) explain the law of large numbers, which is that the sample mean ($\bar{x}$) of the sampling distribution will equal the mean of the population (μ) and the standard deviation of the sample (SD).

Note that the means of individual samples vary from the population mean and from each other. People who teach statistics know that the sampling distribution of any sample size is based on an infinite number of samples, and overall, the law of averages eventually prevails. *It was stated in Chapter 4 that the $\bar{x}$ takes into account all numerical scores for each of the interval and ratio variables. In turn, the law of averages simply said that samples with lower means and those with higher means cancel each other out when they are averaged together; therefore, the mean of means is exactly the same as the true population mean, no matter what sample size produced the sampling distribution.*

Also, note that is not simply the standard deviation of the samples. This is because sample size and sampling error must be factored into SD. Remember that, as sample size increases, the probability of either drawing all small or all large values decreases.

Hypothesis and Hypothesis Testing

This book defines hypothesis as a statement of an educated hunch or speculation about a presumed relationship in the real world (Lee et al., 2016). In most social science and behavioral research, a hypothesis is used as a prediction for testing in a research project. The prediction can be based on formal observation (i.e., experimental study), informal observation (i.e., hospital records), or a theoretical approach (i.e., behavior modification), either based on previous research or new interest (McDaniel, 2016; Nowaczyk, 1988; Rubin, 2013). Essentially, to discover whether there is a significant difference between educated hunches (i.e., the relationship between the variables), a hypothesis test must be conducted. For example, an educated hunch about child sexual abuse can be drawn with a diagram that looks like this:

Independent variable (IV) (Factors related to child sexual abuse)	Dependent variable (DV) (Child sexual abuse)
Pornographic materials Family history Chemical dependency ⟶	Child sexual abuse

The diagram has three IVs (factors) to test one DV. The goal is to see whether the IVs are significantly related to child sexual abuse. One of the keys focuses of hypothesis testing is the distinction between population and sample, as discussed previously in this chapter. *A systematic procedure decides whether the results of a research study, which examines the sample, support the predictions.*

More specifically, hypothesis testing provides a more precise decision-making framework for determining whether an estimated value for a given population parameter is reasonable. Hypothesis testing is done because of the need to generalize research outcomes beyond the sample group and its face value and to make sure that the significant difference was not produced by chance or sampling error (Aron et al., 2011; Freeman et al., 1978). *When the data are not correct—that is, not representative of the population from which the sample was drawn—researchers tend to explain the nonsignificant finding as sampling error. Sampling error is the degree of error to be expected for a given research study based on probability theory, as discussed in the section on probability.*

When conducting a *hypothesis test or test of significance*, statisticians suggest paying attention to the statistical assumptions, summarized as follows (Lee et al., 2016):

- The *level of measurement of the variable*. Essentially, researchers must clearly understand the level of measurement for each and every one of the variables in the research project. This way, the researchers are able to tell whether the data are nominal, ordinal, interval, or ratio level.

- The *method of sampling or sampling design*. Researchers must be able to explain whether the data were collected from a probability sampling design like simple random sampling or nonrandom (nonprobability) sampling, such as convenience sampling, snowball sampling, or purposive sampling. *Note that all statistical tests assume random sampling; therefore, when data are collected from nonrandom sampling, researchers need to clearly discuss the nonprobability sampling.*

- The *shape of the distribution*. The shape of the distribution influences the outcome of the study. Researchers must consider whether the shape of the distribution is normally distributed and whether it is positively or negatively skewed.
- *Sample size and tests of mean difference*. Statistical significance with fewer subjects may be less meaningful than with a larger sample size (see Chapter 9).
- Tests of mean differences always assume interval and ratio data, particularly for the DV.
- State the null hypotheses (H_o) first and then state the alternative hypothesis (H_a) Alternative hypothesis and null hypothesis are discussed in the next section.

Note that although most of the time, researchers are focused on the alternative hypothesis; however, it really depends on the situation. In a situation like racial equality, of course, the focus is on the null hypothesis. The researchers want to test the hypothesis that regardless of race, gender, ethnicity, or type of religion, everyone is being treated equally. In other instances, such as health and well-being and community cohesion, the focus is on the alternative hypothesis. In these situations, researchers want to test the hypothesis that better health care leads to stronger well-being and that strong community cohesion is strongly correlated to less racism or sexism.

Many students find that the most difficult part of mastering inferential statistics is to understand two complementary, yet mutually exclusive, concepts regarding the predicted value of the targeted population parameter. These two complementary concepts are *types of hypothesis* and *directions of the hypothesis*.

TYPES OF HYPOTHESES

Whether one is doing research for a living or is a student learning, they should know that there are *two types of hypotheses or two tests of significance that are related to the study, and they are called research hypothesis and null hypothesis* (McDaniel, 2016; Rubin, 2013; Welkowitz et al., ,2006). This book uses the alternative hypothesis in place of the research hypothesis. It is called the alternative hypothesis because it is an alternative to the null hypothesis (Lee et al., 2016).

The Alternative Hypothesis

In research, the major aim of the research question (not the questionnaire) is often stated as a predictive direction or solution about one or more presumed relationships. It is a wishful declarative statement about the outcome of the research study (Hays, 1994). This type of statement is known as an alternative hypothesis (often designated with either an H_1 or an H_a). H_1 *as designated for the primary hypothesis. Depending on the researchers' definitions, H_1 and H_a can be used interchangeably. In this book, H_a represents the alternative research hypothesis.* Why is it called an alternative hypothesis? Because the null hypothesis, to be discussed later, *states that regardless of situations or conditions, there is no significant difference between the variables.*

Furtheremore, the term *alternative* is used interchangeably with the term *research hypothesis*, and it is a declarative sentence that states or predicts how changes in one variable (usually the antecedent or IVs) are proposed to cause or explain changes in another variable (usually the DV or outcome variable). The following examples illustrate this type of declarative predictive statement:

1. Parental temper tantrum is strongly correlated to child physical abuse.
2. People who complete a 4-year college degree are more likely to have monthly earnings higher than minimum wage; in turn, their chances of living in conditions below the poverty line will be less.
3. It is predicted that domestic violence perpetrators who received social service interventions will be less likely to reoffend than perpetrators who did not receive treatment.

Why are these three statements called alternative or research hypotheses (H_a)? Let us examine the first statement more closely by using the definitions about the DV and IV from Chapter 3. The DV is child physical abuse, and the IV is temper tantrum. If the hypothesis is based on an actual research study, then researchers are examining the various methods to assist parents in managing their anger. One of the methods could be anger management. Another method could be training on the parent-child relationship. And an additional method could be the rights of a child based on cultural sensitivity. *Typically, a temper tantrum (the cause) occurred before child physical abuse (the outcome or the problem).*

The Null Hypothesis

The opposite of the alternative hypothesis is called the *null hypothesis, which is normally designated with an* H_o. Some statistics texts also use H_2, which indicates the secondary hypothesis. *This type of declarative statement states, despite what the sample data suggest, after taking into account sampling errors or chance fluctuations, no real relationship or significant difference exists between the hypothesized statements* (Hays, 1994). Examples of statements using the null hypothesis include the following:

1. Temper tantrum is not related to child physical abuse.
2. There is no relationship between wage earning and 4-year college degree completion.
3. There is not a significant difference between domestic violence perpetrators who received social service interventions and those who did not receive them.

All three statements state that after taking into account sampling errors or chance fluctuations, no real relationship or significant difference is observed between the DV and IVs.

DIRECTION OF THE HYPOTHESIS

Direction or tail is directly connected to hypothesis testing. *When testing a hypothesis, one may use a directional (one-tailed) or nondirectional (two-tailed) hypothesis. The terms are not used interchangeably. The direction and position of a hypothesis depend on the prediction and speculation about the probability* that the relationship may exist along the z score (Barry et al., 2004; Coolidge, 2013; Montcalm & Royse, 2002) (see Chapter 5). Let us see how they are different from each other.

Directional (One-Tail) Hypothesis

The term *directional* (one-tailed or one-sided) *hypothesis* is used to test hypotheses that researchers are certain of or able to predict the direction that the relationship of the variable under investigation will fall on the normal curve (Hays, 1994; Lee et al., 2016). When forming a directional hypothesis, the researchers have predicted a significant observation to be either on the left or right side of the normal curve but not both. *Recall in Chapter 5 that the z score is divided into two equal halves, the left half (from 0 to −3 SD or below $\bar{x}$) and the right half (from 0 to +3 SD or above $\bar{x}$).*

If the researchers know or think that the significant difference will be observed only on the left- or right-hand side under the areas of the mean ($\bar{x}$) of a normal curve, then the hypothesis can be tested using a directional declarative statement. Occasionally, researchers do state their hypotheses using the one-tailed test. Figures 6.1(a) and 6.1(b) are used to depict an example of a directional hypothesis for which significant differences can be observed only at the left side or right side of the normal curve.

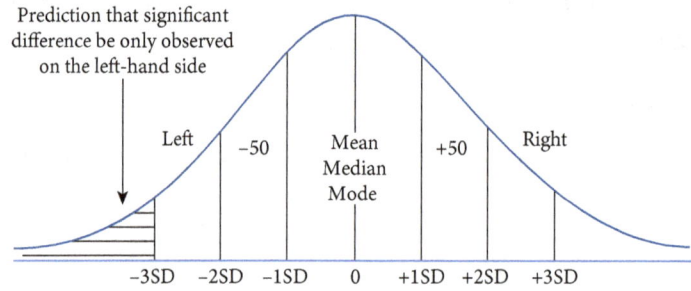

FIGURE 6.1(A)   Prediction That Significant Differences Are Only Observed on the Left Side

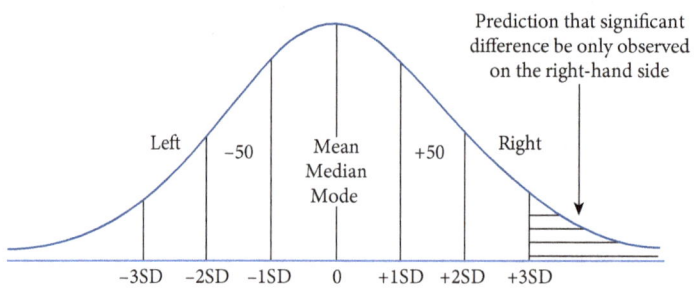

FIGURE 6.1(B)   Prediction That Significant Differences Are Only Observed on the Right Side

An example of a left-side directional hypothesis can be stated as follows:

- Children with very low self-esteem will not have too many friends at school.

An example of a right-side directional hypothesis can be stated as follows:

- There is a strong correlation between parents who are highly supportive of their children both at home and school and parents with outstanding parent-child relationships.

Nondirectional (Two-Tailed) Hypothesis

The term *nondirectional* (two-tailed or two-sided) *hypothesis* is used to test hypotheses for which researchers believe that significant differences do exist but are unsure or unable to predict the direction of the relationship (Hays, 1994; Lee, 2016). Because of the rare use of the directional (one-tailed) hypothesis, both manual and computer applications, such as the *SPSS*, automatically select nondirectional (two-tailed) hypotheses for all tests of statistical significance.

Examples of two-tailed nondirectional hypotheses can be written as the following:

- The research hypothesis is aimed to examine the significant difference on mental health treatments for noncompliant men and women.
- This research study is aimed at examining the significant difference in the parent-child relationship between homeless and non-homeless children.
- The hypothesis states that school bullying is significantly correlated to self-esteem issues for children ages 9–14.

Note that the three examples do not argue that one is better or higher than the other. In summary, when examining an issue within a normal curve, a conclusive prediction regarding whether a significant difference will be observed on the left or right side of the curve is not always possible. Figure 6.2 depicts the significant difference that may occur on either side of the standard normal curve.

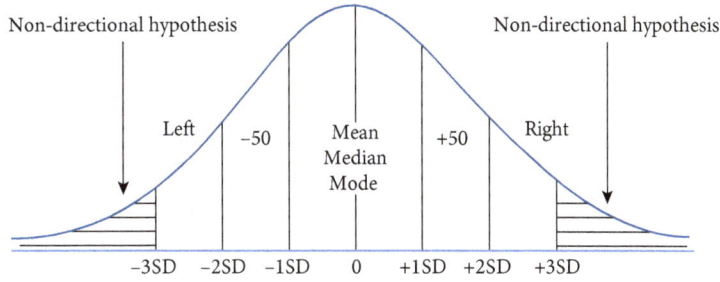

FIGURE 6.2   Nondirectional Hypothesis

CONSTRUCTING THE CONFIDENCE INTERVAL (CI)

Once a tail (direction) of the hypothesis is determined, another helpful activity is to construct a confidence interval estimation for the research project (Figure 6.4). *Because of the advancement of modern technology, researchers generally have no need to construct the CI, but it is important to understand.* From political polls to scientific studies, the term *confidence interval* or *confidence interval estimation* is used throughout various professions. *It is an estimation of how the true population reflects in the interval.*

What Is the Confidence Interval (CI)?

The term *confidence interval* has been briefly discussed elsewhere, especially in Chapter 5. This section provides more detailed information about the CI and how to construct one's own CI using SD areas under the normal curve. The CI is also called the interval estimate because it allows researchers to construct an interval or range of scores around a point estimate (usually around the $\bar{x}$) (Agresti & Finlay, 2009; Leon-Guerrero & Frankfort-Nachmias, 2012). The CI also allows researchers to state a *level of confidence* in how likely it is that the interval contains the population parameters being estimated (King et al., 2011; Welkowitz et al., 2012).

Please note that this book at times uses the *confidence interval* and *level of confidence* interchangeably. Although they are not the same, students have much difficulty differentiating between them. Confidence interval is a *type of estimated statistic* computed from the sample data that provides a range of values between the sample mean and its correspondent standard deviation. On the other hand, it is the *interval* that gives the probability or level of confidence (*p value*) with which the estimation will contain the true parameter. *It is the level of confidence that is always chosen by the investigators/researchers.* For any given estimation (confidence interval) in a given sample, using a higher confidence level (meaning less precise) generates wider confidence interval.

More or less, the CI is the range along the 99.74% discussed in Chapter 5. In that chapter, *it was discussed that the CI is used to calculate the* SD_E *of a sampling distribution and estimate with a certain degree of confidence the closeness of the true population to the* $\bar{x}$. *It was also discussed that the value 99.74% is an ideal percentile that researchers can use to understand the relationship between areas under the normal curve and the standard deviation.* As a matter of fact, the value 99.74% can be either expanded or contracted depending on one's level of confidence. While constructing a CI, a researcher may be only 80% confident that lack of parental support causes children not to perform well in school. Consequently, the researcher may be mistaken 20% of the time. In another instance, 99.9% of the world population will agree that world peace is to keep human beings alive on earth. In this case, the world population is only wrong one one-thousandth (1.00 − .999 = .001) of one percent or one can say that for every 100,000 people, only 100 people will say world peace is not needed $\left(\dfrac{100}{100,000} = .001 \right)$. The number 100 is the interval between 1 and 100,000.

Because of the probability of making mistakes in a research study, researchers must select and construct a CI for the research project. When constructing a CI, the first thing researchers need to do is decide the level of risk of being wrong, as well as how much error can be risked. An estimate is incorrect if the interval developed fails to include the true population parameter. The term *level of significance* or *rejection level* is the probability value used as the criterion in deciding whether an obtained sample statistic (normally the $\bar{x}$) has a low probability of occurring by chance alone if the null hypothesis is true

(King et al., 2011). The *Greek letter alpha (α)* is used to denote the criterion of significance. Sometimes, it is referred to as the power to detect significance or the probability value (*p value*). In most statistical calculations, especially social and behavioral sciences, the accepted cutoff for a criterion of significance is .05 (α = .05). Some people accept a higher cutoff but rarely larger than .07. Alpha is directly related to Type I error (discussed later) and probability.

- Alpha (α) is the threshold the researcher sets the hypothesis or the test of statistics against. Recall that in the bell-shaped curve, the very tail of the normal distribution is labeled the extreme or rejection region. Alpha is used by the researcher to see how extreme the observed result must be to reject the null hypothesis of a significance test. The value of alpha is dependent on the CI set forth by the researcher. In the previous example about world peace, the alpha level of significance was set at $\frac{1}{1,000}$. This means that a true hypothesis will be rejected one out of 1,000 times, which is very small.

- Because there are different statistics tests (Chapters 7 to 11), there are a number of different ways to find a p value. *When conducting hypothesis tests or tests of significance, the tests involve the calculation of a number known as a p value OR selecting it from a standardized table. The number that is calculated or selected is very important to the conclusion of the specific test. This p value gives the researchers a measurement of evidence against the null hypothesis.*

- It was discussed earlier that the null hypothesis assumes that whatever researchers are trying to prove did not happen.

- *When the p value is less than, say .03, the null hypothesis is rejected—stating that there is a significant difference between the variables.* The researchers will explain that there are reasons to believe that something else besides chance alone provided the observed finding.

- *When the p value is greater than say .08, the null hypothesis is supported—stating that there is not a significant difference between the variables.* The researchers will explain that it is reasonable that the findings can be explained by chance alone. Overall, the smaller the p value is, the more difficult it is to claim that a result is statistically significant. In this case, there is a lower probability that what was observed can be attributed to chance. On the other hand, the larger the value of alpha is, the easier it is to claim that a result is statistically significant.

Examples of the confidence interval and level of confidence (p value):

- When the study uses a 99.99% CI, the *p value* is .0001 (1 − .9999 = .0001). The probability that an error will be committed is less than $\frac{1}{10,000}$.

- When the study uses a 98% CI, the *p value* is .02 (1 − .98 = .02). The probability that an error will be committed is less than $\frac{1}{50}$.

- When the study uses a 95% CI, the *p value* is .05 (1 − .95 = .05). The probability that an error will be committed is less than $\frac{1}{20}$.

In the literature, statements such as the following may appear: "There is a strong correlation between self-care and longevity, $p < .05$." The p (as required by the APA) in this case stands for the p value, and the expression itself is a shorthand way of saying that the estimated errors between self-care and longevity are expected to occur by chance less than 5% of the time. To put it another way, the researcher is confident that the relationship between self-care and longevity is 95% or higher (i.e., people that take better care of themselves are likely to live longer). By convention, researchers can accept a 5% chance of committing a statistical error; or there should be a 5% chance that the results from the sample data are due to sampling error (see the discussion of types of error in a further section of the chapter).

Interpreting Results of Statistical Tests

One of the most difficult aspects of learning statistics is not just doing the calculations but also explaining the results. Even during the examination, some students did better on the multiple-choice questions while others did better on the calculations and explaining the results. To help ease the difficulties, please closely follow the instructions that follow. *These instructions should be used as the guiding principles for reporting research findings. Either in an introductory course such as this one or in an advanced statistics course, the same reporting guidelines are used.* This section should help clear up the confusion about p value. The following guidelines should ease tensions and confusion (Lee et al., 2016):

1. As discussed earlier, the level of confidence is chosen by the researchers. Even if a computer application presets the alpha level to a specific level, the researchers can change it.
2. When manually calculating the result of a statistical test of significance or a hypothesis test, visually compare the calculated values (result of the calculation) with the critical value (value obtained from the chart/table of a statistics book). If the calculated value is larger than the critical value, state that *there is a significant finding*. When reporting the research finding and depending on the type of inferential statistics—such as correlation, test of association, and mean difference—replace the word *finding* with the appropriate term being discussed. *This is to state that the null hypothesis has been rejected and that the alternative hypothesis has been supported.* When the opposite result occurs, then change the discussions accordingly. Essentially, when the calculate value is less than the critical value, state the *contrary*.
3. When computing the result of a statistical test of significance or a hypothesis test using a software application such as SPSS, *look for the p value computed by that application* (see Table 6.1). Some software applications do not provide the p value. If the application does not provide the p value, it cannot be used to conduct a hypothesis test. Most software applications, including SPSS, preset the CI to 95% (*p value* = .05) or 99% (*p value* = .01). When the sample is sufficiently large and based on the SD equaling 0 and SD equaling 1, the software application will sometimes compute and provide a new p value for the preset CI. Use the p value given by the computer program and make decisions accordingly. Normally, the p value is labeled "Significance" or simply "Sig." When "Significance" or "Sig." falls between *.000 and .05, accept that there is a statistical significance.* For any p value that is larger than .05, most social and behavioral scientists, like social workers and psychologists, automatically retained the H_o or *state that the researcher has failed to reject the null hypothesis.*

4. Either manually calculated or computed by a software application, as an APA condition, when H_o *is retained*, use the notation "*p* > #," and when H_o *is rejected*, use "*p* < #." The italicized p stands for probability of committing an error, especially retaining the false null hypothesis. The greater than (>) symbol stands for *"not a significant difference"* and the less than (<) symbol stands for a "significant difference" between the variables.
5. *The number symbol (#) is where the researcher will insert either the self-selected level of significance from a standardized table or the one given by the software application.* If manually calculated—suppose that the researcher uses a 95% confidence interval two-tailed test—then the .05 is used. When a software application is used, such as in Table 6.1, then the author will insert .073. The .073 is the new p value produced by SPSS.

TABLE 6.1   Sample Two-Tailed Hypothesis and a New P Value

	Value	df	Asymptotic Significance (2-Sided)
Pearson Chi-Square	6.964[a]	3	**.073**
Likelihood Ratio	8.958	3	.030
Linear-by-Linear Association	.448	1	.503

CONSTRUCTING THE CONFIDENCE INTERVAL USING Z SCORE

Once the confidence interval is selected, such as the one discussed on how college students rated their self-care per month, the researcher may want to transform the selected proportion (percentile) into a z score. The statistical rule for converting a particular level of confidence into a z score is simple and presented in the next section. While the rule for converting a proportion to a z score may be stated differently by people who teach statistics, the transformation remains the same.

Statistical Rules on Converting Proportion Into a Z Score

For a two-tailed hypothesis test or test of significance, do the following:
1. Depending on the z score table, subtract the selected proportion from 100% (if the book uses percent) or 1.0 (if the book uses decimals). If the p value is given by the authors, say .023 in a journal article, skip step 2. Use the number reported by the article and subtract 2.3% (.023 x 100% = 2.3%) from 50% (Step 3). Be consistent.
2. Divide the difference from the subtraction by 2 (because of a two-tailed or nondirectional hypothesis).
3. Subtract the #2 result from 50% or .50 (one-half of the standard score).

4. Use the result from the final subtraction to find the z score. Refer back to Table 5.2 for the proper rule in reading the correct z score.
5. The z score found from the *Percentage Area Under the Normal Curve Between the Mean and z* table (Table 5.3) is the z score needed for the situation under investigation. Recall that once the z score is located, it is equated to the standardized unit, which is the SD.

Practice Example 1 for Two-Tailed Hypothesis

Let us say that a researcher states that they used a 95% CI to conduct the hypothesis test about world peace and racial justice. Without any other information, the researcher wanted their research assistant to calculate the SD for the two-tailed hypothesis that was used for the test of significance. To answer the researcher's question, simply follow the previous five statistical procedures for the two-tailed hypothesis.

- First, subtract 95% from 100% (100 − 95 = 5%).
- Second, divide 5 by 2 (5/2 = 2.50%).
- Third, subtract the difference from 50% (50 − 2.50 = 47.50).
- Fourth, use 47.50% to find the needed z score from Table 5.2.
- Lastly, now notice that 47.50% corresponds to a z score of 1.96. As a result of the two-tailed hypothesis test at a 95% confidence interval, a z score of ±1.96 (plus and minus for the two-tailed hypothesis) is needed. Recall that once the z score is calculated, it is comparable to the estimated population standard deviation (μ). Therefore, the student assistant now knows that the researcher used an SD of ±1.96 for the study about world peace and racial justice (see Figure 6.3). Notice that even at 95% confidence interval, two-tailed test, there are huge proportions on the left and right side under the areas of the normal curve that are not covered.

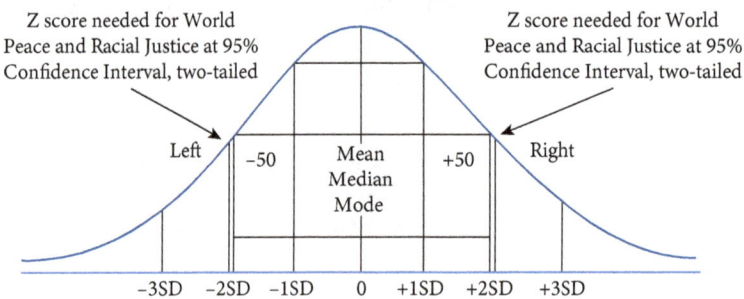

FIGURE 6.3 Z Score Needed to Construct 95% Confidence Interval (p value = .05)

For a one-tailed hypothesis test or test of significance, proceed as follows:

1. Subtract the selected proportion from 100% or 1.0. Again, be consistent with the numeric format.
2. Subtract the first subtraction's difference from 50% or .50.
3. Use the result from the final subtraction to find the z score (Table 5.2) needed for the situation under investigation.

Practice Example 2 for One-Tailed Hypothesis

In another instance, a social work researcher states that recently an experimental research project was completed on the effectiveness of narrative therapy with a large sample of drug-addicted clients. It was found that narrative therapy was very highly effective at a 99.9% confidence interval. Please use the one-tailed hypothesis to calculate the SD that occurred for this instance. To find the SD, simply follow the three steps stated earlier.

- First, subtract 99.9% from 100% (100 − 99.9 = 0.1%).
- Second, subtract the difference from 50% (50 − 0.1 = 49.90).
- Third, use 49.90% to find the z score needed from Table 5.2.

Since the social work researcher stated, *"very highly effective at the 99.9%,"* the value 49.90 is closest to a positive z score of 3.0 (z = +3.00). Again, once calculated, the z score is comparable to the SD. In turn, the social work researcher's computed SD was a +3 SD (see Figure 6.4). Notice that when conducting a hypothesis test, even a 99.9% CI one-tailed test, there is still a good proportion on the right side of the areas under the normal curve that remains uncovered.

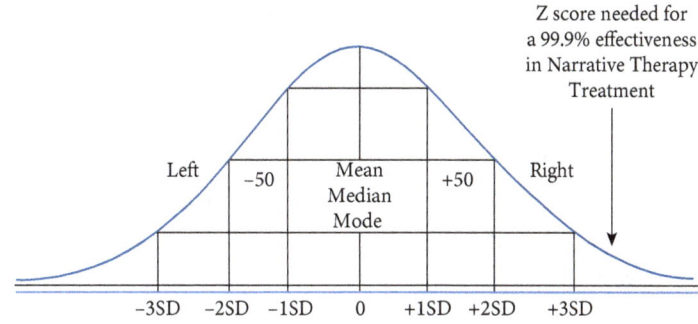

FIGURE 6.4 Z Score Needed to Construction a 99.9% Confidence Interval (p value = .001)

ERROR IN HYPOTHESIS TEST AND ALTERNATIVE EXPLANATION

In social and behavioral sciences, when conducting a hypothesis test or a test of significance researchers need to be aware that conclusions about the research study are based only on available data. Compared to the medical sciences, there are no standardized measuring instruments that accurately measure human services issues, particularly in social services. *Most often, in social services, the degree of effectiveness or severity of an issue can only be measured based on perceptions, views, and level of needs.* Because social services issues and needs are not like diseases that can accurately be diagnosed using specific diagnostic tools or devices, confidence in retaining or rejecting H_0 cannot be guaranteed. For example, in a hypothesis test, a researcher may claim with 99% confidence that chemical dependency affects personal functioning—but such a conclusion may not come from a true result. In measuring social problems, for example, a conclusion about the null hypothesis on domestic violence and poverty can be both true and false. Because of the potential true and false conclusions in research findings, researchers must take into consideration the types of errors that can occur in all research projects. *Errors in statistics are called Type I and Type II errors.*

Type I and Type II Errors

In social services research, one of the most common fears is committing a Type I error. At times, social workers can make the wrong assumptions that child maltreatment only occurs among poor parents and caretakers. The honest truth is that child maltreatment disregards race, gender, ethnicity, or socioeconomic status.

The Type I error occurs when the null hypothesis is true but researchers reject it. Essentially, researchers rejected the wrong portion of the null hypothesis. The explanation should state that there is not a significant difference, but it was concluded that there is, so the researchers rejected the null hypothesis (Hays, 1994; Nowaczyk, 1988). *The problem for a Type II error is the opposite of that for a Type I error. Type II error occurs when the null hypothesis is false, and researchers fail to reject it.* The researchers are supposed to explain that there is a significant finding, but instead, they accept (some statisticians call it retain) the null hypothesis and claim that there is no significant difference. Table 6.2 illustrates the four possible outcomes associated with hypothesis testing (Geber & Hall, 2014).

One helpful hint in reducing the Type I error is to increase the sample size. When the sample size increases, the chance of committing a Type I error decreases. This is one of the reasons why in a research methods course, quantitative instructors usually recommend a minimum sample size of 30, a good sample size of 50, and a very good sample size of 100.

TABLE 6.2 The Four Possible Outcomes Associated With Hypothesis Testing

Decision Regarding the Null Hypothesis (H_o)	Truth Regarding the Alternative Hypothesis (H_a)	
Reject H_o	If H_a is true, the correct decision was made	If H_a is false, made Type I error
Fail to reject H_o	If H_a is false, made Type II error	If H_a is true, the correct decision was made

ALTERNATIVE EXPLANATIONS

In daily life when things do not go as expected, people can come up with all sorts of creative explanations. However, in research, there are specific ways of explaining the results, especially when the findings are not consistent with the expected outcomes or the stated hypotheses cannot be confirmed. *A common explanation includes the researchers addressing concerns regarding the Type I error and Type II error.* In case the researchers still want to provide additional explanations, then they must discuss one or more of the following issues (Engel & Schutt; 2013; Rubin & Babbie, 2017) :

- *Rival Hypotheses.* Rival hypotheses are often referred to as the other variables that were not a part of the research. Because of rival hypotheses, variables being observed may cause a relationship to occur, but outcomes may not be representative of the purposes of H_o and H_a. This occurs when something unknown is not measured or results are positive for something that has no bearing on what is being tested.

- *Design Flaws.* Design flaws usually occur when the researchers are not careful with the measuring instruments (questionnaires) and sampling bias. For example, when studying depression, the questionnaire may be constructed to focus largely on anxiety syndrome. Even though there are co-occurring anxiety symptoms in depressed persons, there are depressive symptoms remarkably different from people who are suffering from anxiety.

- *Sampling Error.* Sampling error could happen with any research project. Usually, sampling error occurs because of unequal size, small sample, changes in data collection procedures, and natural disaster incidents. In the last example, while data collection is being conducted, there could be a major earthquake, a war just started, or a major pandemic is happening. In these situations, instead of responding to the questions as originally intended, the subjects' responses may reflect the event that is occurring.

USING SPSS TO CONSTRUCT CONFIDENCE INTERVAL

This practice example is an illustration of how to use SPSS to construct a confidence interval. Recall in Chapter 5 why the CI is needed. It was stated that the CI is used to understand how the true population reflects in the interval. It was also stated in Chapter 4 the reason APA requires both the $\bar{x}$ and SD to be reported together when discussing the research findings,

The reason for doing so is to get researchers who are knowledgeable in statistics to use the x and SD to estimate the lower bound (lower limit) and upper bound (upper limit) for the distribution set. This practice example is an illustration of how to use SPSS to construct a 99% CI, mainly finding the lower bound, upper bound, and the SD_E for the true population as portrayed in Table 3.1 on the "*Self-are*" variable. To complete the process, open the SPSS file constructed for Table 3.1 and follow these steps:

- On the SPSS drop-down ribbons, select *Analyze*, move the cursor to *Descriptive Statistics*, and then select *Explore*.
- A new mini window like the one that follows will pop up. Select and move the "*Self-Care*" variable to the *Dependent List*.

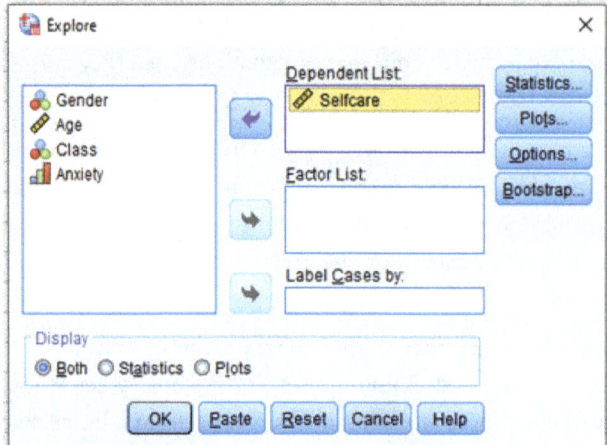

Image 6.1

- Click on *Statistics* (upper right corner). On *Confidence Interval for Mean*, change the preset from 95% to 99%. Hit the *Continue* button.
- Click *Ok*. Momentarily, Table 6.3 will pop up.
- SPSS now produced an output table with the lower bound and upper bound with the SD_E. In generalizing this sample to the population from which it was drawn at a typical $\bar{x}$ of 0 and SD of 1, the population has the lowest self-care per month at .53 and highest at 2.53. Using Formula 6.0, the SD_E on average of self-care per month is .336 $\left(\sqrt{\dfrac{1.695}{15}} = .336\right)$. It also shows a trimmed mean of 1.48 (see Chapter 4 in how to calculate the trimmed mean based on 5%).

TABLE 6.3 Constructing a Confidence Interval Using SPSS

			Statistic	Std. Error
Frequencies of self-care per month	Mean		1.53	.336
	99% Confidence Interval for Mean	Lower Bound	.53	
		Upper Bound	2.53	
	5% Trimmed Mean		1.48	
	Median		1.00	
	Variance		1.695	

SUMMARY

Chapters 5 and 6 provide valuable information concerning some aspects of hypothesis testing. More specifically, Chapter 6 discusses the sampling distributions of the means, types of hypotheses, directions of hypotheses, how to interpret results of statistical tests using the confidence interval, and types of statistical error commonly found in research. The summary that follows should enable learners and users to complete hypothesis tests without difficulty:

- Clearly understand the level of measurement for the data set and define the dependent and independent variable(s). Note that at times, several scale variables are added as a DV, and other variables are grouped as the IVs.
- Make assumptions about the research purposes and specify the variables that will be used to answer the assumptions.
- Clearly state the null and alternative hypotheses. Consider stating one null hypothesis and two or three alternative hypotheses. DO NOT state too many hypotheses because when discussing the results, it may be confusing to explain them all.
- Do not just be dependent on the preset confidence interval set by the software application. Select a confidence interval of your own. Based on the selected confidence interval, the α coefficient needs to draw conclusions and determines the results of the study.
- Calculate the chosen statistical tests. If done by hand, pay attention to the selected p value from a standardized table. If the test is done using a software application, pay attention to the level of significance computed by it.
- When reporting and interpreting the findings, *do not elaborate beyond the evidence presented*. False and invalid reports can occur by exaggerating the results.
- Besides taking the levels of measurement as the "Statistics Bible," the section titled "Interpreting Results of Statistical Tests" is another verse in the Statistics Bible. Not paying attention to the guidelines specified in this chapter will most likely lead to confusing presentations of research findings.

Study Questions

Multiple Choice. The study questions in this chapter should enable learners and users to understand the meaning of probability and hypothesis testing.

The first three questions involve the following statement: Suppose that a researcher is interested in investigating the perceptions that college students have about parents who refused to have their children vaccinated against COVID-19. Assume that a city listed 29,345 K–12 students. Of the given list, the researcher decided to randomly select 275 as student participants.

1. The population parameter of the research project is
   a. permission given by the campus to survey students.
   b. the students' perceptions about parents who refused to have their children vaccinated.
   c. 29,345.
   d. 275.

2. The DV for the research project is
   a. permission given by the parents of the students.
   b. the parents' perceptions about the danger of COVID-19 vaccines.
   c. 29,345.
   d. 275.

3. The sample for the research project is
   a. permission given by the parents of the students.
   b. the parents' perceptions about the danger of COVID-19 vaccines.
   c. 29,345.
   d. 275.

4. Which of the following statements best describe the term *"probability?"*
   a. It is a mathematical equation that shows the proportion of times a particular outcome will occur.
   b. It is a sampling approach that selects only a specific portion of the population.
   c. It is a value that shows that the observed statistic occurred and that it occurred by chance alone.
   d. The threshold the researcher sets the hypothesis or the test of statistics against.

5. Which of the following statements is true about the p value?
   a. It is a mathematical equation that shows the proportion of times a particular outcome will occur.
   b. It is a sampling approach that selects only a specific portion of the population.
   c. It is a value that shows that the observed statistic occurred and that it occurred by chance alone.
   d. It is a number selected as the measurement of evidence against the null hypothesis.

6. Which of the following statements is not associated with the term *sampling distribution of the means*?
   a. It is a social construct.
   b. It is similar to the z score.
   c. It is unrelated to the central limit theorem.
   d. It is a probability theory.

7. If your instructor provides $z = 2.19$, what is the standard deviation for the same situation?
   a. Unknown

b. −2.19
   c. 2.19
   d. 1.48

8. The symbol *p* < is used in a research report to denote what type of meaning?
   a. There is a significant difference between the variables.
   b. There is not a significant difference between the variables.
   c. The variables are less likely to occur again.

9. When testing hypotheses, whether written or not, which type of hypothesis must the research always focus on first?
   a. Null hypothesis
   b. Research hypothesis
   c. Direction of the hypothesis

10. The term *hypothesis* refers to which of the following statements?
    a. A variable about the social world.
    b. A hunch on what things ought to be in the real world.
    c. A statement about the distinction between probability and alpha.

11. When conducting a hypothesis test, which of the following statistical assumptions is not very important?
    a. Random sampling
    b. Normal distribution
    c. Sampling design
    d. Questionnaire construction

12. In a statement, *"People who have higher self-esteem tend to have more friends,"* the statement itself is best described as the
    a. null hypothesis.
    b. research hypothesis.
    c. either one is correct.

13. In regard to the direction of the hypothesis, Question 12 is best described as a
    a. directional hypothesis.
    b. nondirectional hypothesis.
    c. either one is correct.

14. Researchers often provide alternative technical explanations to support their research findings. Which of the following explanations is not important?
    a. Rival hypothesis
    b. Design flaw
    c. Random error
    d. Lack of comparative sample

15. When cognitive-behavioral approaches are done correctly, men and women will have the same benefits. This type of hypothesis is called a
    a. one-tailed hypothesis.
    b. two-tailed hypothesis.
    c. either one is correct.

16. It is stated by the author that when the calculated value of an inferential statistic is larger than its critical value, researchers must
    a. retain the null hypothesis.
    b. reject the null hypothesis.
    c. either rejecting or retaining is up to the researcher.

17. If given a confidence interval of 98%, what is the p value for the situation?
    a. .2
    b. .02
    c. .1
    d. .01

18. In Question 17, what would be the z score if the instructor asks their students to calculate the z score for a two-tailed hypothesis?
    a. 2.31
    b. 2.32
    c. 2.33
    d. 2.34

Answers to Study Questions

QUESTION	ANSWER	QUESTION	ANSWER
1	c	10	b
2	b	11	d
3	d	12	b
4	a	13	a
5	d	14	d
6	c	15	b
7	c	16	b
8	a	17	b
9	a	18	c

CHAPTER 7

Inferential Statistics
Cross-Tabulation and Chi-Square

OVERVIEW

This chapter introduces inferential statistics. As discussed in Chapter 1, inferential statistics are used for hypothesis testing. The first inferential statistics are known as cross-tabulation and chi-square.

THE MEANING OF BIVARIATE ANALYSIS

As stated thus far, the basic foundation for understanding inferential statistics is called bivariate analysis, which is used to analyze the relationship between two variables. Analyzing three or more variables all at once is beyond the scope of this book. Only in Chapter 11 will there be some presentations about the means test, which is when there is one DV but two or more IVs are compared. Other than that, no other advanced inferential statistics are discussed.

The prefix bi- here means two variables. These variables can be a combination of two variables of the same scale (same type) or one level of measurement versus all others. This chapter focuses only on the association of two nominal variables. As a result, the ordinal-, interval-, or ratio-level data are not applicable to this chapter. Additionally, due to the length of the book, situations such as changing the values of interval or ratio variables into dichotomous categories are not applicable to this chapter either. Dichotomy means the values of a variable are divided into only two categories.

WHAT ARE CROSS-TABULATION AND CHI-SQUARE?

In statistics, cross-tabulation (crosstab for short) is one of the bivariate analyses. *It is called cross-tabulation because the goal is to break down the values of two nominal variables or to do a comparison when two samples are not drawn from the same population.* Crosstab is an inferential statistic used to summarize categorical data to create a contingency table (Montcalm & Royse, 2002; Welkowitz et al., 2006;Wesleyan University, 2021). *Contingency means that event or prediction cannot be made from the table.* Although event and prediction cannot be made from the table, it provides an extremely clear picture of the interrelation between two nominal or categorical variables and helps find an interaction between them. This is the reason why crosstab is heavily used in all branches of research, including engineering and pure science.

Examples of crosstab hypothesis test may include statements like:

- Is there any significant association between types of religion and race?
- What is the significant difference between the experimental and placeboes interaction effects for ethnic minority and non-minority groups in terms of trustworthiness toward COVID-19 vaccines?
- Anti-Asian hate crime is strongly associated with political party affiliation.
- There is a significant difference in gender and types of popular college degrees.

The test itself is called by several names for different purposes. This book discusses only the one most commonly used, which is the Pearson chi-square (χ^2) test of independence or test of association. The book will also discuss how to measure its strength by using Phi, Lambda, and Gamma.

The Pearson chi-square (χ^2) test of statistics of significance uses a contingency table to examine the relationship between the variables. *The purpose is to examine that when the expected and observed frequencies are squared, does it still hold true for the population? A simpler explanation is that it examines whether the two variables are discretely related (dependent).*

The null hypothesis and the alternative hypothesis can be stated as follows:

H_o : The variables are statiscally independent.

H_a : The variables are statiscally dependent.

English learners, such as the author of this book, may have difficulty understanding "statistically independent" and "statistically dependent" when relating the terms to the null and alternative hypothesis definition. A quick summary would help. An easy way is reversing the thinking process. Statistically dependent means there is no significant difference between the variables, and statistically independent means there is a significant difference between the variables. Why so? In social work, social workers often talk about the significant relationship between mindfulness and good health. This means that mindfulness (e.g., "Yes and No") is strongly correlated (dependent) to being in good health (e.g., "Yes and No") for individuals. In a redundancy manner, the social workers want to advocate to their clients that "yes" practice (dependence) of mindfulness is strongly associated with "yes" in having good health. Independence simply means mindfulness is not related to (independence) good health. I hope you find this helpful.

Social work examples could also include examining the relationship between gender and type of social services or examining college education—one could be interested in examining types of popular college degrees and gender. Elementary school clinical psychologists could examine the association between children with attention deficit and hyperactive disorders (ADHD) who received and did not receive counseling. Note that gender, types of social services, college degree, and did or did not receive counseling are all nominal variables.

There are situations where the categories of values are more than two. Nominal variables such as race, types of employment, college major, and city of residency can contain three or more categories. Race, for example, is a nominal variable, but there are many racial groups within "race." In situations like these, the value categories will be more than two. Keep in mind that the focus is on two variables. Therefore, it does not matter how many categories are there for each of the variables. The only problem is that when there are several categories for the variables, the contingency table can be large, making it a tedious process for manual calculation.

Calculating the chi-square test of independence is simple and straightforward. The following steps are helpful:

1. Either manually or electronically, create a contingency table. Give a label such as 1, 2, 3 to each of the cells. The number 1 is for cell 1, 2 for the second cell, and 3 for the third cell.
2. Calculate the corresponding percentages for each of the cells.
3. Calculate the expected frequencies for the contingency table.
4. Calculate the chi-square (χ^2) statistic.
5. Calculate the degrees of freedom for the situation under investigation. Pay attention to the total columns and rows.
6. Interpreting the chi-square statistic by comparing the result of the calculation with the numbers found from a standardized table such as Table 7.5. When using a computer application, find the p value provided by the program as instructed in the section in Chapter 6, "Interpreting the Results of Statistical Tests."

Practice Example

Table 7.1 displays a hypothetical large research project about three groups of people on the importance of practicing mindfulness for healthy living. First, notice that there are two variables. Race is one of the variables, and mindfulness is the other. There are three groups of participants (i.e., Asian, Latino, and White) and there are also three responses (i.e., Yes, No, and Decline). This is called a 3 × 3 study because the contingency table contains three columns and three rows. The null hypothesis and alternative hypothesis for all three groups of research participants can be stated as:

H_o : Healthy living is independent on mindfulness practice.

H_a : Healthy living is dependent on mindfulness practice.

CI = 99.9%, two − tailed (equate to p value of .001)

Note that the purpose for the research study is to test the hypothesis that the practice of mindfulness is important (*dependent*) to the three groups of subjects. In case, the null hypothesis is ruled out, then the result will be generalized (advocated) to the general population about the usefulness of mindfulness practice. In contemporary social work practice, such a study project is very important for evidence-based practice. Social work educators and practitioners want to advocate for people in the community to practice mindfulness for personal well-being.

TABLE 7.1 **Mindfulness Practice Is Good for Healthy Living**

Mindfulness Good for Health	Racial Background of Respondent			
	Asian	Latino	White	Rows Total
Yes	250(a)	200(b)	325(c)	775 (R_1) **a + b + c = R**
No	75(d)	40(e)	90(f)	205 (R_2) **d + e + f = R**
Decline	15(g)	30(h)	60(i)	105 (R_3) **g + h + i = R**
Columns Total	340 (C_1) **a + d + g = C**	270 (C_2) **b + e + h = C**	475 (C_3) **c + f + i = C**	1085 (N) **Grand total**

By following the previously suggested steps, Table 7.1 can be completed with the following tasks:

1. Create the contingency table.
2. Calculate the expected frequencies for all nine cells.
3. Calculate the respective degrees of freedom for the situation under investigation.
4. Interpret the chi-square statistic using the critical values from Table 7.1.

Constructing a Contingency Table

Before conducting the null and alternative hypothesis tests for the two nominal variables, the most helpful way to understand the values and variables is to transform the raw scores into a contingency table. Displaying data this way is called a cross-tabulation or crosstab for short. Table 7.1 summarized the values from two nominal variables that have 1,085 (N = 1,085) respondents who participated in the research project. If all of the scores are display on a sheet of paper, they will be long and confusing. To make it easier for the naked eye, a crosstab table is created. The purpose is to be able to visualize the values of the variables individually in each of the cells, as well as the total scores for the distribution set. Typically, in crosstab tables, frequency distributions can be summarized based on columns (sum downward), rows (sum across), and total (N) with their respective percentages placed immediately below the scores (see Table 7.2). The original scores, 250, 200, 325, 75, and so on, are called *observed frequencies*, either designated with an f_o or just an O.

The crosstab table also makes it easier to complete the manual calculation. All one does is calculate it cell by cell. The letter assignments make it easier to identify the cells as cell a, cell b, cell c, and so on instead of having to refer to the values as 250, 200, 325, and the like. When adding the values of each cell across (horizontally), the crosstab table, such as a + b + c, it is called *Marginal Rows Total* (designated with an R). When adding the values downward (vertically), it is called *Marginal Columns Total* (designated with a C). When the total scores are added together—either horizontally or vertically—the summation is called *Grand Total*, designated with an N. The capital letter N is used because the Pearson chi-square is based on the total numbers of participants rather than just a subset of the respondents.

More specifically, when adding 250 to 200 and 325, the summation for this row is labeled R_1, second row R_2, and third row R_3 (see Rows Total). Repeat the same process for the columns. They are now designated with C_1, C_2, and C_3 (see Columns Total).

Calculating Percentages

Once the crosstab table is constructed, the first comparison for the individual cells is calculating their respective percentages. To calculate the corresponding percentages, simply do the same calculations as one would do for any percent. Take the sum of the frequency count and divide it by the total subjects. For example, to know the proportion of the Asian respondents who said the practice of mindfulness is important to be in good health, divide 250 by 1085, then multiply the result by 100%: $\left(\dfrac{250}{1085}\right) \times 100\% = 23.04\%$

Repeat the same process for each of the cells. When finished, the results will look just like Table 7.2. Be mindful that percentages can be calculated based on the total subjects or just the summation of a particular row or column.

The percentages show that 23.04% of the Asian respondents stated that mindfulness contributes to good health, followed by Latino at 18.43%, and White at 29.95%. Of the three groups, White respondents show the highest percentages that mindfulness contributes to healthy living. Latino is the group that least concurred with the usefulness of mindfulness. By examining the entire table, Asian was the group that least decline to state that mindfulness is related to healthy living at 1.38% (n = 15). If the variables were independent, the percentages would be equaled or nearly equaled to one another. In this preliminary percentages examination, the results have already indicated that the variables are dependent (significant), but the percentages are not scientific. The research project still needs to prove that it is in fact dependent (significant).

TABLE 7.2 Percentages State That Mindfulness Is Good for Healthy Living

Mindfulness Good for Health	Racial Background of Respondent			
	Asian	Latino	White	Rows Total
Yes	250(a) 23.04%	200(b) 18.43%	325(c) 29.95%	775 (R_1) **a + b + c = R**
No	75(d) 6.91%	40(e) 3.69%	90(f) 8.29%	205 (R_2) **d + e + f = R**
Decline	15(g) 1.38%	30(h) 2.76%	60(i) 5.53%	105 (R_3) **g + h + i = R**
Columns Total	340 (C_1) **a + d + g = C**	270 (C_2) **b + e + h = C**	475 (C_3) **c + f + i = C**	1085 (N) **Grand total**

Formula for the Chi-Square (χ^2)

Table 7.3 shows the formula for calculating the Pearson chi-square (χ^2) statistic. The formula in Table 7.3 and the statistical symbols presented in Table 7.1 have insufficient information for completing the chi-square. The formula states that when f_e is subtracted from f_o, the difference is squared and then divided by f_e (Wesleyan University, 2021). The latest symbol cannot be found anywhere among all the statistical symbols discussed thus far in this chapter.

The letter f_e stands for the expected frequencies for each of the cells in a crosstab table. It is also called the unknown frequency. The letter f_o stands for the observed frequencies, which are the scores that are already displayed in each of the cells. In the example about race and mindfulness, f_o are the scores from cell a to i. Note that some statistics books, including the first edition of this book, use O for observed frequencies and E for expected frequencies. The expectation is that to retain the null hypothesis (H_o), the numerical scores for each cell must be statistically independent.

TABLE 7.3 **Hypotheses for Calculating the Pearson Chi-Square (χ^2)**

Purpose	Null Hypothesis (H_o)	Alternative Hypothesis (H_a)
Test the association between two nominal variables	There is no significant association between the variables in the population; therefore, the variables are statistically independent.	There is a significant association between the variables in the population; therefore, the variables are statistically dependent.

Assume that the probability value (p value) is self-selected at a 95% CI or higher. The chi-square test of independence can be calculated by Formula 7.0.

Formula 7.0 is as follows:

$$\chi^2 = \sum \frac{(f_o - f_e)^2}{f_e},$$

where

χ^2 = The Pearson chi-square coefficient (also called Pearson's chi-square coefficient),
f_o = Observed frequency (the raw score in each individual cell), and
f_e = Expected frequency (also called unknown frequency).
Since f_e is unknown or expected, it must be calculated by Formula 7.1.
Formula 7.1 is as follows:

$$f_e = \frac{(C)(R)}{N},$$

where
C = Marginal columns total,
R = Marginal rows total, and
N = Grand total.

By looking closely at the statistical symbols displayed in Table 7.1 and the formula for calculating the expected (unknown) frequency, the Pearson chi-square coefficient can now be calculated.

Calculating the Chi-Square

Earlier, it was stated that once the contingency table is created, the next step is calculating the percentages. This step is already done, as shown in Table 7.2. The next step is to calculate the expected frequencies. To calculate the expected frequencies, simply use Formula 7.1. The first step is calculating the expected frequency. The subscript is used to indicate which cell is being calculated.

To calculate the expected frequency for cell a ($Cell_a$), expand the generic Formula 7.1 to look like this: $Cell_a = \frac{(C_1)(R_1)}{N}$. Make sure to follow the notations labeled for Table 7.1.

$$Cell_a = \frac{(340)(775)}{1085} = 242.86$$

Expected frequency for cell b ($Cell_b$) is now expanded as $= \frac{(C_2)(R_1)}{N}$

$$Cell_b = \frac{(270)(775)}{1085} = 192.86$$

Expected frequency for cell i ($Cell_i$) $= \frac{(C_2)(R_3)}{N}$

$$Cell_i = \frac{(475)(105)}{1085} = 45.97$$

Students always get confused in this part of the process. Remember to always use the Marginal Rows Total (R), the Marginal Columns Total (C), and the Grand Total (N) to calculate the expected frequencies. It is always helpful to mark the cells being calculated. Move the fingers horizontally to find the Marginal Rows Total and move the fingers vertically to find the Marginal Columns Total. Use the same guideline to complete the expected frequencies for all nine cells.

After the expected frequencies are finished and displayed on top of each other as completed for percentages, the results look similar to Table 7.4. The table is now ready to be used to calculate the Pearson chi-square statistic.

Now, the last step in calculating the chi-square is using the values in Table 7.4 for Formula 7.0. Keep in mind that Formula 7.0 is the generic formula. Depending on the contingency table created based on the result of the research study, the chi-square formula may be expanded. This is the reason why the sigma sign (Σ) is placed in front of the formula.

TABLE 7.4 Observed Frequencies and Expected Frequencies for Mindfulness and Race

Mindfulness Good for Health	Racial Background of Respondent			Rows Total
	Asian	Latino	White	
Yes	250(a) 242.86	200(b) 192.86	325(c) 339.29	775 (R_1)
No	75(d) 64.24	40(e) 51.01	90(f) 89.75	205 (R_2)
Decline	15(g) 32.90	30(h) 26.13	60(i) 45.97	105 (R_3)
Columns Total	340 (C_1)	270 (C_2)	475 (C_3)	1085 (N)

$$(\chi^2) = \frac{(250-242.86)^2}{242.86} + \frac{(200-192.86)^2}{192.86} + \frac{(325-339.29)^2}{339.29} + \frac{(75-64.24)^2}{64.24} + \frac{(40-51.01)^2}{51.01} +$$

$$\frac{(90-89.75)^2}{89.75} + \frac{(15-32.90)^2}{32.90} + \frac{(30-26.13)^2}{26.13} + \frac{(60-45.97)^2}{45.97}$$

$$\chi^2_{calculated} = 19.85 \text{ (This is the calculated value or the chi-square coefficient)}$$

The subscript "calculated" is inserted as a shorthand symbol for the calculated value, and the summation of all nine chi-squares is the grand total for the chi-square coefficient. The summation is used to determine whether there is a significant difference between the variables. Based on the tables concerning the practice of mindfulness and race, the calculated Pearson chi-square coefficient still says nothing about the relationship between the variables. *To either retain or reject the null hypothesis, the critical value for the respective chi-square coefficient and its magnitude must be known. In fact, the magnitude must be known before the critical value for a specific level of confidence can be found.* The magnitude is called degrees of freedom (df).

Interpreting the Chi-Square Result

To interpret the result of any chi-square coefficient, its df must be calculated, and these are slightly different from one statistical test to another. Normally, degrees of freedom are the attributes that are free to vary in a population or sample. For the Pearson chi-square coefficient, it is used to correct the number of cells in a contingency table. Essentially, degrees of freedom are used to reduce the number of cells in columns and rows. The formula for degrees of freedom for the chi-square is calculated using Formula 7.3.

Formula 7.3 Calculating the degrees of freedom (df) for the Pearson chi-square:

$$df = (C - 1)(R - 1),$$

where

C = Marginal columns total (number of actual values/categories for the column), and

R = Marginal rows total (number of actual values/categories for the row).

Therefore, the degrees of freedom (df) for mindfulness and race are calculated by

$$df = (3 - 1)(3 - 1),$$

$$df = 4.$$

Earlier in the chapter, the null hypothesis stated that the variables were independent of each other. The alternative hypothesis stated that the variables were strongly dependent on each other based on a 99.9% confidence interval, which gives a p value of .001 on a two-tailed hypothesis test. Please note that most statisticians agree that the Pearson chi-square is always conducted with a two-tailed test. Why? Because the χ^2 statistic does not depend on which is the IV and which is the DV. In simple terms, there is no way to predict the direction for the H_o.

To get the critical value for the calculated chi-square coefficient, use the df and the self-selected p value (based on the confidence interval of 99.9%). Now take a look at Table 7.5. At 4 degrees of freedom (df = 4) and a p value of .001, the critical value is 18.46.

In Chapter 6, under the section "Interpreting Results of Statistical Tests," it was stated that if the calculated value is larger than the critical value, state that there is a significant finding. Depending on the type of inferential statistics, such as correlation, test of association, and mean difference, when reporting the research finding, replace the word "finding" with the appropriate term being discussed. This is to state that the null hypothesis has been rejected and that the alternative hypothesis has been supported. When the opposite result occurs, then change the discussions accordingly.

In the case of mindfulness and race, at a 99.9% CI, 4 df, the calculated value (19.85) exceeded the critical value (18.46). In this case, H_o has been rejected and the H_a has been supported by concluding that health and well-being of racial groups is associated with the practice of mindfulness (χ^2 = 19.85, df = 4, p < .001). Note that the chi-square statistic by itself does not indicate the strength of the association. It indicates only whether the association occurred. In case the researchers still want to know the strength of the association, additional statistics are needed as discussed next. *The statistical notations inside the parenthesis are format and style conditions required by APA.*

TABLE 7.5 Critical Value of Chi-Square

	Level of Significance					
df	.20	.10	.05	.02	.01	.001
1	1.64	2.71	3.84	5.41	6.63	10.83
2	3.22	4.61	5.99	7.82	9.21	13.82
3	4.64	6.25	7.82	9.84	11.34	16.27

(Continued)

TABLE 7.5 (Continued)

	Level of Significance					
df	.20	.10	.05	.02	.01	.001
4	5.99	7.78	9.49	11.67	13.28	18.46
5	7.29	9.24	11.07	13.39	15.09	20.52
6	8.56	10.64	12.59	15.03	16.81	22.46
7	9.80	12.02	14.07	16.62	18.48	24.32
8	11.03	13.36	15.51	18.17	20.09	26.12
9	12.24	14.68	16.92	19.68	21.67	27.88
10	13.44	15.99	18.31	21.16	23.21	29.59
11	14.63	17.28	19.68	22.62	24.72	31.26
12	15.81	18.55	21.03	24.05	26.22	32.91
13	16.98	19.81	22.36	25.47	27.69	34.53
14	18.15	21.06	23.68	26.87	29.14	36.12
15	19.31	22.31	25.00	28.26	30.58	37.70
16	20.46	23.54	26.30	29.63	32.00	39.25
17	21.62	24.77	27.59	31.00	33.41	40.79
18	22.76	25.99	28.87	32.35	34.81	42.31
19	23.90	27.20	30.14	33.69	36.19	43.82
20	25.04	28.41	31.41	35.02	37.57	45.32
21	26.17	29.62	32.67	36.34	38.93	46.80
22	27.30	30.81	33.92	37.66	40.29	48.27
23	28.43	32.01	35.17	38.97	41.64	49.73
24	29.55	33.20	36.42	40.27	42.98	51.18
25	30.68	34.38	37.65	41.57	44.31	52.62

26	31.80	35.56	38.89	42.86	45.64	54.05
27	32.91	36.74	40.11	44.14	46.96	55.48
28	34.03	37.92	41.34	45.42	48.28	56.89
29	35.14	39.09	42.56	46.69	49.59	58.30
30	36.25	40.26	43.77	47.96	50.89	59.70

Adapted from Welkowitz, J., Cohen, B. H., & Lea B. R. (2012). Introductory statistics for the behavioral sciences (7th ed.). John Wiley & Sons.

Note About a 2 x 2 Study

This section highlights some common issues concerning studies that use only two columns and two rows for the nominal variables. A 2 x 2, also called *dichotomous study* is very common in social and behavioral sciences (Hays, 1994; Zeitlin & Auerbach, 2019). In situations like mental health treatment compliance, the therapist may ask both female and male clients for a yes or a no answer on the recommended type of intervention, child protective social workers may want to know whether parents want to reunite with their children, and clinical psychologists may want opinions from parents about whether Ritalin is helpful or hurtful to children with ADHD. Please also note that some statistics books state that when the observed frequencies for any cell are less than 5, the cell must be combined with other cells.

In any event, when the social workers and therapists use a "Yes and No" answer, a "Helpful and a Not Helpful," and responses from the same clients at two different periods of time, such research tends to have a very small sample size. For this reason, besides calculating the chi-square statistic, consider taking the following additional statistics to examine the strength of association between the variables.

MEASURING THE STRENGTH OF ASSOCIATION

The Phi (Φ)

One of the widely used measures of association with 2 × 2 tables is the Phi (Φ). Phi is used to examine how the calculated chi-square is proportional to the sample size (King et al., 2011; Mogull, 2004). The formula for Phi is

$$\text{Phi } (\Phi) = \sqrt{\frac{\chi^2}{n}}$$

Let's say that there are 15 parents who have lost parental rights to their children because of substantiated cases of physical abuse. The parents were asked by the county CPS and the county juvenile court in a survey questionnaire whether the court can make a unilateral decision about their children. The county juvenile court used a 99% CI to examine the result of the survey. Their responses are displayed in Table 7.6.

TABLE 7.6 Two-Parent Families Who Have Lost Parental Rights to Child in the District Juvenile Court

Willing to Work on Court-Mandated Requirements to Get Back the Children	Parents		
	Father	Mother	Total
Yes	7(a) 6.93	6(b) 6.07	13 (R_1)
No	1(d) 1.07	1(e) .93	2 (R_2)
Total	8 (C_1)	7 (C_2)	15 (N)

Follow the same procedures for calculating the expected frequencies as discussed in Table 7.3. The chi-square statistic can now be calculated as

$$\chi^2 = \Sigma \frac{(8-6.93)^2}{6.93} + \frac{(6-6.07)^2}{6.07} + \frac{(1-1.07)^2}{1.07} + \frac{(1-.93)^2}{.93}$$

$$\chi^2_{Calculated} = .17$$

At 1 df and a p value of .01, the critical value for chi-square is 6.63. The county DSS failed to support the research hypothesis. It has been concluded that the parents' and court's unilateral decisions are independent of each other.

To examine the strength of the hypothesis test, the Phi can now be calculated as

$$\text{Phi }(\Phi) = \sqrt{\frac{.17}{15}}$$

$$\text{Phi }(\Phi) = .106$$

The result for Phi is similar to the Pearson correlation coefficient to be discussed in Chapter 8. A perfect correlation is between −1.0 and +1.0 (±1.0). The closer the result of the calculated value gets to ±1.0, the stronger the relationship is. In this particular example, the result for Phi is quite far from ±1.0; therefore, the relationship is very weak. In turn, the association between parents that have lost parental rights and the juvenile court's unilateral decision is also extremely weak. The result essentially shows that for the sake of the child, the court must work closely with the parents, even after they have lost their parental rights.

The Cramer's V

Another measure of association is Cramer's V. Continuing on with the same case scenario, the formula for Cramer's V is

$$\text{Cramer's V} = \sqrt{\frac{\chi^2}{n(k-1)}}$$

where

K is used for the group.

N is the sample size.

The result for Kramer's V can now be calculated by

$$\text{Kramer's V} = \sqrt{\frac{.17}{15(2-1)}}$$

$$\text{Kramer's V} = .106$$

In this case, both Phi and Kramer's V produced the same results. The reason is that the court's unilateral decisions only provided a "Yes and No" answer option (two categories).

Two other tests on the strength of association are Lambda (l) and Gamma (g). Because of the length of the chapter, the formulas for Lambda and Gamma will not be shown. Instead, they will be shown later by using SPSS. Important note about Lambda and Gamma. Lambda is used to measure association known as proportional reduction error when one of the nominal variables is chosen as the DV and the other nominal variable is chosen as the IV (Zeitlin & Auerbach, 2019). Zeitlin and Auerbach add that Gamma is the preferred method of measuring the strength and direction of an ordinal variable arranged in a contingency table or with dichotomous nominal variables (p. 178).

Practice Example 2

A very large school district is interested in knowing more about the overprescription of Ritalin to treat children with ADHD. For this reason, they decided to send a survey to all current and previous parents whose children were prescribed Ritalin. The goal is to test the hypothesis (H_a) that Ritalin is not the only method to treat children with ADHD. If it is found that children's behaviors are dependent on Ritalin (H_a), then the school will want to increase the number of school social workers to provide counseling rather than depend solely on Ritalin. The school district is using a 99% CI, two-tailed hypothesis.

After the surveys were returned, a contingency table was constructed, as shown in Table 7.7.

TABLE 7.7 Parental Perceptions on the Effectiveness of Ritalin on ADHD Kids

Parental Perceptions	Parent's Racial Identity					
	Asian	African	Latino	White	Other	Total
Ritalin is absolutely effective	85 49.77	18 14.82	20 23.15	38 62.27	25 36	186
Ritalin is somewhat effective	105 89.1	25 26.52	30 41.44	121 111.48	52 64.44	333
Alternative methods such as counseling are highly recommended	240 291.13	85 86.66	150 135.41	379 364.25	234 210.56	1088
Total	430	128	200	538	311	1,607

$$\chi^2 = \sum \frac{(85-49.77)^2}{49.77} + \frac{(18-14.82)^2}{14.82} + \frac{(20-23.15)^2}{23.15} + \frac{(38-62.27)^2}{62.27} + \frac{(25-36)^2}{36} +$$

$$\frac{(105-89.1)^2}{89.1} + \frac{(25-26.52)^2}{26.52} + \frac{(30-41.44)^2}{41.44} + \frac{(121-111.48)^2}{111.48} + \frac{(52-64.44)^2}{64.44} +$$

$$\frac{(240-291.13)^2}{291.13} + \frac{(85-86.66)^2}{86.66} + \frac{(150-135.41)^2}{135.41} + \frac{(379-364.25)^2}{364.25} + \frac{(234-210.56)^2}{210.56}$$

$$\chi^2 = 61.96$$

The degrees of freedom can be calculated by

$$df = (5-1)(3-1),$$

$$df = 8.$$

At 8 df and a p value of .01, the critical value for chi-square is equal to 20.09.
The calculated chi-square ($\chi^2_{Calculated}$ = 61.96) is much larger than the critical value ($\chi^2_{Critical}$ = 20.09), thus the null hypothesis is rejected. The finding shows that parent participants do not want children who are diagnosed with ADHD to be solely dependent on Ritalin; in turn, the school district needs to find an alternative method of intervention (χ^2 = 61.96, df = 8, p < .01). In fact, 67.7% (1088/1607 = .677) of the research subjects stated the alternative methods.

USING SPSS TO COMPUTE CHI-SQUARE

The functionalities of statistical applications like SPSS make it very simple to do the crosstab and compute the chi-square hypothesis test. To calculate the crosstab and chi-square for the data file for the variable "Gender" and "Current class standing" for Table 3.1, simply follow these steps:

First, pull down the *Analyze* ribbon, move the cursor to *Descriptive Statistics,* and then choose *Crosstabs* (see the following image). If it is a nonparametric statistic, move the cursor further down to *Nonparametric Tests*, and on *Legacy Dialogs*, choose *Chi-Square*. Please note that this book is not about nonparametric statistics.

- Some users select *Column* to display the DV and *Row* for the IV and vice versa. In case a category is chosen as the DV, please state it clearly. *Again, please note that chi-square is almost always a non-directional hypothesis test.* Also, note that chi-square is a bivariate analysis, so select one variable for *Row* and one for *Column*.

- To continue the practice from Table 3.1, select the variable "*Gender*" for *Column(s)* and "*Class*" for *Row(s)*.

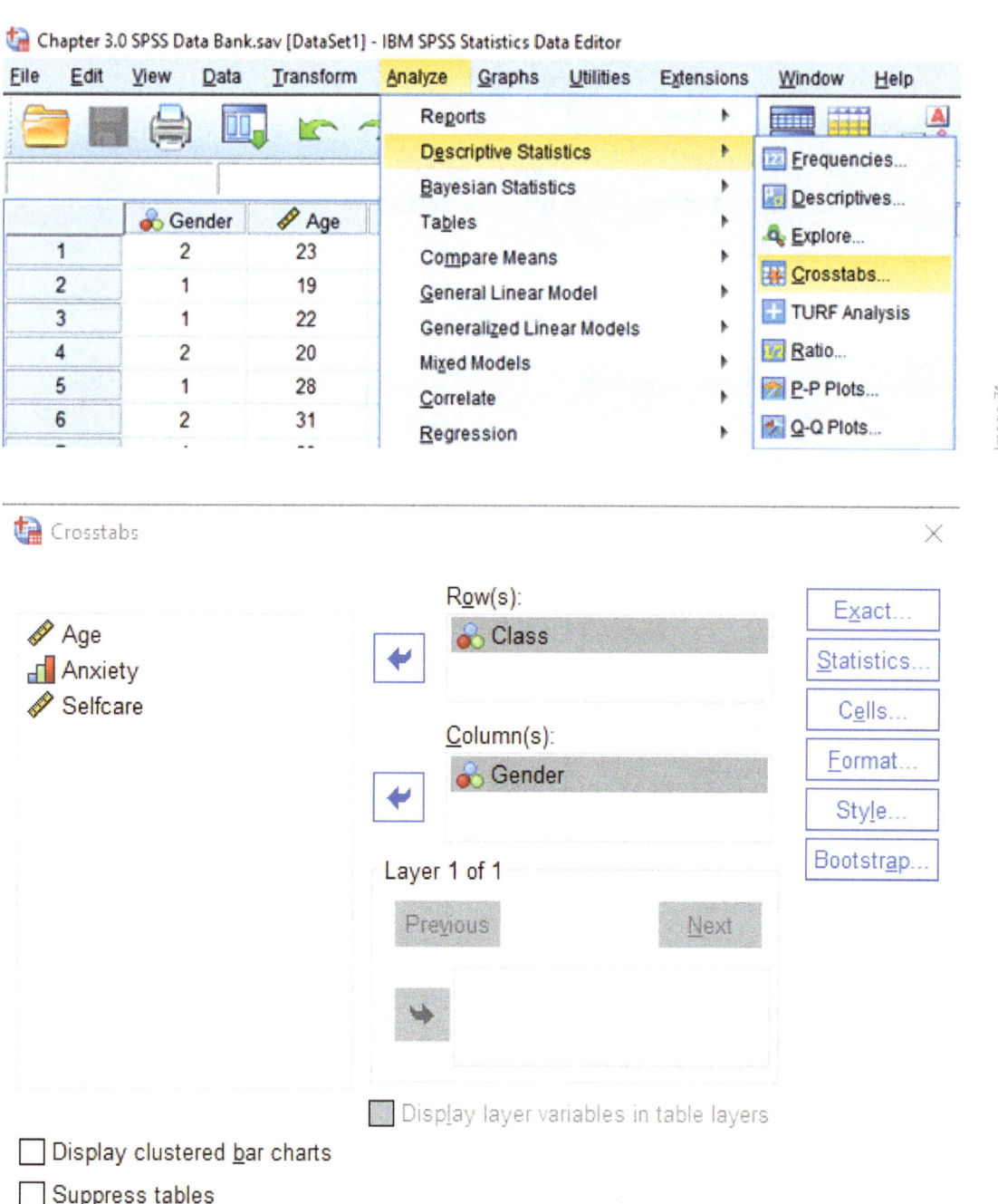

- Next, click *Statistics*, check *Chi-Square, Phi and Cramer's V, Lambda, and Gamma*. Then click *Continue* to exit.

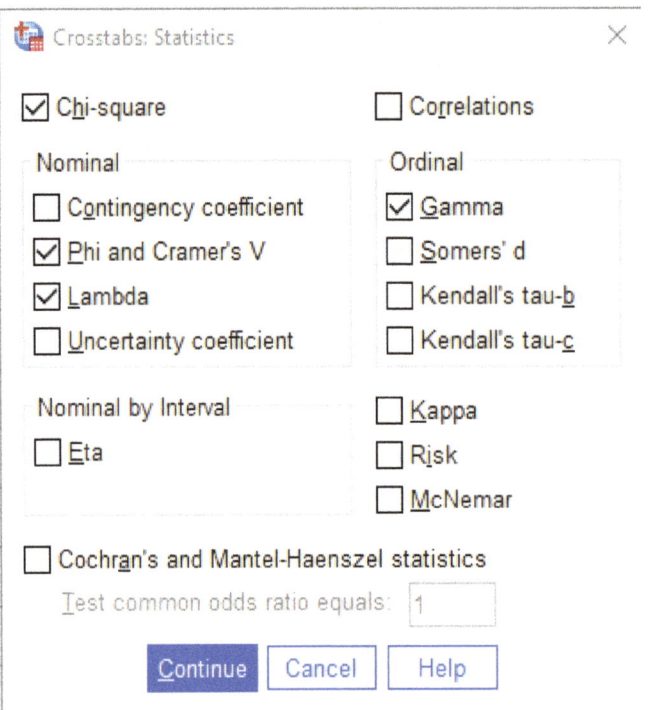

Image 7.3

- To get the *Expected Frequencies* and *Total Percentages* for the output table, click *Cells* and then select them as shown in the following image. Click *Continue* to exit. Note that the *Observed Frequencies* have already been preset by SPSS.

- Click *OK* and momentarily, the information shown in Tables 7.8a and 7.8b will appear.

- *For an actual research report, the user must include both Tables 7.8(a) and 7.8(b) with the report. Table 7.8(c) and 7.8(d) are not necessary.* Without the two former tables, even statisticians will be at a loss to explain the findings.

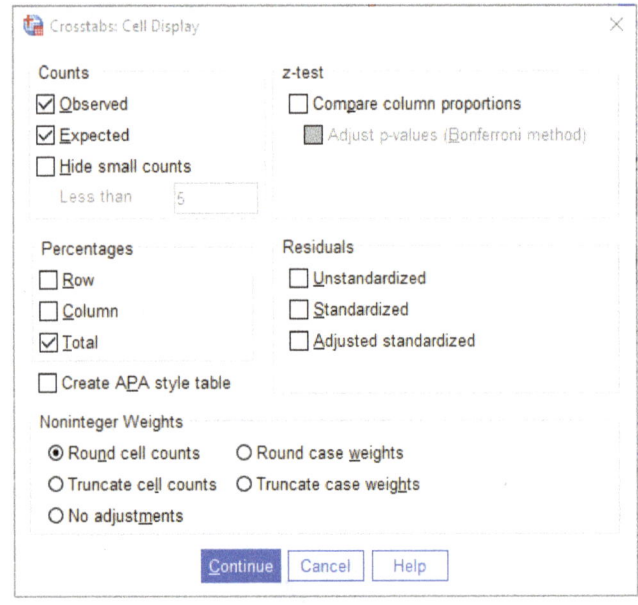

Image 7.4

TABLE 7.8(A) Students' Class Level * Gender of Respondent Cross-Tabulation

			Gender of Respondent		Total
			Female	Male	
The students' class level	Freshman	Count	1	1	2
		Expected Count	.9	1.1	2.0
		% of Total	6.7%	6.7%	13.3%
	Sophomore	Count	0	1	1
		Expected Count	.5	.5	1.0
		% of Total	0.0%	6.7%	6.7%
	Junior	Count	4	0	4
		Expected Count	1.9	2.1	4.0
		% of Total	26.7%	0.0%	26.7%
	Senior	Count	2	6	8
		Expected Count	3.7	4.3	8.0
		% of Total	13.3%	40.0%	53.3%
Total		Count	7	8	15
		Expected Count	7.0	8.0	15.0

TABLE 7.8(B) Chi-Square Tests

	Value	df	Asymptotic Significance (2-sided)
Pearson Chi-Square	6.964a	3	.073
Likelihood Ratio	8.958	3	.030
Linear-by-Linear Association	.448	1	.503

Table 7.8(a) shows the observed (*count*), expected frequencies (*expected count*), and the corresponding percentages *(% of total cell)* for each of the cells. *Table 7.8(b) is the result for the hypothesis test and*

its result is generalizable to the population from which the sample was drawn. The row labeled "Pearson Chi-Square" is what the researcher must report. The "*Value*" is the calculated chi-square, *df* is the degrees of freedom, and *asymptotic significance* is the p value. *Asymptotic is symmetrical of the variable.* In Chapter 6, it was stated that when *"Significance" or "Sig."* falls between .000 and .05, accept that there is a statistical significance. For any p value that is larger than .05, most social and behavioral scientists, like social workers and psychologists, automatically retain the H_0 or state that the researchers have failed to reject the null hypothesis.

TABLE 7.8(C)   **Measures on Strength of Association**

		Value	Asymptotic Standard Error[a]	Approximate T[b]	Approximate Significance
Nominal by Lambda	Symmetric	.429	.243	1.430	.153
Nominal	The students' class level Dependent	.286	.296	.835	.404
	Gender of respondent Dependent	.571	.229	1.801	.072
	Gender of respondent Dependent	.464	.152		.090c

TABLE 7.8(D)   **Symmetric Measures**

		Value	Asymptotic Standard Error[a]	Approximate T[b]	Approximate Significance
Nominal by Nominal	Phi	.681			.073
	Cramer's V	.681			.073
Ordinal by Ordinal	Gamma	.442	.345	1.237	.216
N of Valid Cases		15			

Tables 7.8(c) and (d) show the Lambda, Phi, and Gamma values. Take a look at the last column in Table 7.8(d). SPSS calculated the probability of committing a Type I error that is larger than the acceptable p value of .000 to .05. Because of this, the null hypothesis is retained.

In this case, the null hypothesis for the association between gender and the respondents' class standing is retained ($\chi^2 = 6.964$, df = 3, $p > .073$). By using Phi and Kramer's V alone, the strength of the association still shows a weak relationship (F = .681, $p > .073$). The research study outcome failed to support the alternative hypothesis.

In an opposite scenario, Table 7.9 shows a hypothetical result for the Pearson chi-square to indicate that the alternative hypothesis is supported. How does one know it? Because the p value given by SPSS is .000.

TABLE 7.9 Sample Chi-Square Tests When the Alternative Hypothesis Is Supported

	Value	df	Asymptotic Significance (Two-Sided)
Pearson Chi-Square	248.340	6	.000
Likelihood Ratio	270.959	86	.000
Linear-by-Linear Association	12.446	1	.000
N of Valid Cases	1,408		

SUMMARY

This chapter shows how to calculate the first inferential statistic, the Pearson chi-square independence test. Calculating the chi-square test of independence is simple and straightforward. The following steps are helpful:

1. Either manually or electronically, create a contingency table. Give a label such as 1, 2, 3 to each of the cells. The number 1 is for cell 1, 2 for the second cell, and 3 for the third cell.
2. Calculate the corresponding percentages for each of the cells.
3. Calculate the expected frequencies for the contingency table.
4. Calculate the chi-square (χ^2) statistic.
5. Calculate the degrees of freedom for the situation under investigation. Pay attention to the total columns and rows.
6. Interpret the chi-square statistic by comparing the result of the calculation with the numbers found from a standardized table such as Table 7.5. When using a computer application, find the p value provided by the program, as instructed in the Chapter 6 section, "Interpreting the Results of Statistical Tests."

The chi-square also shows that even in nominal variables, the Phi and Kramer's V can be used to examine the strength of the association or interrelation between the variables. It is also demonstrated that SPSS can easily be used to compute the chi-square. Chapter 8 will introduce correlation analysis.

Study Questions

Multiple Choice. The following study questions can be really helpful to statistics learners who want to know more about the application of the chi-square statistic.

The first several questions focus on this statement: Suppose that in past years, one observed that mental health clients who received mental health treatments, such as medication or individual and group counseling, significantly improved in how they felt about themselves. Because of this observation, a person wanted to test a hypothesis focusing on gender and treatment types to see if there was any association between the variables. Among the 3,000 clients, 750 females stated having received only medication, and 1,250 females indicated getting both medication and counseling. Of those who identified as male, 480 received only medication, while 520 received medication and counseling. The research is based on a 99.9% confidence interval, two-tailed hypothesis.

1. The scores 750, 1,250, 480, and 520 in this contingency table are called
    a. raw scores.
    b. observed frequencies.
    c. expected frequencies.
    d. unknown frequencies.

2. The variables "Medication Only" and "Medication and Counseling" are based on what level of measurement?
    a. Nominal
    b. Ordinal
    c. Interval
    d. Ratio

3. Assume that gender is displayed as columns and treatment type is designated for rows. The summation for medication only is called
    a. column scores.
    b. grand columns.
    c. column summation.
    d. marginal columns total.

4. The reason the expected frequencies are needed for the chi-square statistic is because
    a. they are needed to understand the total scores obtained from the research project.
    b. they are needed to understand the distributive scores for each cell.
    c. they are the scores expected for each of the cells in a cross-tabulation table.
    d. they are the unexpected scores for each of the cells in a cross-tabulation table.

5. Out of the total number of clients, the proportion of the male respondents who received medications and counseling is

   a. 16%.
   b. 33%.
   c. 41.7%.
   d. 17.3%.

6. The degree of freedom (df) for the statistical analysis is

   a. 3.
   b. 2.
   c. 1.

7. The expected frequencies for the females who received only medication is

   a. 750.
   b. 1,230.
   c. 410.
   d. 820.

8. The chi-square test of association for the scenario is

   a. unable to determined.
   b. 5.98.
   c. 11.95.
   d. 30.38.
   e. 8.31.

9. What would you say about the result of the hypothesis test? Would you say

   a. that treatment type is independent of gender?
   b. that treatment type and gender are significantly dependent on each other?
   c. that the study is inconclusive?

10. What would you say about the H_0? Would you say

    a. it is retained?
    b. it is rejected?
    c. it is either retained or rejected as long as the explanation is understandable?

11. What is the acceptable way to display the statistical notations for the research project as required by APA?

    a. ($\chi^2 = 30.39$, $df = 1$, $p < .001$)
    b. ($\chi^2 = 30.39$, $df = 1$, $p > .001$)
    c. ($\chi^2 = 30.39$, $p < .001$)
    d. ($\chi = 30.39$, $p > .001$)

12. Under what statistical assumption should the chi-square test of independence not be used?

    a. In a 2 × 2, at least one cell has an expected frequency of more than 5.
    b. In a 2 × 2, at least one cell has an expected frequency of less than 5.
    c. In a table that is larger than 2 × 2, more than 20% of the observed cells have an expected frequency of less than 5.

13. Suppose that you are given $\chi^2 = 12.59$, $df = 10$, $p > .08$. Even not knowing how the results were calculated, you can easily state that

    a. the null hypothesis is retained.
    b. the alternative hypothesis is retained.
    c. there is insufficient information.

14. In Question 13, what would you say about how the degrees of freedom were calculated? They were calculated based on

    a. 2 × 5 or 5 × 2.
    b. 2 × 6 or 6 × 2.
    c. 3 × 6 or 6 × 3.

15. Which of the following statistical assumptions is correct about cross-tabulation?

    a. It is used to examine the relationship between interval- and ratio-level data.
    b. It is used to examine the relationship between ordinal-level data.
    c. It is used to examine the association between nominal-level data.
    d. It is used to examine the frequency distribution between the variables.

16. If you are given a chi-square of 3.16 with a sample size of 19, what is the value of Phi?

    a. 40.78
    b. 4.078
    c. .4078
    d. .0407

Answers to Study Questions

QUESTION	ANSWER	QUESTION	ANSWER
1	b	9	b
2	a	10	b
3	d	11	a
4	c	12	a
5	d	13	a
6	c	14	c
7	d	15	c
8	d	16	c

CHAPTER 8

Inferential Statistics

Correlation

OVERVIEW

Similar to Chapter 7, this chapter involves bivariate analysis that is particularly on correlation for interval and ratio data (variables). Knowledge of advanced data manipulation, which is not the subject of this book, is necessary to test hypotheses with nominal and ordinal data using correlation.

INTRODUCTION TO CORRELATION

What Is Correlation?

In academic arenas, such as social work and health services, correlation is commonly used to study numerical statements about the relationship between two interval and ratio variables that are classified as continuous variables. More specifically, in professional settings, such as social work and nursing, correlation is applied to two continuous variables. For example, social work professors may talk about the relationship between years spent in college and the probability of their future wage earnings. County social workers may talk about the relationship between knowledge of domestic violence and the probability of spousal abuse. Nurses may talk about the amount of junk food that children consume per week and the risk of child obesity.

The key focus for correlation is examining the strengths and variations of the relationship between two interval- or ratio-level variables (Aron et al., 2011; Freeman et al., 1978; Montcalm & Royse, 2002). More specifically, correlation is used to examine the statistical significance of randomized interval and ratio variables. When two variables are correlated (from this point in the chapter, the plural "variables" refer to the relationship between a DV and another DV, a DV and an IV, or an IV and another IV), the Pearson correlation coefficient (Pearson r) is used.

The Pearson correlation is commonly represented by the lowercase letter r, and it is called the Pearson correlation coefficient or just Pearson's r. As cited by King et al. (2011), in 1896, Karl Pearson developed the correlation formula by studying the relationship between the height of parents and their offspring. The Pearson r is also called the linear or product-moment correlation coefficient.

The manual calculation to be discussed later includes two formulas. Formula 8.0 shows the Pearson product-moment correlation coefficient when "normality is not assumed." Formula 8.1 shows the Pearson correlation when "normality is assumed." For the SPSS illustrations, it illustrates Pearson's r, Kendall's tau b, Spearman's rho, and the meaning of "controlling variable" by using partial correlation. *Normality* means that the researchers should try to make sure that the data set is normally distributed to the left and right sides of $\bar{x}$ inside the bell curve before completing certain statistical tests, such as correlation, regression, and t-tests.

When the values between two interval or ratio variables are accurately displayed on a graph, assuming that there is no variability, the data set will produce a graph with a straight line. Sometimes, however, the general relationship between two variables does not follow a straight line, so it is called a *curvilinear correlation*. Table 8.1 depicts the normal distribution of the variable years spent in college and the probability of an hourly wage among 30 research subjects.

TABLE 8.1 Relationship Between Years Spent in College and Hourly Wage

ID	Years Spent in College (X)	Hourly Wage (Y)
1	12	15
2	16	20
3	18	32
4	21	60
5	14	17
6	18	35
7	20	62
8	21	65
9	18	35
10	19	30
11	12	14
12	14	18
13	18	40

14	16	25
15	21	72
16	12	14
17	13	17
18	16	26
19	18	38
20	21	55
21	13	15
22	16	29
23	18	35
24	21	56
25	12	14
26	16	33
27	15	30
28	18	38
29	18	42
30	21	55

Graphical Display of Direction of Correlation

How does one know that Pearson's r is positive or negative? When the values of interval/ratio variables move in the same direction (either increase or decrease together), the result is a *positive correlation coefficient (r = +)*. A *negative* or *inverse correlation coefficient (r = −)* means that as the values of one variable (i.e., IV) decrease, the values of the other variable (i.e., DV) increase, or vice versa. In short, the values of the variables under investigation go in opposite directions (see Figures 8.1(a) and (b)).

In a scatterplot—when there is a DV and an IV—the DV is normally displayed on the ordinate (the vertical or y-axis), and the IV is displayed on the abscissa (the horizontal or x-axis). This facilitates a visual determination regarding whether a plausible relationship exists between the two variables or whether to make predictions about the possible effect the IV has on the DV. When the two variables are displayed in this way, *the DV is better conceptualized as the criterion variable and the IV as the predictor variable*. Why is the IV classified as the predictor variable? Because in a real research study, the

PI wants to examine how the IV either affected or influenced the issue under investigation (called the outcome or DV in statistics).

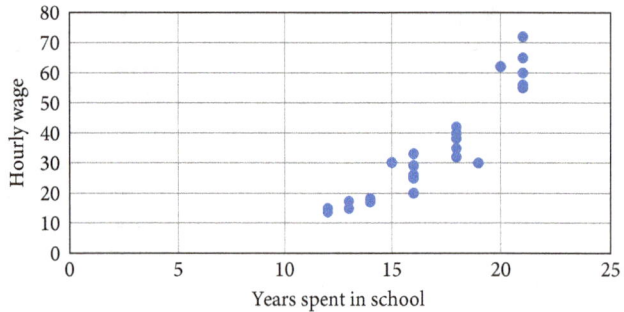

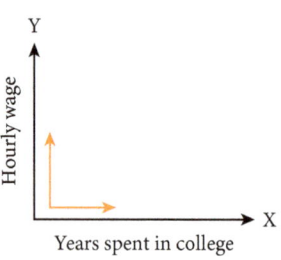

FIGURE 8.1(A) Sample Scatterplot With Positive Correlation for Table 8.1

FIGURE 8.1(B) Diagram Depicting Positive Correlation

Figure 8.1(a) depicts a positive correlation coefficient with an interpolation line. The interpolation line is pointing upward at a 45° angle. *When the interpolation line is pointing upward or somewhat upward, one should already know that the result for the Pearson correlation coefficient will be positive (r = +).* Another visualization is depicted in Figure 8.1(b). Notice that in positive correlation, the values of the variables move in the same direction. For example, when the value for the y-axis is pointing upward or downward, the values for the x-axis are also pointing outward or inward.

Figure 8.2(a) depicts a negative correlation with an interpolation line pointing downward toward the x-axis—indicating that the more knowledge on domestic violence, the less likely domestic violence will occur. Pearson's r will be negative (r = −). The diagram in Figure 8.2(b) shows that the values of the variables point in the opposite direction. For example, when the values for the y-axis increase, the values for the x-axis decrease and vice versa.

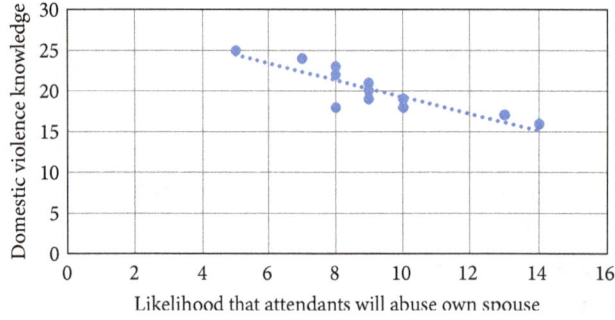

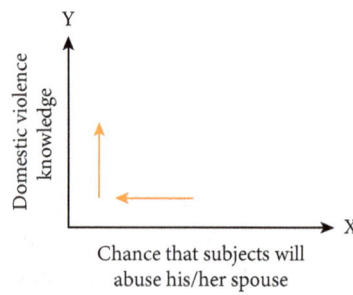

FIGURE 8.2(A) Scatterplot Depicting a Negative Correlation

FIGURE 8.2(B) Depicting Negative Correlation

Figure 8.3(a) displays the hypothetical variable *"Gross monthly salary"* and *"Percent of client below poverty level."* When the interpolation line is flat or almost flat like this, do not complete the Pearson correlation coefficient (r = *very close to 0*). Figure 8.3(b) shows the diagram in which the direction for the correlation coefficient is close to zero or unknown. *Notice that the arrows inside the y- and x-axis do not point in any direction.*

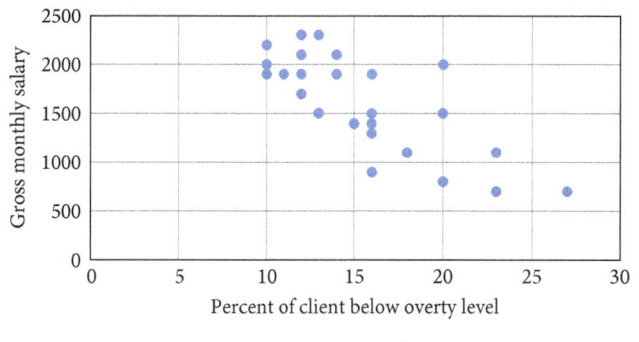

FIGURE 8.3(A)   Scatterplot Depicting a No (Zero) Correlation

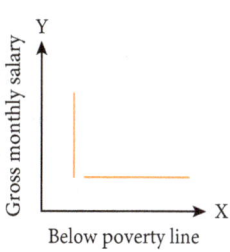

FIGURE 8.3(B)   Diagram Depicting No Correlation

Is a Positive, Negative, or Zero Correlation a Better Coefficient?

One may ask, "Is a *positive, negative, or no correlation* better?" The correct answer really depends on the research interest and the social behavior under investigation.

When empirically studying human behavior in the social environment, the purpose may be to obtain a positive correlation. Another study may wish for a negative or zero correlation. King et al. (2011) state that a positive or negative correlation is used only to indicate the direction of the correlation, not its degree of severity. The calculated Pearson correlation coefficient (Pearson's r) is never used to explain that a positive correlation is better than a negative correlation or vice versa.

Certainly, in situations like equal work with equal pay—regardless of race or gender—the strongest desired in American society is a zero or a near-zero correlation. In other situations, like the relationship in the amount of chemical dependency and level of personal functioning or the relationship between depression score and doses of antidepressant, the desired outcome is a strong negative correlation. For example, when people use fewer illegal drugs or less alcohol (values of the IV decrease), they are more likely to spend quality time with their loved ones (values of the DV increase). If this occurs, the values of the IV decrease and family relationships (outcome) become stronger. Therefore, a negative correlation is more desirable to the researchers and practitioners. Of course, results like this could be important in evidence-based practice.

In some research studies, such as the relationship between income and years spent in college or depression score and lower doses of antidepressants, a strong positive correlation is preferred. Take the latter for example. Clinical social workers anticipate seeing lower depression scores or depression scores drop (DV) so that they can ask the psychiatrist to reduce or lower the doses (IV) of antidepressant drugs their clients take. Another strong expectation for evidence-based practice.

Value of the Pearson Correlation Coefficient (Pearson's)

Regardless of the sample size, whether a research project has 52 or 50,002 subjects, the result of the statistical computation will always produce a correlation coefficient ranging from –1.00 to +1.00 (Hays,

1994; Trochin, 2020). *The value of –1.00 represents a perfect negative correlation, while a value of +1.00 represents a perfect positive correlation. With the perfect correlation, there is no variation in the variables. A value of 0.00 represents a complete lack of (zero) correlation.* When completed, the correlation coefficient for the data set depicted in Figures 8.3(a) and (b) will be very close to 0.

A correlation coefficient that gets closer to either end of –1.00 and +1.00 indicates a stronger relationship. For example, when examining the relationship between the self-esteem of youth and their antisocial behaviors, a negative correlation coefficient of –0.467 is observed. Seeing this coefficient, people that know statistics already have the hunch that the null hypothesis may be rejected. Why? Because every statistician knows that based on the sample size, the researchers are trying to get their calculated value much closer to the ±1.0.

The Strength of the Correlation Coefficient Range

When the scatterplot displays a straight horizontal interpolation line, then it is just a matter of explaining that there is no correlation between the variables. *However, when this is not the case, how does one use terms such as weak, moderate, strong, and very (extremely) strong relationship or correlation?* What range of the calculated correlation coefficient (r_{cal}) must exist to support the use of such terminology? Because there is no consensus among statisticians, explaining the result is up to the researchers. The following are some suggested guidelines (Lee et al., 2016; Weinbach & Grinnell, 2015):

1. Use the calculated Pearson correlation coefficient as determinants.
    - When the calculated correlation coefficient (r_{cal}) is .89 or larger, use "extremely" strong relationship between the variables.
    - When r_{cal} is between .70 to .88, use "very strong" relationship between the variables.
    - When r_{cal} is between .60 to .69, use "there is a moderate" relationship between the variables.
    - When r_{cal} is between .50 to .59, use "a significant" relationship between the variables.
    - When r_{cal} is between .30 to .49, use "weak" relationship between the variables.
    - When r_{cal} is .30 or less, state that "there is no relationship between the variables."
2. The suggested ranges in #1 sound interesting, but that is not always the case, especially in large sample sizes. The calculated Pearson correlation coefficient could be very small, say .25. Situations like this happen more often than not. For such situations, use the p value produced by the software application. Keep in mind that as the p value decreases (CI increases), the chance of random error decreases. For example, a p value of .001 (CI = 99.9%) is stronger than .01 (CI = 99%). As a result, when the p value becomes larger, then chances of rejecting H_o become stronger. In turn, with a study project that has 100 or more participants, if the computer program gives a p value of .000 and a correlation coefficient of .25, one can certainly state that "there is a very strong" relationship between the variables, in contrast to a p value of .05. For the p value of .05, one could just say that "there is" a significant difference between the variables.
3. Always factor the sample size into findings. When the sample size *n* is small, a larger coefficient is needed to reject H_o. Table 8.6 shows that as the sample size (N) increases, the correlation

coefficient becomes smaller. Therefore, for a research project that has 100 or more participants, a much smaller correlation coefficient is needed to reject the null hypothesis. Be mindful that even if the null hypothesis can be rejected with a very small coefficient, the relationship between the variables may not be strong. Why? Because there is too much variability between the values of the variables (see coefficient of determination later in the chapter).

CORRELATION IS NOT CAUSATION

Before calculating Pearson's r, it is of utmost importance to be aware that correlation is not used to examine or establish cause. Among statisticians, Weinbach and Grinnell (2015) state that the correlation coefficient cannot reveal whether the values of the criterion outcome (DV) variable have been caused by the values of the predictor (IV) variable. Weinbach and Grinnell further state that *Pearson's r reveals only the pattern of a relationship and variations in the predictor variable, which is beyond the researchers' control.* Essentially, variations are observed after the fact. Thus, any interpretation of correlation that implies causation is incorrect, so the result of a correlation coefficient is never acceptable as proof of causality.

Another important note about correlation is that when only two variables are being examined at a time, it is highly likely that other variables may also have an effect. This is often referred to as *spurious association* (Agresti & Finlay, 2009). For instance, excessive drinking tends to lead to depression. Long-term alcohol dependency often leads to the development of depressive syndromes, but the syndromes can be developed by many other stress-producing factors, such as genetics, financial crisis, and relationship issues.

Lastly, even though the variations are always observed after the fact, the number of variations observed can be used to make a prediction about the effects they have on the criterion (DV) variable. This prediction is further discussed in Chapter 10 on regression.

USEFULNESS OF CORRELATION IN SOCIAL WORK AND BEHAVIORAL SETTINGS

Either intentionally or unintentionally, correlations are frequently used by people in social work and behavioral sciences. For example, at CPS, social workers may want to know the relationship between parental styles and risk factors toward child maltreatment. School psychologists may want to investigate the relationship between child delinquency and street gangs in a particular region of the country.

A correlation study examining these two particular topics may provide sufficient information about (a) the strength of parental styles and risk toward child maltreatment and (b) child delinquency and street gangs. While in school, college students—such as those in social work, nursing, and psychology—can use correlation to examine various curriculum issues pertaining to their college education. Possible topics for student researchers could include one or more of the following:

- The relationship between study hours and GPA.
- The relationship between enrollment units per term and time spent to obtain a diploma or degree.
- The rigor of an academic program and perceived student appreciation of programs and their respective professors.

FORMULA FOR CALCULATING THE CORRELATION COEFFICIENT

The computational formula for the Pearson correlation coefficient is found in Formulas 8.1 and 8.2. For the manual calculations, this book shows the product-moment correlation coefficient in Formula 8.1 and the Pearson correlation coefficient when normality is assumed in Formula 8.2. They both produced nearly identical results. As stated in the overview, the SPSS illustrations show the product-moment correlation coefficient, Kendal's tau, Spearman's rho, and partial correlation. The product-moment correlation coefficient is also known as the computational formula—which can be produced by any statistical software program—meaning that either by hand or technology, the same result is produced Hays, 1994; Meyers et al., 2006).

Formula 8.1

Pearson's Product-Moment Correlation Coefficient (Pearson's r) When Normality Is Not Assumed

$$r_{xy} = \frac{N\left(\sum XY\right) - \left(\sum X\right)\left(\sum Y\right)}{\sqrt{\left[N\sum X^2 - \left(\sum X\right)^2\right]\left[N\sum Y^2 - \left(\sum Y\right)^2\right]}}$$

$\sum X$ = The summation of the X column
$\sum Y$ = The summation of the Y column
$\sum X^2$ = The sum of the square of X
$\sum Y^2$ = The sum of the square of Y
$\left(\sum X\right)^2$ = Squaring the sum of the scores of X
$\left(\sum Y\right)^2$ = Squaring the sum of the scores of Y

where

r_{xy} = The correlation coefficient (Pearson's r),
N = Sample size, and
$\sum XY$ = The sum of the product of X and Y

Formula 8.2

Pearson Correlation Coefficient (Pearson's r) When Normality Is Assumed

Unbiased Formula:

$$r_{xy} = \frac{\frac{1}{N-1}(\sum XY - N(\bar{X})(\bar{Y}))}{(SD_x)(SD_y)}$$

N = Sample size
$\sum XY$ = The sum of the product of X and Y
$(\bar{X})$ = The mean for column X
$(\bar{Y})$ = The mean for column Y
SD_x = Standard deviation for column X
SD_y = Standard deviation for column Y

where

- the numerator measures the covariance of the variables,

- the denominator measures the product of the standard deviations, and

r_{xy} = Pearson's r for unbiased calculation.

Practice Example 1

Table 8.1 displays a hypothetical data set depicting hourly wage as the DV (criterion) variable and years spent in college as the IV (predictor) variable. *The goal is to achieve two major objectives: (a) find a relationship between the criterion and predictor variables and (b) discover how much of the variance in the criterion variable could be explained by the predictor variable.* To achieve the objectives, let us assume that a research study uses a two-tailed test with a 99% CI. The hypotheses can be stated as follows:

H_o = There is no relationship between hourly wage and years spent in college.

H_a = There is a significant relationship between hourly wage and years spent in college.

By glancing at the Pearson's r formula, the original scores in Table 8.1 can now be expanded as in Table 8.2.

The *product-moment correlation coefficient (Pearson's r)* can be completed as follows:

$$r_{xy} = \frac{30(18,911) - (506)(1037)}{\sqrt{[30(8,810) - (506)^2][30(44,361) - (1037)^2]}}$$

$$r_{xy} = \frac{567,330 - 524,722}{\sqrt{[264,300 - 256,036][1,330,830 - 1,075,369]}}$$

$$r_{xy} = \frac{42,608}{\sqrt{(8,264)(255,461)}}$$

$$r_{xy} = \frac{42,608}{\sqrt{2,111,129,704}}$$

r_{xy} = .927 (This is the calculated correlation coefficient or $[r_{calculated}]$).

TABLE 8.2 Expanding Table 8.1 Into Segments for the Pearson's r Calculation

ID	X	X²	Y	Y²	XY
01	12	144	15	225	180
02	16	256	20	400	320
03	18	324	32	1,024	576
04	21	441	60	3,600	1,260
05	14	196	17	289	238
06	18	324	35	1,225	630
07	20	400	62	3,844	1,240
08	21	441	65	4,225	1,365
09	18	324	35	1,225	630
10	19	361	30	900	570
11	12	122	14	196	168
12	14	196	18	324	252
13	18	324	40	1,600	720
14	16	256	25	625	400
15	21	441	72	5,184	1,512
16	12	144	14	196	168
17	13	169	17	289	221
18	16	256	26	676	416
19	18	324	38	1,444	684
20	21	441	55	3,025	1,155
21	13	169	15	225	195
22	16	256	29	841	464
23	18	324	35	1,225	630

24	21	441	56	3,136	1,176
25	12	144	14	196	168
26	16	256	33	1,089	528
27	15	225	30	900	450
28	18	324	38	1,444	684
29	18	324	42	1,764	756
30	21	441	55	3,025	1,155
N = 30	$\Sigma X = 506$	$\Sigma X^2 = 8,810$	$\Sigma Y = 1037$	$\Sigma Y^2 = 44,361$	$\Sigma XY = 18,911$
	$\bar{X} = 16.87$		$\bar{Y} = 34.57$		
	Variance = 9.499		Variance = 293.633		
	$SD_x = 3.082$		$SD_y = 17.136$		

Note. *The symbols can be arranged in any order. Keep it clear that Y is used for the DV.*

The result for Pearson's r is quite strong. It is very close to a perfect correlation of 1.0. However, at this point, one still cannot state whether the null hypothesis or the alternative hypothesis has been supported. In order to conclude the result, one still needs to get the critical value of r ($r_{critical}$). At the self-selected CI stated previously for a two-tailed hypothesis, the critical value of r can be found by using Table 8.3. With a sample size of 30 (N = 30) and a two-tailed hypothesis at a 99% CI (p value = .01), the critical value is .449. Please note that some statistics books used four decimal places, while this book and others use three decimal places. The reason for this is that currently, SPSS and some other software applications only display three digits for Pearson's r.

First, notice that the calculated value of .927 (r_{cal}) is larger than the critical values (r_{crit}) of .449. Next, use the statistical rule discussed in Chapter 6 (see the section "Interpreting Results of Statistical Tests"), which stated that when calculating quantitative data by hand, the calculated value must be compared with the critical value based on the self-selected tail of the hypothesis and the p value; otherwise, there is no possible way to tell whether to retain or reject H_o. *If the calculated value is larger than the critical value, state that there is a significant finding.*

Therefore, in the case of an hourly wage, it is safe to conclude that based on a 99% CI and two-tailed hypothesis, there was a very strong correlation between the variables (r = .927, p < .01). The symbols inside the parenthesis are the statistical notations required by the APA and other publication outlets.

WHAT IS THE COEFFICIENT OF DETERMINATION (r^2)?

The correlation coefficient (Pearson's r) represents the strength and variation of the relationship between two continuous variables. In Chapter 4, the concept of variability was introduced, mainly focusing on the variance. For a single variable, *the variance* or *sum of squares* is used to calculate the standardized unit of measurement, which is the SD.

However, when two variables are correlated, what is the role of the SS^2 in this situation? Essentially, what is the role of the *sum of squares* in this situation? *When the correlation coefficient is squared* (r^2) *(in SPSS, see R-squared) and then multiplied by 100%, the product becomes known as the coefficient of determination*. This transformation to the r^2 represents *the proportion of SS^2 in the DV that is explained by the IV.* The r^2 is also called the *"strength"* or *"magnitude"* of the research outcome. When reporting results from the correlation analysis, it is important that the r^2 be taken into consideration. With all this background knowledge, the Pearson correlation coefficient can now be calculated.

USING r^2 TO DETERMINE VARIATION

The result indicates that there is a very strong correlation between hourly wage and years spent in college, but the amount of variation among the values of the variables is unknown. *More specifically, the amount of variation in the DV that can be explained by the IV is unknown*—that is, the number of years spent in college that actually contributed to wage earning. The *coefficient of determination*, which is squaring *r* and then multiplying the result by 100%, was discussed earlier (Monette et al., 2005; Rubin, 2013; Zeitlin & Auerbach, 2019).

In Practice Example 1, if the calculated correlation coefficient is squared and multiplied by 100% [$(.927)^2(100\%)$], the result is 85.93%. *Based on this transformation, it can be stated that years spent in college explained 85.93% of people's hourly wage. However, the other 14.07% (100 − 75.43 = 14.07) of the factors affecting hourly wage cannot be explained.* The remaining factors may be due to environmental factors, such as geographical location, being new employees, and so forth.

Note that even in this scenario, where years spent in college were purportedly predicted as having a very strong relationship to hourly wage, a great amount of the variation is still unaccounted for. Suppose that a different variable was computed, and the correlation coefficient equated to .300 (r_{cal} = .300), then the IV can only explain 9% of the variation. The other 91% of the variation was not accounted for. *This is why r^2 is also called the magnitude for Pearson's r.*

TABLE 8.3 Critical Value of *r*

	Level of Significance for One-Tailed Test				
	.05	.025	.01	.05	.005
	Level of Significance for Two-Tailed Test				
N	.10	.05	.02	.01	.001
1	0.988	0.997	0.9995	0.9999	0.99999
2	0.900	0.950	0.980	0.990	0.999
3	0.805	0.878	0.934	0.959	0.991
4	0.729	0.811	0.882	0.917	0.974
5	0.669	0.755	0.833	0.875	0.951
6	0.621	0.707	0.789	0.834	0.925
7	0.582	0.666	0.750	0.798	0.898
8	0.549	0.632	0.715	0.765	0.872
9	0.521	0.602	0.685	0.735	0.847
10	0.497	0.576	0.658	0.708	0.823
11	0.476	0.553	0.634	0.684	0.801
12	0.457	0.532	0.612	0.661	0.780
13	0.441	0.514	0.592	0.641	0.760
14	0.426	0.497	0.574	0.623	0.742
15	0.412	0.482	0.558	0.606	0.725
16	0.400	0.468	0.542	0.590	0.708
17	0.389	0.456	0.529	0.575	0.693
18	0.378	0.444	0.515	0.561	0.679
19	0.369	0.433	0.503	0.549	0.665
20	0.360	0.423	0.492	0.537	0.652

(*Continued*)

TABLE 8.3 (Continued)

	Level of Significance for One-Tailed Test				
	.05	.025	.01	.05	.005
	Level of Significance for Two-Tailed Test				
N	.10	.05	.02	.01	.001
21	0.352	0.413	0.482	0.526	0.640
22	0.344	0.404	0.472	0.515	0.629
23	0.337	0.396	0.462	0.505	0.618
24	0.330	0.388	0.453	0.496	0.607
25	0.323	0.381	0.445	0.487	0.597
26	0.317	0.374	0.437	0.479	0.588
27	0.311	0.367	0.430	0.471	0.579
28	0.306	0.361	0.423	0.463	0.570
29	0.301	0.355	0.416	0.456	0.562
30	0.296	0.349	0.409	0.449	0.554
40	0.257	0.304	0.358	0.393	0.490
60	0.211	0.250	0.295	0.325	0.408
120	0.150	0.178	0.210	0.232	0.294
∞	0.073	0.087	0.103	0.114	0.146

Reconstructed from Welkowitz, J., Cohen, B. H., & Lea, B. R. (2012). Introductory statistics for the behavioral sciences (7th ed.). Wiley. With permission from Wiley & Sons.

CALCULATING PEARSON'S R USING AN UNBIASED FORMULA

Now that the product-moment correlation coefficient is completed, assume that the researchers still want proof from an unbiased test of the relationship between hourly wage and years spent in college (Welkowitz, 2006; Witte, 1993). The unbiased formula is shown in Formula 8.1. The expanded Table 8.3 also shows the sample means and the standard deviations for the variables (see columns 2 and 4).

$$r_{xy} = \frac{\frac{1}{30-1}[(18{,}911 - 30(16.87)(34.57))]}{(3.082)(17.136)}$$

$$r_{xy} = \frac{\frac{1}{29}[18{,}911 - 17{,}495.88]}{52.813}$$

$$r_{xy} = \frac{\frac{1}{29}(1{,}415.12)}{52.813}$$

$$r_{xy} = \frac{48.797}{52.813}$$

$$r_{xy} = .924$$

Even with the unbiased formula, Pearson's r still shows a very strong relationship between hourly wage and years spent in college ($r = .924$, $p < .01$). The only difference between the product-moment correlation coefficient and the unbiased formula is that the unbiased formula always produces a conservative result, which is always slightly less than Pearson's r.

Practice Example 2

For another practice example, the county DSS is interested in investigating the inverse relationship between knowledge gained from a domestic violence training program and the probability that if they gain more in-depth knowledge, domestic violence perpetrators may not become repeated offenders. The county social services administrators believe that if the perpetrators are more educated about the social and psychological effects domestic violence has on their spouses, then the degrees of spousal abuse in the community will decline.

To pursue this interest, social services administrators approached the county courthouse to mandate that 20 individuals who were arrested for domestic violence attend a domestic violence training program. Assume that two instruments were used to measure the effectiveness of the training program. One of these two instruments was designed to measure the participants' level of knowledge gained concerning social and psychological effects commonly encountered by victims of domestic violence. The other instrument was a scale used to measure the likelihood that participants will physically abuse a spouse at least once in the next 2 years. Both measuring instruments were based on five items (five statements), with scores ranging from 1 to 5. For the knowledge scale, which was the outcome variable (y), higher scores indicate more knowledge. For the predictor variable (x), lower scores indicate lesser degrees of domestic violence in the next 2 years. Since there were five statements for each of the variables, by summing the total scores for each of the variables, the lowest score was 5 and the highest score was 25.

Table 8.4 shows the results for the county's social services' domestic violence training program. *Assume that the social services program is using a 99.9% CI, the null hypothesis and the alternative hypothesis for Pearson's r can now be stated and calculated as follows:*

H_o = There is no relationship between the domestic violence knowledge training program and the probability of reducing future domestic violence incidences.

H_a = There is a significant relationship between the domestic violence training program and the probability of reducing future domestic violence incidences.

$$r_{xy} = \frac{20(3,316)-(399)(170)}{\sqrt{[20(8,081)-(399)^2][20(1,546)-(170)^2]}}$$

$$x_{xy} = \frac{66,320-67,830}{\sqrt{[161,620-159,201][30,920-28,900]}}$$

$$x_{xy} = \frac{-1,510}{\sqrt{(2,419)(2,020)}}$$

$$r_{xy} = \frac{-1,510}{\sqrt{4,886,380}}$$

$$r_{xy} = \frac{-1,510}{2,210.52}$$

$$r_{xy} = -.683$$

The calculation results in a correlation coefficient of –.683 (r_{cal}). Based on the specified CI of 99.9% ($p = .001$) as previously stated, a two-tailed hypothesis, and a sample size of 20, the critical value is .652 (see Table 8.3). It is now safe to conclude that there is a moderate relationship between the educational training program on domestic violence and the likelihood that the participants will not abuse their spouses in the future ($r = -.683, p < .001$). Essentially, H_o was rejected, and H_a has been supported.

Remember that the negative sign is used to indicate the inverse function (direction) of the variables. It is not used to indicate that the calculated value is less than the critical value. In turn, the negative correlation indicates that as perpetrators become more knowledgeable about the social and psychological effects encountered by victims of domestic violence, they are less likely to abuse their spouses in the future. Assume that instead of the study being based on a sample of 20, the research questionnaire was in fact randomly administered to 150 married people in the general public; then the finding is generalizable to the population in which the sample was drawn. In turn, this is a clear evidence-based practice situation.

TABLE 8.4 Domestic Violence Educational Training

ID	X	X²	Y	Y²	XY
01	21	441	9	81	189
02	19	361	10	100	190
03	20	400	9	81	180
04	17	289	13	169	221
05	24	576	7	49	168
06	23	529	8	64	184
07	20	400	9	81	180
08	25	625	5	25	125
09	18	324	7	49	126
10	16	256	12	144	192
11	22	484	8	64	176
12	21	441	5	25	105
13	18	324	9	81	162
14	19	361	8	64	152
15	20	400	10	100	200
16	23	529	6	36	138
17	20	400	5	25	100
18	19	361	8	64	152
19	16	256	10	100	160
20	18	324	12	144	216
N = 20	$\sum X = 399$	$\sum X^2 = 8{,}081$	$\sum Y = 170$	$\sum Y^2 = 1{,}546$	$\sum XY = 3{,}316$

In addition, the coefficient of determination can also be calculated by

$$r^2 = (-.683)^2(100\%)$$

$$= 46.65\%$$

The result for the coefficient of determination indicates that domestic violence training explained about 46.65% of domestic violence incidences or reduced the amount of domestic violence. In turn, the magnitude of the domestic violence training program is significant, but it is only a partial explanation of factors to reduce it. In fact, this type of training program accounts for less than half of the amount of variation used to alleviate domestic violence incidences. If the county DSS really wants to reduce domestic violence incidences, then they must search for other variables to explain the remaining 53.35% of domestic violence issues.

UNDERSTANDING KENDALL'S TAU B, SPEARMAN'S RHO, AND PARTIAL CORRELATION COEFFICIENT

Beyond Pearson's r and the unbiased formula, there are additional correlation coefficients that can be used. Each is used for a slightly different statistical criterion. This last part of the chapter discusses three other correlation coefficients that are commonly used in both practice and research: Kendall's tau b, Spearman's rho, and partial correlation. Because of the length of the chapter, SPSS is used to depict the results for these three computations. Just to make sure that everyone is comfortable reporting outcomes from these three correlation coefficients, the statistical criteria are discussed next.

Kendall's tau b and Spearman's rho are referred to as nonparametric statistics. Partial Correlation is similar to Pearson's r, but it is used when the researchers want to control one or more of the predictor variables (see the following explanation).

Typically, *nonparametric statistics are used with ordinal-level data or in advanced statistics courses where the values of interval/ratio variables are reduced to rank order.* For example, income, which is a ratio variable, can be recoded into these values: upper, upper-middle, middle, lower-middle, and lower class. The most important part of nonparametric statistics is that the set of parameters, mainly the population mean (μ) and population variance (σ^2), are no longer being assumed—*making them simple to understand.* In a typical research study, the researchers assume normal distribution, and they use the known sample mean, median, mode, standard deviation, and variance to estimate the unknown population parameters (μ) and population variance (σ^2). Nonparametric statistics do not factor all these descriptive statistics into the findings.

Furthermore, *nonparametric statistics make no assumptions about the sample size and do not assume that the data set comes from a normally distributed population.* The result is easy to calculate but the explanations, especially for how the IV affects the DV, are difficult to understand. For example, the rank order of a mental health treatment program sets the metrics as 1 = strongly disagree, 2 = disagree,

3 = agree, and 4 = strongly agree. Assume a correlation coefficient of .418 is obtained. The difficulty is which part of the metrics really explains the effectiveness of the mental health treatment? Is it all of them or only the ones that state, *"Agree"* and *"Strongly agree"*?

Kendall's Tau B and Spearman's Rho

The two popular and accepted measures of nonparametric rank correlations are Kendall's tau and Spearman's rho correlation coefficient. Remember that correlation analyses measure the strength of the relationship between two interval or ratio variables. Both Kendall's tau b and Spearman's rank correlation coefficient are used to assess statistical associations based on the ranks of the data. Ranking data are carried out on the variables that are separately put in order and are numbered (Agresti & Finlay, 2009). Agresti and Finlay provide the following summary about the usefulness of Kendall's tau b and Spearman's rho (p. 243):

- *Ordinal measures of association take values between –1 and +1. The signs tell us whether the association is positive or negative.*
- *If the variables are statistically dependent, the population values of ordinal measures equal 0.*
- *The stronger the association, the larger the absolute value of the measure. Value 1.0 and –1.0 represent the strong association.*

With these statistical guidelines, the purpose of Kendall's tau b and Spearman's rho is to investigate the possible association in the underlying variables. *It is incorrect to write in the report that the null hypothesis has no rank correlation between the variables. Another thing to remember is that the result for Kendall's tau b is usually smaller than for Spearman's rho, which means that when examining associations between or among rank-order variables, Spearman's rho is preferred over Kendall's tau b* (see Table 8.6). Why? Because Spearman's rho uses a more conservative formula.

Partial Correlation Coefficient

There are limitations in using the product-moment correlation coefficient. Regardless of the number of predictor variables, Pearson's r always correlates two variables. Take the Beck Depression Inventory-II (BDI-II), which is freely available online, as an example. It has 21 items measuring generalized depression using the predictor variables from *"sadness"* to *"loss of interest in sex."* One can add the values of all 21 items to get the total depression score, or one can correlate two of the predictor variables and see how they correlate with each other. *While correlating the predictor variables, researchers may also want to control for one or more of the predictor variables to see how the predictor variables are associated. This is when the partial correlation coefficient can be used.*

The partial correlations procedure computes partial correlation coefficients that describe the linear relationship between two variables while controlling for the effects of one or more additional variables. Correlations are measures of linear association. *Two variables can be perfectly related, but if the relationship is not linear, then a correlation coefficient is not an appropriate statistical tool for measuring their association*. For example, while examining a linear relationship among the BDI-II items, one may want to control the items on "*Self-critical*," "*Indecisiveness*," and "*Loss of interest in sex*."

USING SPSS TO CALCULATE PEARSON'S r

In Tables 8.1 to 8.3, Pearson's r was manually calculated and interpreted. Now, let's use SPSS to create a data file for the predictor (X) and criterion (Y) variables. *Refer to Appendix A and Chapter 3 for how to create an SPSS data file.*

After the SPSS file is created, *Pearson's r, Kendall's tau b, and Spearman's rho* can be computed by following these steps:

- First, pull down the *Analyze* ribbon. Move the cursor down to *Correlate*. Choose *Bivariate*. Review Chapters 3 and 7 to become familiar with these ribbons and mini windows.

- Although not demonstrated here, but if there are multiple variables and the researcher is interested in *partial correlation,* they can see the sample box that follows. Instead of selecting *Bivariate*, choose *Partial* right below it. Enter the predictor variables into the first box (mini window) and then enter the variable(s) being controlled by the box below it.

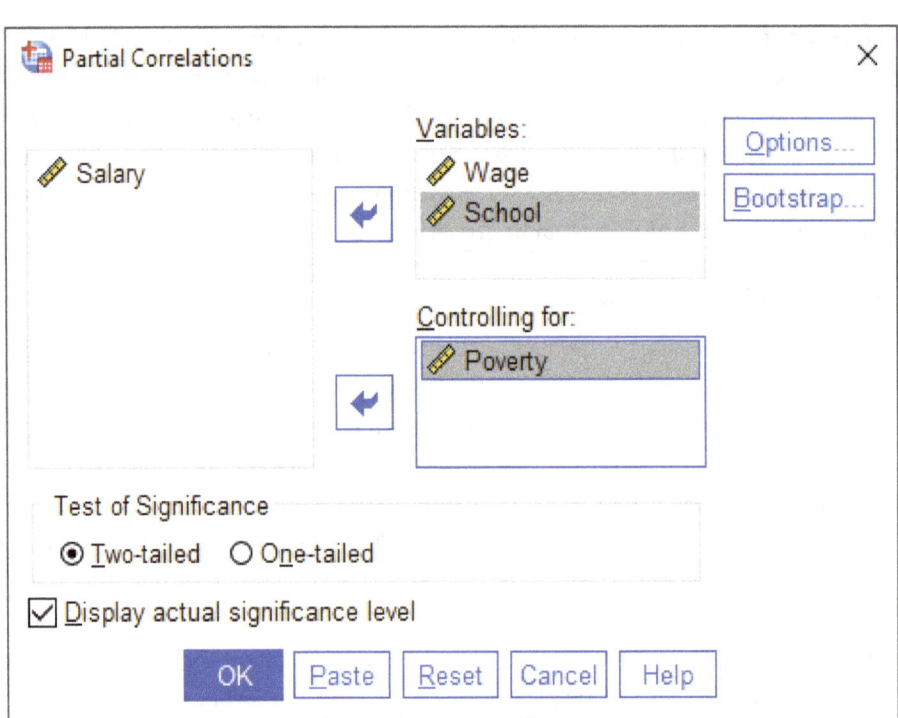

Image 8.1

- To compute Pearson's r for Table 8.1, select and hit the forward arrow (→) the variable that was created for "*Years spent in college,*" and the variable created for "*Hourly wage.*" The selection will appear as follows.

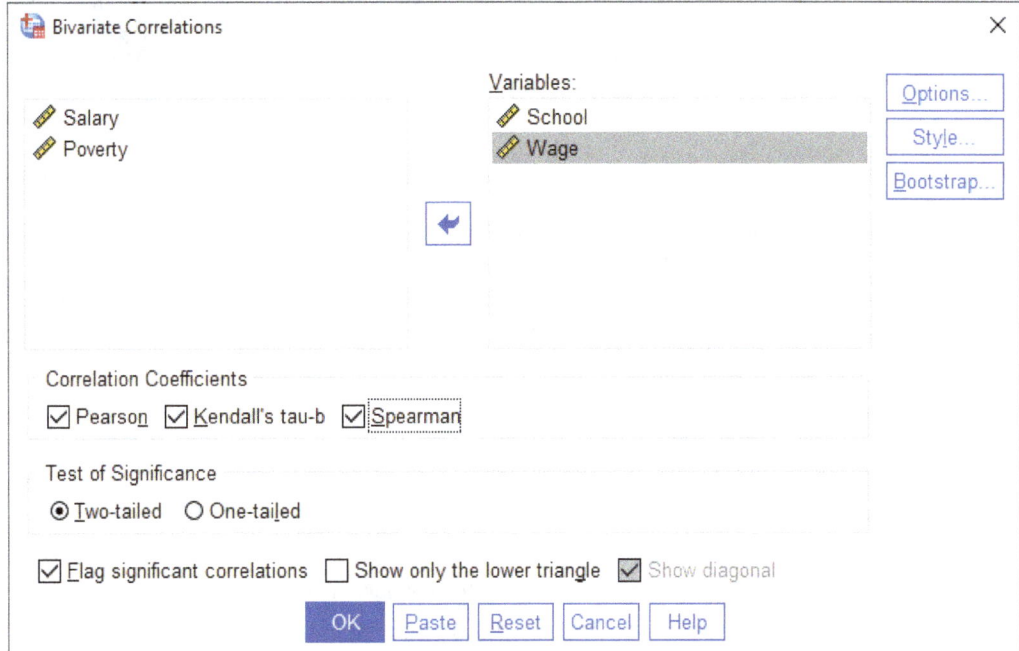

Image 8.2

- In the middle of the screen on *Correlation Coefficient*, notice that *Pearson* was automatically checked. Kendall's tau b and Spearman's rho are listed next to it. Also, notice that on *Test of Significance*, *two-tailed* was automatically highlighted. Should the user have a personal research project, if the choice is *one-tailed*, undo the two-tailed option.
- Select Kendall's tau b and Spearman's rho.
- Click *Bootstrap* to change the confidence interval if so desired.
- Click *OK*. Momentarily, the results will be displayed like in Table 8.5. This table confirms the manual calculation for Pearson's r for Table 8.1.

TABLE 8.5 A Hypothetical Rank Correlation Using Kendall's Tau B and Spearman's Rho on the Use of Social Work Values and Ethical Practice.

		Years Spent in School
Years spent in school	Pearson Correlation	1
	Sig. (two-tailed)	
	N	30
Hourly wage	Pearson Correlation	.927**
	Sig. (two-tailed)	**.000**
	N	30

**Correlation is significant at the 0.01 level (two-tailed).

Similar to the manual calculation, Pearson's correlation matrix shows a significant relationship between hourly wage and years spent in college ($r = .927$, $p < .000$). As stated in Chapters 6 and 7, when calculating solutions by computer pay attention to the computed p value. Whenever the computed p value *falls between .000 and .05*, the users can conclude that the finding is *significant* and then substitute the word *finding* with the appropriate concept, such as relationship, association, or cause and effect. Because the p value computed for Table 8.1 is *.000*, the users can conclude that there is a very strong relationship between the variables. Please note that the *coefficient of determination* (r^2) or (R^2) can be computed under linear regression (see Chapter 10).

Table 8.6 shows the values of two hypothetical variables. One is on the use of social work values and the other is on ethical practice in social work. Both variables asked undergraduate students to rank how well they were prepared for graduate study. The rank metric was set on "*Unprepared, Poorly prepared, Adequately prepared, Well prepared, and Excellently prepared.*" *As noted previously, Spearman's rho shows a higher association between the rank-order variables.* Based on a sample size of 55 and a p value of .000, one can conclude that there is a very strong association between social work values and social work ethics ($r = .781$, $p < .000$).

TABLE 8.6 Rank Correlation Coefficient

			Use of Social Work Values
Kendall's Tau B	Use of Social Work Values	Correlation Coefficient	
		Sig. (two-tailed)	.
		N	55
	Ethical Practice	Correlation Coefficient	.712**
		Sig. (two-tailed)	.000
		N	55
Spearman's Rho	Use of Social Work Values	Correlation Coefficient	
		Sig. (two-tailed)	.
		N	55
	Ethical Practice	Correlation Coefficient	.781**
		Sig. (two-tailed)	.000
		N	55

SUMMARY

This chapter introduced the basic function of correlation analysis, Pearson's r. Pearson's r is widely used in examining the interrelatedness of two interval-/ratio-level data in a linear relationship. This relationship indicates the strengths and variations between the criterion and predictor variables ranging between ±1.0 and when there is no linear relationship, 0. The reason for this is that as the calculated correlation coefficient gets closer to ±1.0, the relationship between the variables becomes stronger. Pearson's r can be used when normality is not assumed and when normality is assumed. The formula for normality tends to produce a slightly more conservative result than when the formula for normality is not assumed.

In conjunction with Pearson's r, the coefficient of determination (r^2) is often used to examine the magnitude of strength. Essentially, the coefficient of determination represents the proportion of variance in the DV that is explained by the IV. The coefficient of determination is also called the "strength" or "magnitude" of the research outcome.

There are a few other formulas for correlation analysis. These formulas include Kendall's tau b and Spearman's rho, and they are referred to as nonparametric statistics. Another computation formula for correlation is the partial correlation. Partial correlation is similar to Pearson's r, but it is used when the researchers want to control one or more of the predictor variables.

Similarly, correlation can be used as a parametric or nonparametric statistic. Parametric statistics are the types of inferential statistics that assume normal distribution and random sampling. Nonparametric statistics are the types of inferential statistics that do not assume normal distribution. Typically, nonparametric statistics are used with ordinal-level data or in advanced statistics courses where the values of interval/ratio variables are reduced to rank order. For example, income, which is a ratio variable, can be recoded into these values: upper, upper-middle, middle, lower-middle, and lower class. The most important part of nonparametric statistics is that the set of parameters, mainly the population mean (μ) and population variance (σ^2), are no longer being assumed—making them simple to understand. In a typical research study, the researchers assume normal distribution, and they use the known sample mean, median, mode, standard deviation, and variance to estimate the unknown population parameters (μ) and population variance (σ^2). Nonparametric statistics do not factor all these descriptive statistics into the findings.

Study Questions

Multiple Choice. Please use the following study questions to enhance your learning.

1. Under correlation, the DV is better conceptualized as
   a. the predictor variable.
   b. the criterion variable.
   c. the correlated variable.

2. Pearson's *r* correlation coefficient requires that the dependent and independent variables must meet specific statistical assumptions. Which of the following assumptions is incorrect?
   a. Normal distribution, random sampling, nominal data
   b. Normal distribution, random sampling, ordinal data
   c. Normal distribution, random sampling, interval or ratio data
   d. All of the above

3. The statement that reads "*larger family size results in more family support*" can best be conceptualized as
   a. zero correlation.
   b. positive correlation.
   c. negative correlation.
   d. family support.

4. The statement that reads *"As depression scores dropped, self-esteem score increased"* can best be conceptualized as

    a. no correlation.
    b. positive correlation.
    c. negative correlation.

5. The term *correlation* is used to

    a. explain a causal relationship.
    b. explain the association between or among nominal variables.
    c. explain the relationship between interval and ratio variables.

6. If you are given the result $r = .653$, what is the coefficient of determination for the research project?

    a. 42.63%
    b. 42.64%
    c. 65.30%
    d. .653%

7. In correlation analysis, the coefficient of determination explains which of the following variability?

    a. The number of variations in the criterion variable that can be explained by the predictor variable.
    b. The number of variations in the predictor variable that can be explained by the criterion variable.
    c. The coefficient of variation.

8. In a hypothetical situation, if r is given as $.712, p < .01$, what would you conclude about this research outcome? Would you say that

    a. there is no significant relationship between the variables?
    b. there is a significant relationship between the variables?
    c. either one is correct?

9. Similarly, based on the information provided in Question 8, what would you say about the research hypothesis (H_a)?

    a. The research hypothesis has been supported.
    b. The research hypothesis has been rejected.
    c. The research hypothesis cannot be explained.

10. Prior to calculating Pearson's r, assume that the scores are unevenly scattered along the x- and y-axes. What would you say about the correlation coefficient for a situation like this?

    a. There is a positive correlation.
    b. There is a negative correlation.
    c. There is no correlation or zero correlation.
    d. More information is needed.

11. If two variables are correlated and one can always speculate that there is a chance other variables may also have an effect on the outcome of the variables, what do you call this possible effect?

    a. Cause and effect
    b. Strong correlation
    c. Association
    d. Spurious

12. Which of the following variables can be correlated using Pearson's r?

    a. Family size and level of happiness
    b. Family size and monthly food expenditures
    c. Place of residency and level of happiness
    d. All
    e. Only a and b

13. Suppose that two correlation coefficients are given. The first correlation coefficient was calculated from a sample size of 537 (r_1 = .472, p < .001), and the second coefficient is based on a sample size of 35 (r_2 = .552, p < .001). Which correlation coefficient shows the strongest relationship? Hint: Consider the scientific merit.

    a. The first coefficient
    b. The second coefficient
    c. They are equally strong

14. If X = 24, 30, 23, 32, 28, 31, 25, and 30 and Y = 5, 10, 4, 10, 7, 9, 6, and 8, what is Pearson's r for this situation?

    a. .861
    b. .970
    c. .961

15. In Question 14, if p = .01, two-tailed, what would you say about the finding?

    a. There is no correlation between the variables.
    b. There is a significant correlation between the variables.
    c. Either one is correct.

16. Which of the following statements is correct about partial correlation?

    a. It is used to examine the strength of a correlation coefficient.
    b. It is used to do a partial analysis of the coefficient of determination.
    c. It is used to control one or more predictor variables.
    d. All of the above

17. Kendall's tau b and Spearman's rho are mainly used to complete which of the following?

    a. Examine the association between nominal variables
    b. Examine the association between rank-order variables

    c. Examine the association between interval and ratio variables
    d. All of the above

18. What is the major difference between the product-moment correlation coefficient and the unbiased formula for correlation?
    a. The product-moment correlation is the more conservative coefficient.
    b. The unbiased formula for correlation is the more conservative coefficient.
    c. The product-moment correlation formula is easier to compute solutions.
    d. All of the above.

Answers to Study Questions

QUESTION	ANSWER	QUESTION	ANSWER
1	b	10	c
2	c	11	d
3	b	12	e
4	c	13	a
5	c	14	c
6	b	15	b
7	a	16	c
8	b	17	b
9	a	18	b

CHAPTER 9

Inferential Statistics
The T-Tests

OVERVIEW

Chapters 7 and 8 introduced procedures for conducting basic hypothesis tests. These procedures normally involve comparing two nominal scores (Chapter 7) or two interval-/ratio-level scores (Chapter 8) with each other. Now, suppose there is one nominal variable and one interval/ratio variable, what would be a good statistical tool for finding any significant differences between the variables? For example, a college professor wants to examine the level of happiness among their students. Assume that happiness is weighed on a scale from 0 to 5 (ratio-level data) and the students are graduates and undergraduates (nominal data). Neither the chi-square nor the correlation computation is applicable to this situation. Indeed, a computer application will compute solutions for the situation if used, but those who know statistics will condemn the results as absolutely wrong. Let us try to look at four different scenarios:

1. The goal is to test a hypothesis on weight (interval data) differences between people in minority and nonminority status groups (two nominal categories) in a particular region of the country. When the term *weight* is brought up, which group's (nominal) weight (interval) is being referenced?
2. The goal is to see whether there is a significant difference between income (ratio) for racial groups (nominal).
3. The goal is to test the hypothesis on degrees of self-care (interval or ratio) among people in a particular location (nominal).
4. The goal is to examine the statistical significance of the willingness to take the COVID-19 vaccination shots (interval/ratio) among people of color (nominal).

All four statements show only one interval/ratio value but indicate there might be one or more nominal values or categories. For example, in statement #4, the term *people of color* can be two or more categories. People of color usually refer to ethnic minority groups. In this case, there could be even 10 or more groups.

When testing hypotheses that compare interval/ratio-level data with nominal data, the hypothesis test is called the *means test* (Hays, 1994; Welkowitz et al., 2012; Witte, 1993). The means test falls into three major classifications: (1) the basic means test is called *t-statistics*, or simply *t-tests*. Notice that the term "tests" is plural. This indicates that there is more than one basic mean tests for the first classification. The rest of this chapter is about t-tests. The terms *t-test, t-statistic,* and *calculated t* are used interchangeably. (2) When comparing one interval/ratio value with three to four (maximum at 5) value categories, the means test becomes known as a *simple analysis of variance* (ANOVA). And (3) when comparing two or more interval/ratio values with five or more value categories, the statistical calculation becomes known as *multiple analysis of variance* (MANOVA) (Hays, 1994; Mogull, 2004). ANOVA is discussed in Chapter 11. MANOVA must be taken in an advanced statistics course. To grasp the meaning of the means test, the term *"mean(s)" is/are used for the DV and value categories are for the IVs*. Write this *italicized* sentence into a song lyric to help you remember the means test. One cannot (it is even illegal to) switch them.

THE MEANING OF T-TESTS

Like chi-square and correlation, t-tests are tools for bivariate analyses and are used to test for statistical differences between the means ($\bar{x}$) of two groups (k = 2).

The groups (k is used in place of group) could be the sample and the population, two related or unrelated groups, or the experimental and control group. When there are three or more groups for a single DV, the application changes to ANOVA (Chapter 11). And when there are two or more DVs and multiple IVs under each DV, it is called MANOVA (which is beyond the scope of this book).

Essentially, *t-tests are tests of statistical significance that can be used to compare the differences between two means while factoring in sampling error* (Witte, 1993). Witte explained that, theoretically, sampling is based on the null hypothesis that there is no difference between the two means in the two populations from which the samples were drawn. Conceptually, the means from any two groups must be thought of as drawn from the distribution of all possible samples. This is so because the theoretical sampling distribution of the null hypothesis assumes no difference between the group means in the population. Therefore, the mean of that population should equal 0, or the difference between the sampling distribution and the population parameter is 0 (King et al., 2011; Witte, 1993). In summary, t-tests include the following computational conditions (Lee et al., 2016):

1. The level of measurement for the DV must be interval or ratio. Therefore, weight, income, degrees of self-care, and level of trustworthiness toward COVID-19 vaccination shots, as presented in the overview, can be used as DVs.

2. The level of measurement for the IV must be nominal. Therefore, the possible concepts are "minority and nonminority groups" for the first statement, "race" for the second statement, "gender or race" for the third statement, and "people of color" for the fourth statement.

Just as in computing the SD, data analyses using the t-tests can be complex and time-consuming if one is making calculations by hand. There are two major reasons for this complexity (Lee et al., 2016):

1. There are several methods for calculating each of the t-tests; however, there is no universally agreed on computational formula, especially symbols used to designate meanings for the variables and the statistical assumptions in the sample and population. Therefore, researchers must have a clear understanding of the meaning and statistical assumptions regarding each of the t-tests.
2. Because the computational formula for each of the t-tests can be expanded to fit the research objectives as stated in the first reason, the competence of the researcher is critical.

Of course, to alleviate everyone's anxiety whether using a simple formula, complex functions, or a computer application, the same result is obtained. Another way to alleviate anxiety is the use of the estimated standard deviation of the difference scores (SD_{E1-E2}) and the estimated standard error of the difference ($SD_{\bar{D}}$) (see the dependent and independent samples t-tests later in the chapter).

THREE TYPES OF T-TESTS

When testing for mean(s) difference, there are three types of t-tests. Each type is distinctively different from the other. Always pay attention to the meaning and the respective assumptions for each of the tests. *Note that t is always lowercased.*

1. The one-sample t-test.
2. The independent samples t-test.
3. The dependent samples t-test.

Various Statistical Assumptions About the T-Tests

In addition to the two computational reasons stated earlier, several other conditions must be met prior to using the three t-tests. The following are four very important assumptions about the usages of the t-tests:

1. The t-statistic is a part of bivariate analysis, and equal variances using the SS^2 are assumed. This is known as homogeneity of variance. Because most research studies use homogeneity of variance, the focus here is on equal variances. Leon-Guerrero and Frankfort-Nachmias (2012) stated that when the sum of the squares of one sample is twice as large as that from another sample, then unequal variances must be assumed. Research outcomes rarely result in one project having twice the variances of another, so the focus of this chapter is on equal variances.
2. The samples drawn at random from the population may or may not be equal (see the computation in this chapter for the estimated standard error when equal variances are assumed). If random

selection is not possible for independent and dependent samples t-tests, then a random assignment may be considered. Random assignment simply means dividing the participants into two groups with some sort of random draw.

3. The t-tests are statistical tools used to compare either the sample mean with the population mean (μ) or two related or unrelated means ($\bar{x}$). *They are not intended to test for relationship/ association or treatment effects. Even when a significant difference is detected, it shows only that one mean is significantly different from the other.*

4. In the case of the dependent and independent samples t-tests, the researcher must assume that the first sample mean is greater than the second mean ($\bar{x}_1 > \bar{x}_2$) and that the sample means are greater than the population mean ($\bar{x} > \mu$). In the discussion, make it very clear which is the first mean, which is the second mean, and which is the population mean. The reason for this assumption is that the researcher must be able to recognize and clearly explain the findings about the group that did better under specific interventions. For example, the researcher must be able to explain clearly whether the experimental group or the control group improved under certain conditions. The positive and negative sign (±) is used to describe this condition.

Let us now examine each of the t-tests.

The One-Sample T-Test

The one-sample t-test or one-sample statistic is used for two different purposes (Welkowitz et al., 2006):

1. It can be used to determine if the sample is large enough to represent the population parameter.
2. Rather than base findings on frequency distributions and variability, the desire is to conduct an inferential test for the sampling distribution.

In the first instance, when conducting the t-test with a sample size of 30 and a sample size of 300 participants, there will be different results for the hypothesis test. The significantly different results are due to sample size. When sample sizes (n) are large, the values of the sample standard error (SD_E) will be close to that of the population standard error (SD_μ), and the distribution of the t-statistic will be very nearly normal. On the other hand, when the sample size (n) is small, the values of SD_E may vary considerably from the population mean ($\mu_{\bar{x}}$) or the hypothesized population parameter ($\mu_{hypothesized}$). The t-distribution may also depart considerably from that of the normal distribution of z. This is based on the validation that was completed by William S. Gosset (as cited by King et al., 2011), who published an article anonymously in 1899 using the name "Student" in Dublin, Ireland, while teaching at the University College and working for the Guinness brewery company.

For either purpose, the one-sample t-test can be used to compare a sample mean or sample statistic ($\bar{x}$) to a population mean ($\mu_{\bar{x}}$) or the hypothesized mean ($\mu_{hypothesized}$). The lowercase Greek mu (μ) sign, pronounced mu, is typically used to represent the term *population parameter* and $\bar{x}$ is used for the term *sample mean* or *sample statistic*. King et al. (2011) stated that to use the one-sample t-test, users first must know the population parameter (μ). However, in most situations, either the population means ($\mu_{\bar{x}}$) or the population standard deviation (μ_{SD}) will not be known. Because μ is rarely known, the researcher must *estimate the sample standard error of the difference in mean* (SD_E) *using the sample standard deviation (SD)*. The formula to estimate μ from the sample standard deviation is

$$SD_E = \frac{SD}{\sqrt{n}}$$

where

SD_E = Estimated standard error of the mean,
SD = Sample standard deviation, and
n = Sample size.

Therefore, the one-sample t-test is calculated by the formula

$$t = \frac{\bar{x} - \mu_{\bar{x}}}{SD_E}$$

or, in simplified form, it is calculated by

$$t = \frac{\bar{x} - \mu_{\bar{x}}}{SD/\sqrt{n}}$$

where

t = t-statistic,
$\bar{x}$ = the sample mean, and
$\mu_{\bar{x}}$ = Population mean or the hypothesized parameter for the t-statistic.

Practice Situation Using One-Sample T-Tests

Suppose that the state DSS reported that in the past 3 years there were 4,526 children temporarily or permanently removed from the custody of their parents or caretakers because of abuse and neglect. Of the children removed, your county averaged ($\bar{x}$) 328 children per year for the reporting period. DSS states that on average ($\mu_{\bar{x}}$) of 439 children were removed from every county in the past 3 years with an SD of 87. By reviewing the numbers (scores), it is evident that your home county's removal of 328 children was slightly below the state's overall average of 439 but probably within 1 SD. Because of this, it is desirable to examine further whether your county is statistically different from other counties based on a 95% CI, two-tailed hypothesis. The stated hypotheses are as follows:

H_0: *There is no significant difference in average child removal between your home county and the overall state average.*
H_a: *There is a significant difference in average child removal between your home county and the overall state average.*

Based on the statewide report, the data can be summarized as follows:

Your home county's average ($\bar{x}$) = 328
DSS's overall average ($\mu_{\bar{x}}$) = 439
State's total removal (n) = 4,526
State's overall standard deviation (SD_{state}) = 87

Now, *the t contribution can be calculated by*

$$t = \frac{328 - 439}{87 / \sqrt{4,526}}$$

$$t = \frac{-111}{87 / \sqrt{4,526}}$$

$$t = -85.834$$

Similar to chi-square (Chapter 7) and correlation (Chapter 8) statistical tests, the calculated t-statistic of −85.834 still does not explain anything about the population from which the sample was drawn, particularly the null hypothesis (H_o). *To retain or reject the null hypothesis, one still needs to find the critical value to compare it with the calculated value.* In the scientific community, results must be scientifically based before one can generalize findings from a sample to the population. This scientific method of conclusion is done by comparing the calculated values with some type of standardized values within the normal curve. For this t-test—before retaining or rejecting $\dot{H}_o$—see Table 9.1, which provides critical values of the t-distribution to determine whether the calculated t-statistic is such that the null hypothesis is rejected.

To find the critical values of the t-distribution, two important pieces of information are required.

1. The tail of the hypothesis
2. The degrees of freedom (*df*) involved in the research project

In calculating the t-statistic, statisticians recommend that one of the scores be allowed to vary. The reason is that in human society, everyone has their own biases; therefore, to minimize biases, it is best that one respondent's/participant's scores be allowed to vary. The degrees of freedom are then computed by

$$df = (n - 1)$$

In turn, the degrees of freedom for the practical situation are computed as

$$df = (4,526 - 1)$$

$$df = 4,525$$

TABLE 9.1 Critical Value of t

df	Level of Significance for One-Tailed Test					
	.10	.05	.025	.01	.005	.0005
	Level of Significance for Two-Tailed Test					
	.20	.10	.05	.02	.01	.001
1	3.078	6.314	12.706	31.821	63.657	636.619
2	1.886	2.920	4.303	6.965	9.925	31.598
3	1.638	2.343	3.182	4.541	5.841	12.941
4	1.533	2.132	2.776	3.747	4.604	8.610
5	1.476	2.015	2.571	3.365	4.032	6.859
6	1.440	1.943	2.447	3.143	3.707	5.959
7	1.415	1.895	2.365	2.998	3.449	5.405
8	1.397	1.860	2.306	2.896	3.355	5.041
9	1.383	1.833	2.262	2.821	3.250	4.781
10	1.372	1.812	2.228	2.764	3.169	4.587
11	1.363	1.796	2.201	2.718	3.106	4.437
12	1.356	1.782	2.179	2.681	3.055	4.318
13	1.350	1.771	2.160	2.650	3.012	4.221
14	1.345	1.761	2.145	2.624	2.977	4.140
15	1.341	1.753	2.131	2.602	2.947	4.073
16	1.337	1.746	2.120	2.583	2.921	4.015
17	1.333	1.740	2.110	2.567	2.898	3.965
18	1.330	1.734	2.101	2.552	2.878	3.922
19	1.328	1.729	2.093	2.539	2.861	3.883
20	1.325	1.725	2.086	2.528	2.845	3.850
21	1.323	1.721	2.080	2.518	2.831	3.819

(*Continued*)

TABLE 9.1 (Continued)

df	Level of Significance for One-Tailed Test					
	.10	.05	.025	.01	.005	.0005
	Level of Significance for Two-Tailed Test					
	.20	.10	.05	.02	.01	.001
22	1.321	1.717	2.074	2.508	2.819	3.792
23	1.319	1.714	2.069	2.500	2.807	3.767
24	1.318	1.711	2.064	2.492	2.797	3.745
25	1.316	1.708	2.060	2.485	2.787	3.725
26	1.315	1.706	2.056	2.479	2.779	3.707
27	1.314	1.703	2.052	2.473	2.771	3.690
28	1.313	1.701	2.048	2.467	2.763	3.674
29	1.311	1.699	2.045	2.462	2.756	3.659
30	1.310	1.697	2.042	2.457	2.750	3.646
40	1.303	1.684	2.021	2.423	2.704	3.551
60	1.296	1.671	2.000	2.390	2.660	3.460
120	1.289	1.658	1.980	2.358	2.617	3.373
∞	1.282	1.645	1.960	2.326	2.576	3.291

Adapted from Welkowitz, J., Cohen, B. H., & Lea, B. R. (2012). Introductory statistics for the behavioral sciences (7th ed.). John Wiley & Sons.

Notice that at 4,525 degrees of freedom, the *df* for Table 9.1 only goes up to 120. Because the table goes only as far as 120, use the last row (∞) on the table, 95% CI ($p = .05$) and two-tailed hypothesis, for the critical value of *t*. The critical value of the *t*-distribution is equal to 1.960. Notice that some statistics books call it the t-distribution. Do not confuse the negative sign of −85.834. As previously stated, assumption number 4 states that when completing the t-test, the researchers must assume that the first sample mean is greater than the second mean ($\bar{x}_1 > \bar{x}_2$) and that the sample means are greater than the population mean ($\bar{x} > \mu$). The negative sign simply helps researchers to explain which mean is greater than which. Because the calculated *t*-statistic is much larger than the critical values (ignoring the negative sign in front of *t*), the H_o hypothesis is rejected and H_a is supported.

In summary, the finding from the one-sample *t*-statistic indicates that the number of children removed by DSS was statistically different from one county to another ($t = -85.834$, $df = 4,525$, $p < .05$). The negative calculated *t*-statistic also indicates that your county had significantly fewer children removed by CPS compared to the overall average of all counties. Because of the negative calculated *t*, the population mean ($\mu_{\bar{x}}$) is larger than the sample mean ($\bar{x}$). As explained in the last two chapters, the statistical configurations (i.e., *t* = –85.83, *df* = 4,525, *p* < .05) are conditions required by APA style.

The Independent Samples T-Test and Its Relation to Social Work

Different than the one-sample t-test, the independent samples t-test can be used to evaluate the differences in means ($\bar{x}$) between two unrelated, unconnected groups or unmatched pairs that are selected at random from the population (Tokunaga, 2018; Witte, 1993; Zeitlin & Auerbach, 2019).

Examples of two unrelated groups include the following:

- The study focuses on the difference between two groups of individuals who are diagnosed with major depression. One of the groups received Western-style psychotherapy (i.e., cognitive-behavioral modification) as an experimental group, and another group was encouraged to apply natural styles of healing as the control group.
- A research study focuses on two randomized samples of Asian and White youth pertaining to behavioral modification.
- A researcher is interested to examine the knowledge men and women have about ADHD in children.
- A research project targets the PTSD of female and male veterans that served in foreign wars.

The prospective participants in these four hypothetical scenarios are unrelated. In the first scenario, Western-style psychotherapy is different from natural styles of healing. In the second scenario, Asian and White are two very different groups. In the third example, men and women are separate categories. And in the last scenario, female and male are two separate veteran groups.

Formula for the Independent Samples T-Test

As in all inferential statistics, there are two key purposes for testing hypotheses for the independent samples t-test. The two key purposes are as follows (Lee et al., 2016):

1. Is the difference between the two sample means statistically significant? Be aware that in statistical analyses, differences among a set of scores or some percentage change may or may not be enough to show statistically significant differences between or among the variables under investigation.
2. If there is statistical significance, how will the results of the research study be generalized to the population from which the sample was randomly drawn? Recall that in Chapter 6, the terms *generalize* and *infer* apply to the degrees of confidence in the sample being representative of the population from which it was drawn.

For these two reasons, the goal of conducting hypothesis testing on the criminal youth helpfulness treatment scale is to see whether the two means are statistically different. If they are, are the gaps between the means ($\bar{X}_S$) for Asian and Caucasian youth groups representative of all youth? The terms *youth* and *population* are evidence-based concepts used to describe adolescents locally, nationally, or internationally, depending on where and how the study is conducted.

Remember that most population parameters for the t-test are not known (μ_1 & $\mu_2 = 0$ or unknown). Because the population parameters are not known, the standard error is unknown as well ($SD_E = 0$). However, the sample standard error of the difference in the two means (SD_{E1-E2}) can be estimated. *Some people call this "pooled variances."* The way to estimate the standard error for the two independent means is slightly complicated (see the following). The formula for estimating the *t*-statistic for independent samples t-test is

$$t = \frac{\bar{x}_1 - \bar{x}_2}{SD_{E1-E2}}$$

where

$\bar{x}_1$ = Sample mean for Group 1,
$\bar{x}_2$ = Sample mean for Group 2, and
SD_{E1-E2} = Estimated standard error of the difference in the two samples (pooled variances)

When equal variances (homogeneity of variance) are assumed ($n_1 = n_2$ or $\mu_1 = \mu_2$), the estimated standard error is computed by

$$SD_{E1-E2} = \sqrt{\frac{SS_1^2 + SS_2^2}{(n_1 + n_2) - 2}\left(\frac{1}{n_1} + \frac{1}{n_2}\right)}$$

In turn, the formula for the independent samples t-test is calculated by

$$t = \frac{\bar{x}_1 - \bar{x}_2}{\sqrt{\frac{SS_1^2 + SS_2^2}{(n_1 + n_2) - 2}\left(\frac{1}{n_1} + \frac{1}{n_2}\right)}}$$

where

SS_1^2 = Sum of the square (variance) for Group 1 (pooled variance 1),
SS_2^2 = Sum of the square (variance) for Group 2 (pooled variance 2),
n_1 = Sample size for Group 1, and
n_2 = Sample size for Group 2.

Note that even though equal sample size and equal variances are assumed, in actual research studies, it is highly probable that they are not going to be equal. The formula for calculating the estimated standard error between the two independent means looks a bit intimidating, but the calculation is not that complicated.

With the aforementioned formula, the independent t-test for the case scenario about behavior modification for criminal youth offenders to reduce recidivism rates can now be calculated as follows. *In manual calculations, pay close attention to the algebraic operations.*

Practice Example Using Independent Samples T-Test

Suppose that two criminal youth groups (k = 2) were randomly drawn from the juvenile justice crime system to participate in a behavior modification program as a way to investigate whether this type of treatment is significantly different for juvenile crime recidivism. One of the groups was Asian (k_1) and the other group was Black (k_2). Assume that each group (k) comprised 50 youth (n_1 = 50; n_2 = 50). Without going through the long and tedious calculations, assume that the treatment helpfulness behavior modification measure was based on a metric scale from 1 (not helpful at all) to 10 (extremely helpful). At the end of the program, the Asian youth averaged 8.82 ($\bar{x}_{k1}$) on the treatment helpfulness scale with the sum of the squares (SS^2_{Asian}) of 4,897, and the Black youth averaged 9.65 ($\bar{x}_{k2}$) with a sum of the squares (SS^2_{Black}) of 5,210 (see Chapter 4 on how to calculate SS^2). The entire scenario can be summarized in Table 9.2. Assuming that this is based on a 99% CI, two-tailed test, the null hypothesis and the alternative *hypothesis can be stated as follows:*

H_o = *There is no mean difference for youth offenders who received behavior modifications.*
H_a = *There is a significant mean difference for youth who received behavior modifications.*

TABLE 9.2 Behavior Modification Treatment for Asian and Black Youth

Concept	Race	
	Asian	Black
Sample size (n)	50	50
Sample mean ($\bar{x}$) on a scale from 1 to 10	8.82	9.65
Sum of squares (SS^2) for total (variances)	4,897	5,210

$$t = \frac{7.82 - 9.65}{\sqrt{\frac{4,897 + 5,210}{(50+50)-2}\left(\frac{1}{50} + \frac{1}{50}\right)}}$$

$$t = \frac{-1.83}{\sqrt{\frac{10,107}{98}(.02 + .02)}}$$

$$t = \frac{-1.83}{\sqrt{(103.31)(.04)}}$$

$$t = -0.901$$

Similar to the one-sample t-test, once the calculated statistic is known, one still needs to calculate its degrees of freedom (df). The degrees of freedom for the independent samples t-test are computed as

$$df = (n_1 + n_2 - 2).$$

In the case of the youth recidivism rate, the degrees of freedom are computed as

$$df = (50 + 50 - 2)$$

$$= 98.$$

The calculated t-statistic is −0.901, with 98 degrees of freedom. As stated earlier, the scenario assumed a 99% CI (p value = .01) two-tailed hypothesis to examine the result of this study. With a 99% CI two-tailed hypothesis, the closest critical value is equal to 2.167 (see Table 9.1). The conclusion is that at the 99% CI, there is no statistically significant difference in means between Asian and Black youth (t = −0.901, df = 98, p > .01). In this case, the null hypothesis is retained, or the researcher failed to reject the . The negative sign is used to show that the Black youth group has a slightly higher mean score, but it is insufficient to demonstrate statistical difference.

Furthermore, *it is unknown whether behavior modification was or was not effective in helping the two youth groups in recidivism.* Sometimes people use the sample mean to argue that it is effective, but to truly justify the effectiveness of behavior modification, other statistical results are required—such as variability (Chapter 4) or the effect size (discussed at the end of this chapter). Just to reiterate, *the independent t-test simply indicates that there is or there is not a statistically significant difference between two independent means.*

The Dependent Samples T-Test

The *dependent samples t-test is an appropriate statistical procedure for comparing the means ($\bar{x}$) of two groups (k = 2) selected at random from the population that fall under one of these concepts: connected, correlated, or related to each other; matched pairs; or repeated-measure design* (Tokunaga, 2018; Witte, 1993; Zeitlin & Auerbach, 2019).

This type of t-test is less common than the independent samples t-test. Typically, the same participants are used in both groups *because the IVs are fixed by nature.*

Examples of dependent sample t-tests include the following:

- A research study focuses on the level of happiness among Native American high school students at school A and school B.
- A study aims at the knowledge gained by master's degree social work students at two accredited social work programs.

- An experimental research project aims to examine the effectiveness of the Pfizer vaccine in protecting against COVID-19 and other diseases in children and adults.
- A researcher is interested in the effectiveness of the practice of mindfulness on females and males.

In the first example, even though there are different tribal groups, the US census always lumps Native Americans as a single entity so that they are considered related or can be matched. In the second example, accredited social work programs must follow the same educational policy and accreditation standards. In turn, it is assumed that graduate students gained the same types of knowledge. In the third example, the Pfizer vaccine is the main focus. And in the last example, mindfulness is a health and well-being practice modality that health and human services workers encourage individuals and families to practice.

Formula for the dependent samples t-test is a bit more confusing than the independent samples t-test. For this, please pay attention to the following steps. As usual, the null and alternative hypotheses can be stated as

$$H_o : \bar{x}_1 = \bar{x}_2$$

$$H_a : \bar{x}_1 > \bar{x}_2$$

$$t = \frac{\bar{x}_1 - \bar{x}_2}{\sqrt{\frac{\Sigma D^2 - \frac{(\Sigma D)^2}{N}}{N(N-1)}}}$$

where

$\bar{x}_1$ = the mean of the pretest scores or characteristic 1,
$\bar{x}_2$ = the mean of the posttest scores or characteristic 2,
ΣD^2 = the sum of the squares of the differences between pretest and posttest scores or characteristics 1 and 2,
$(\Sigma D)^2$ = the square of the sum of the differences between pretest and posttest scores or characteristics 1 and 2, and
N = the number of pairs of scores or the total participants.

Practice Example for the Dependent Samples T-Test

This is another example of evidence-based practice. Assume that youth were randomly selected from a large school district to participate in a knowledge-based training program about risk factors that may cause youthful age individuals to commit crimes offered by the county DSS. Before the training, the youth were administered a set of questions assessing their knowledge about various risk factors. After 6 weeks, when the training was completed, the therapist re-administered the same set of questions to the youth.

The before and after training scores are shown in Table 9.3. Assume that the project used a 99.9% CI with a two-tailed test.

The statistical calculations for the dependent samples look a bit intimidating, but they are, in fact, very simple. To complete the dependent samples t-test, simply follow the same guidelines for the Pearson correlation coefficient. Table 9.4 shows how to complete the necessary columns before calculating the t-statistic.

TABLE 9.3   Youth Crime Prevention Success Training Program

ID	Before Training (X)	After Training (Y)
Male	30	50
Female	20	55
Male	35	45
Male	40	65
Female	38	51
Female	27	35
Male	25	45
Male	15	30
Female	17	29
Female	28	32
Male	32	40
Male	21	39
Female	10	35
Male	25	35
Female	36	55
Male	24	48
Male	35	54
Female	29	50
Male	18	35
Female	22	42

TABLE 9.4 The Completed Breakdown Elements for Dependent Samples T-Test

ID	Before Training (x_1)	After Training (x_2)	Difference (D) $D = x_1 - x_2$	Difference Square $(D)^2$ $D^2 = (D)(D)$
Male	30	50	−20	400
Female	20	55	−35	1,225
Male	35	45	−10	100
Male	40	65	−25	625
Female	38	51	−13	169
Female	27	35	−8	64
Male	25	45	−20	400
Male	15	30	−15	225
Female	17	29	−12	144
Female	28	32	−4	16
Male	32	40	−8	64
Male	21	39	−18	324
Female	10	35	−25	625
Male	25	35	−10	100
Female	36	55	−19	361
Male	24	48	−24	576
Male	35	54	−19	361
Female	29	50	−21	441
Male	18	35	−17	289
Female	22	42	−20	400
N= 20	$\bar{x}_1 = 26.35$	$\bar{x}_2 = 43.50$	$\sum D = -343$	$\sum D^2 = 6{,}909$

The dependent samples t-test can now be completed by

$$t = \frac{26.35 - 43.50}{\sqrt{\dfrac{6{,}909 - \dfrac{(-343)^2}{20}}{20(20-1)}}}$$

$$= \frac{-17.15}{\sqrt{\dfrac{6{,}909 - \dfrac{117{,}649}{20}}{20(19)}}}$$

$$= \frac{-17.15}{\sqrt{\dfrac{6{,}909 - 5{,}882.45}{380}}}$$

$$= \frac{-17.15}{\sqrt{2.701}}$$

$$= \frac{-17.15}{1.643}$$

$$= -10.434$$

By glancing at Table 9.1, the degrees of freedom are needed to find the critical value of t. The degrees of freedom for the dependent samples t-test are computed by taking the sample size minus one (df = N − 1). There were 20 youth for the case scenario, so the df are 19. At 19 df, a two-tailed hypothesis, with a 99.9% CI (p value = .001), the critical value for t is 3.850.

Because the calculated t-statistic is much larger than the critical value of the t-distribution (as discussed previously, ignore the negative symbol), H_o is rejected. As stated in Chapter 6 regarding interpreting results of statistical tests, it is safe to conclude that the youth training program for the 20 youth showed a significant difference between the pretest and the posttest scores ($t = -10.434$, $df = 19$, $p < .01$). Again, the symbols inside the parentheses are statistical notations required by the APA. As discussed, do not get confused about the negative sign. The negative t-statistic simply indicates that the posttest scores were higher than the pretest scores. *Essentially, because of the training program, the youth become more aware of risk factors toward criminal conduct (because of a higher mean at posttest).*

THE CORRELATION EFFECT SIZE AND COHEN'S d EFFECT SIZE

For either the independent or dependent samples t-tests, to examine treatment effects, the effect size must be computed. In addition to converting the z score into a percentile and calculating a specific score (see Chapter 5), researchers need to see where the z score falls under the standard normal curve. The z score can also be used to estimate the degree to which treatment effect is present in the population. For example, researchers may want information about the means of two groups in terms of how many standard deviations one group's mean is above or below another group's mean (Weinbach & Grinnell, 2015; King et al., 2011). The difference between the size of the phenomenon in the population and the sample mean is called the effect size.

The correlation coefficient of effect size is used for the independent samples t-test. Similar to the coefficient of determination for correlation, the correlation coefficient of effect size is always positive and ranges from 0 to 1.00. Coolidge (2013) provides the following scale to interpret the magnitude of the effect size for the independent samples t-test.

TABLE 9.5 Correlation Coefficient of Effect Size

Effect Size	Minimum r Value
Small	0.100
Medium	0.243
Large	0.371

The formula to calculate the correlation coefficient (r) of effect size for the independent samples t-test is calculated by

$$r_E = \sqrt{\frac{t^2}{t^2 + df}}$$

where

r_E = Correlation coefficient of the effect size,
t^2 = Square the calculated t-statistic, and
df = Degrees of freedom for the independent samples t-test.

In the first practice example about behavior modification for Asian and Black youth, the effect size is calculated as

$$r_E = \sqrt{\frac{(-.901)^2}{(-.901)^2 + 98}}$$

$$= \sqrt{\frac{.812}{.812 + 98}}$$

$$= \sqrt{\frac{.812}{98.812}}$$

$$= .008$$

The result indicates that not only was there no mean difference between Asian and Black youth who received behavior modification as discussed earlier but now the correlation coefficient of the effect size is extremely small.

The most popular effect size for the dependent samples t-test is the Cohen's d (Coolidge, 2013; Welkowitz et al., 2012). Most importantly, Cohen's d applies the same concept as the z score (Chapter 5). The only difference between the effect size of the z score and Cohen's d is the application of the concept. While the z score is used for many different purposes, Cohen's d is mainly used to compare mean difference between two groups, such as a before and after treatment group. Cohen's d can also be used to examine the mean difference between an experimental and control group. Illustrated here is an effect size for the youth who received training on criminal risk factors. The formula for Cohen's d is

$$d = \frac{\bar{x}_1 - \bar{x}_2}{SD_{all\ participants}}$$

Cohen suggests (as cited by Coolidge, 2013) that the following guidelines can be used to interpret the effect size. Coolidge (2013) also states two aspects about Cohen's d: (1) the value of d can be interpreted as how many standard deviations are the two means different from each other, and (2) unlike the correlation coefficient of effect size, Cohen's d can be greater than 1.0.

TABLE 9.6 Cohen's d Effect Size

Effect Size	Minimum d Value
Small	0.20
Medium	0.50
Large	0.80

The effect size for the DSS youth training program can now be calculated. To avoid the tedious manual calculation for the overall standard deviation, it was computed by SPSS, and it is 12.468. Recall that the mean for the pretest was 26.35 and the mean for the posttest was 43.50.

$$d = \frac{26.35 - 43.50}{12.468}$$

$$= \frac{-17.15}{12.468}$$

$$= -1.38$$

By ignoring the negative sign, the $\bar{x}$ ($\bar{x}_1$) for the pretest and the $\bar{x}$ ($\bar{x}_2$) for the posttest with their respective SD of 12.468, the Cohen's d is 1.38 SDs apart from each other. This means that Cohen's d yields a very large effect size (greater than the amount specified by Cohen's d), which indicates that this type of training can be generalized from the sample to the population from which the sample was drawn.

USING SPSS TO COMPUTE THE T-TESTS

Remember that there are three types of t-tests (one sample, independent samples, and dependent samples). Before using SPSS to do the computations, check to be certain that the type of t-test conforms to the statistical assumptions stated earlier in the chapter. The t-tests are one of the SPSS computations for which the laws of statistics must be obeyed or the results will be inaccurate. *Because of page limitations for the chapter, instructions are provided for all three types of t-tests. However, only the dependent samples t-test is demonstrated here.*

To compute the one-sample t-test, take the following steps:

1. Pull down the *Analyze* ribbon. Move the cursor to *Compare means* and then move the cursor over to the *One-Sample T-Test.* Click it. The following mini window will pop up.

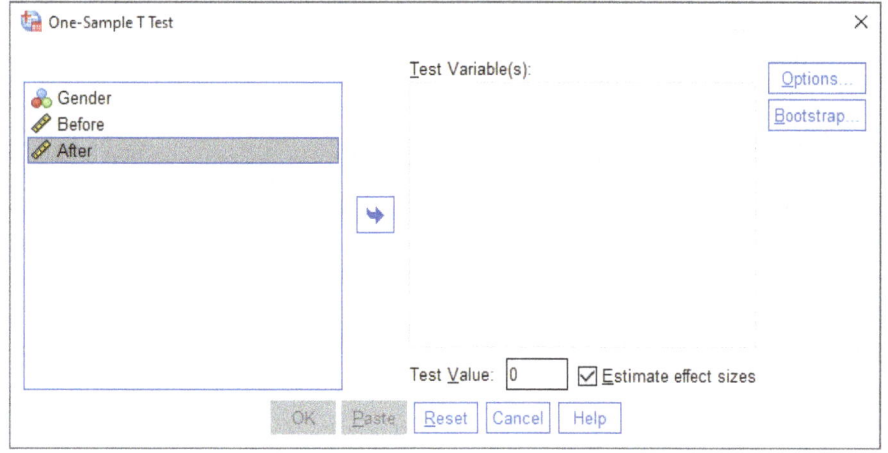

Image 9.1

2. On *Test Variable(s)*, select and hit the forward arrow for the variable(s) being tested. Remember that only interval or ratio variable(s) is/are applicable. Why? Because it is here where SPSS will compute the sample mean ($\bar{x}$). On *Test Value*, enter the population parameter ($\mu_{\bar{x}}$). *Remember that most of the time, the population parameter is unknown; therefore, the researchers may have to hypothesize it.* Check and review the one-sample t-test formula discussed earlier in the chapter.
3. On *Options*, click and insert the preferred confidence interval. Click *OK*. Momentarily, the result for the one-sample t-test will be shown. There are various statistical results shown, but look for the column with t and the *p* value designated with *Sig.*
4. Interpret the result accordingly.

To compute the *independent samples t-test*, take the following steps:

1. Pull down the *Analyze* ribbon. Move the cursor to *Compare means* and then move the cursor over to the *Independent Sample T-Test*. Click it. The following mini window will pop up.

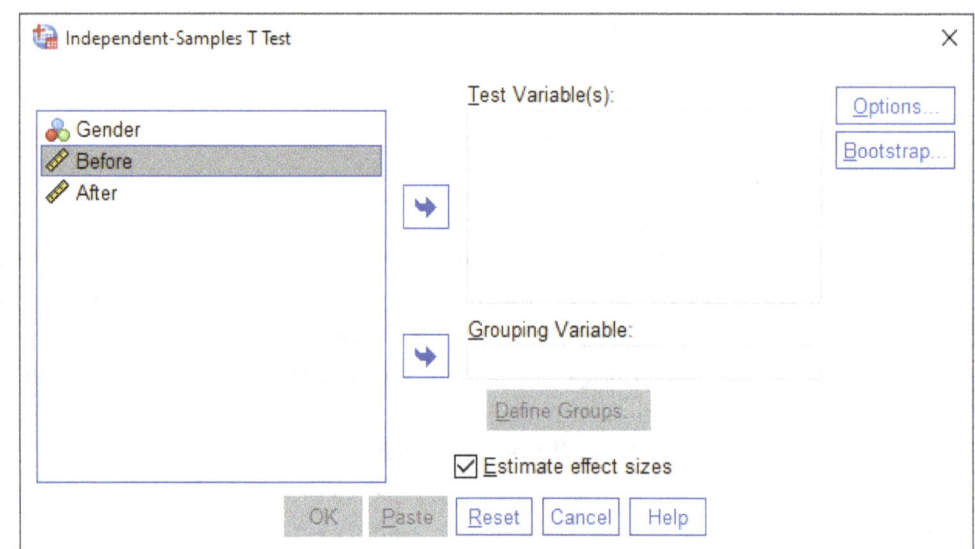

Image 9.2

2. On *Test Variable(s)*, select the interval or ratio variable(s) and hit the forward arrow to move the DV onto it. Here is where the DV must be entered.
3. On *Grouping Variable*, select the variable that is being treated as the IV from the variable list (the first mini window). *Remember that the IV must be nominal* (categorical) and only two categories can be entered. In case the nominal variable being treated as the IV has multiple categories, the user must decide as to which two categories are being examined. As soon as the IV is selected and pasted onto it, the small rectangle below it will turn yellow with a question mark and the function **Define Groups** will be **bolded**.
4. Click *Define Groups* and enter the two categories being examined into *Group 1* and *Group 2*. For example, Group 1 represents the female participants, and Group 2 represents the male participants.

5. Click *Options* to change the confidence interval to one's own self-selected level.
6. Click *OK*. Momentarily the t-test table will be shown. Again, there are various statistical results displayed. Look for the column with *t* and *Sig.* to interpret the result.

For demonstration purposes, the dependent samples t-test is shown next. *Refer to Appendix A and Chapter 3 regarding creating an SPSS data file*. Once the SPSS data file is created, take the following steps to compute the dependent samples t-test:

1. Pull down the *Analyze* ribbon. Move the cursor to *Compare means* and then move the cursor over to the *Paired- Sample T-Test*. Click it. The following mini window will pop up.

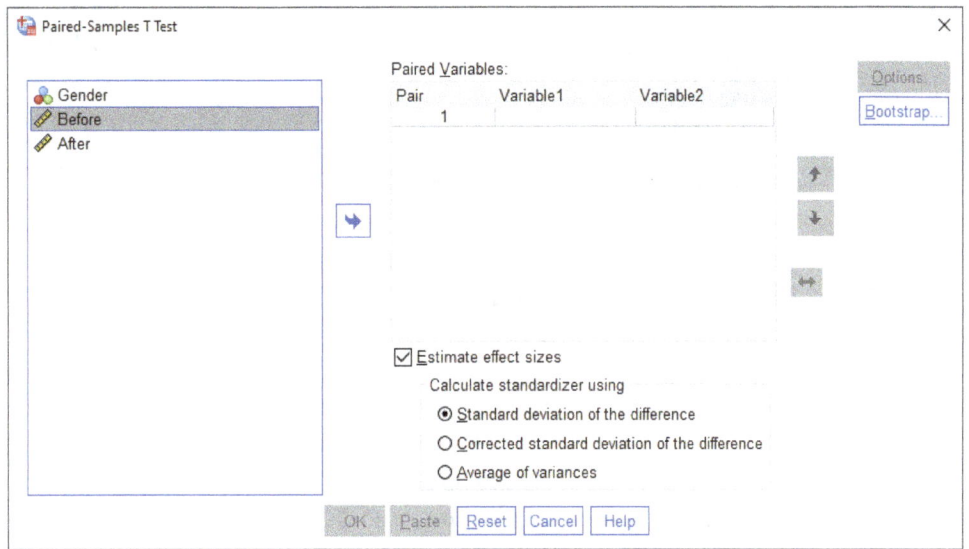

Image 9.3

2. Assume that in your SPSS data file you are using similar variable names for all three variables in Table 9.3. On *Paired Variables*, insert *Before* into *Variable 1* and *After* into *Variable 2*. The before is the risk factor scores before the training was provided, and the after is the risk factor scores after the 6-week training was completed.
3. Click *Options* to enter the self-desired confidence interval.
4. Click *OK*. Momentarily, the following three tables will be shown.

TABLE 9.7 **Paired Samples (Dependent) Statistics**

		Mean	N	Std. Deviation	Std. Error Mean
Pair 1	Total risk factor scores before training	26.35	20	8.177	1.829
	Total risk factor scores after training	43.50	20	9.870	2.207

TABLE 9.8 **Paired Samples Correlations**

		N	Correlation	Sig.
Pair 1	Total risk factor scores before training and total risk factor scores after training	20	.683	.001

TABLE 9.9 **Paired Samples Test**

	Paired Differences					t	df	Sig. (Two-Tailed)
	Mean	Std. Deviation	Std. Error Mean	99% Confidence Interval of the Difference				
				Lower	Upper			
Pair 1 Total risk factor scores before training and total risk factor scores after training	−17.150	7.350	1.644	−21.852	−12.448	−10.434	19	.000

The first part of the table confirms the sample mean for the pretest and posttest scores as manually calculated. Similar to the manual calculation, SPSS also confirms that there is a significant difference in mean scores between the pretest and posttest scores ($t = -10.434$, $df = 19$, $p < .000$). In fact, SPSS increases the CI from 99.9% to 99.99%. If one is to increase the p value to four decimal places, the p value is .0001.

SUMMARY

In this chapter, a brief summary of how t-tests can be applied to various situations and for evaluating one's practice outcome was provided. Overall, the one-sample t-test can be used to examine the following possible health and human services issues:

- Any type of intervention program in which the criterion or DV is interval or ratio; for example, the volume of illegal drug abuse based on specific criteria
- The scale of personal functioning of a sample and the population
- Comparing a sample mean on treatment sessions with the population mean of that group

The independent samples t-test can be used with the following issues:

- Comparing two independently drawn samples with a health and human services program—for example, the effectiveness of an outreach program for children with attention deficit hyperactivity disorder for children groups A and B, for which A and B are not related
- School counseling methods with no more than two methods for children with learning disabilities and for which each method is independently designed
- Self-rated perceptions regarding practice effectiveness of two unrelated groups, such as nurses and social workers

The dependent samples t-test can be used in the following potential situations:

- Comparing two related scores—for example, pretest and posttest scores of psychotherapeutic drugs
- Examining changes in cognitive-behavioral approaches for two related groups
- Examining the degree of job training compliance for two related groups

The correlation coefficient effect size and the Cohen's d effect size can be used to examine the magnitude (i.e., small, medium, large) of the means difference for the independent samples and dependent samples, respectively.

When using SPSS to compute the t-statistic, pay close attention to the required level of measurement for the dependent and independent variables. Take note that the DV must always be interval or ratio and the IV must be nominal or categorical. Anything different will result in the wrong statistic being computed.

Study Questions

Multiple Choice The study questions below should be very helpful for learners to understand the mean tests.

1. Suppose that a survey was completed on 500 people at a local municipality center about the need for an illegal drug recovery center. The DV is the knowledge of the respondents, and the IVs are Native Americans and Latinos. Which type of t-test is suitable for the situation?
    a. One sample
    b. Dependent samples
    c. Independent samples
2. What is the true meaning of the *t*-test?
    a. To analyze the relationship between the variables
    b. To analyze the association between the variables
    c. To compare the mean outcome difference between the variables

3. In regard to the t-statistic, what level of measurement is needed for the IV?

    a. Nominal
    b. Ordinal
    c. Interval and ratio

4. In regard to the t-statistic, how many DV(s) is/are needed?

    a. One
    b. Two
    c. Three or more

5. Suppose that two groups of health and human services workers, nurses, and social workers reported their average daily water consumption of 48 and 56 ounces per day, respectively. According to the laws of statistics, what would you say about the t-test statistic?

    a. The t-statistic is positive.
    b. The t-statistic is negative.
    c. The t-statistic is either positive or negative.
    d. There is insufficient information.

6. The one-sample t-test is most suitable for which of the following situations?

    a. Compares the mean of a DV in the sample with its estimated mean within the population
    b. Compares the means of two related samples
    c. Compares the means of two unrelated samples

7. Suppose that one is interested in examining the number of hours that women from two separate cities spent doing volunteer work in the past 6 months. What is the proper t-statistic?

    a. One-sample t-test
    b. Independent samples t-test
    c. Dependent sample t-test

8. Suppose that $t = 7.120$, $df = 6$, $p < .000$. What can one say about the results of the study?

    a. There is no significant difference in means between the variables.
    b. There is a significant difference in means between the variables.
    c. There is a significant difference in the relationship between the variables.

9. According to statistical assumptions about the t-test for question 8, what would you say about the sample means? Would you say that

    a. mean 1 is greater than mean 2?
    b. mean 2 is greater than mean 1?
    c. the samples have equal means?

10. Assume that there are two sample groups. The first sample is undergraduate social work students at University X, and the second sample is undergraduate nursing students at University Y. Both groups were administered the Level of Commitment to Community Well-Being Scale. What is the type of t-test that must be calculated?

    a. One sample
    b. Independent samples
    c. Dependent samples
    d. All three

11. Which of the following statements is correct about the independent samples t-test?

    a. The samples are related, matched, and connected.
    b. The samples are related, do not match, and are connected.
    c. The samples are unrelated, do not match, and are unconnected.

12. Which of the following statements is correct about the dependent samples t-test?

    a. The samples are related, matched, and connected.
    b. The samples are related, do not match, and are connected.
    c. The samples are unrelated, do not match, and are unconnected.

13. The difference between Cohen's d and the z score is

    a. The z score is used for many different purposes; Cohen's d is used to study the association between variables.
    b. The z score is used for many different purposes; Cohen's d is used to study the relationship between variables.
    c. The z score is used for many different purposes; Cohen's d is used to study the mean difference between two groups.

14. If the result of an independent samples t-test is 7.39 with 18 degrees of freedom. What is the correlation of effect size?

    a. It is .08.
    b. It is .75.
    c. It is .09.
    d. It is .87.

15. According to Coolidge (2013), the correlation of effect size for question 14 is

    a. small.
    b. medium.
    c. large.

16. Which of the following is false about the correlation coefficient of effect size?

    a. It can be larger than 1.0.
    b. It is equaled to 1.0.
    c. It can be negative.
    d. It can range from 0 to 1.0.

Answers to Study Questions

QUESTION	ANSWER	QUESTION	ANSWER
1	c	9	a
2	c	10	b
3	a	11	c
4	a	12	a
5	b	13	c
6	a	14	d
7	b	15	c
8	b	16	d

CHAPTER 10

Inferential Statistics

Simple Linear Regression

OVERVIEW

Certainly, one must be a statistician to fully understand the complex functions of regression. For non-statisticians, such as this author, only survive regression by understanding the basic form of its algorithms. Regression is a statistical technique used to model and analyze the relationships between variables in how they are related in a particular situation. There are as many as 20 types of regression. Stat Analytica (2020) states that regression is one of the branches of the statistics subject that is essential for predicting the analytical data of finance, investments, and other disciplines. Stat Analytica states further that regression is also used to calculate the character and strength of the connection between the DVs with a single or more series of predicting variables.

From business management to engineering and pure social science research, regression is used to make predictions, help make decisions, understand demand and supply, understand the process of different variables affecting outcomes, and manage the issue under investigation. Overall, there are two basic kinds of regression. One is the simple linear regression and the other is multiple linear regression. Simple linear regression is used to make a prediction or explain the result of the DV using a specific IV. Multiple linear regression, such as logistic regression, is used to analyze complex data where there are two or more IVs. Regression by itself is a very difficult statistical method. The statistical computations are complex and time consuming.

To truly understand regression, taking a course in multivariate regression is necessary. It was one of most difficult statistics courses taken by this author while in college. Multivariate means three or more variables, one or two DV and three or more IVs for each of the DVs. Because of the complexity of regression, the manual calculation for this chapter only discusses the simplest method, which is linear regression.

Similarly, on SPSS, only the linear regression model (LRM) and its relevant statistical symbols, meaning, and interpretations are discussed. Questions such as *"What makes people happy?"* will not be discussed. Why? Because there are many IVs that make people happy, which is beyond the scope of this book.

In correlation analysis, it was stated that *x* (IV) may or may not be related to *y* (DV). This chapter will examine various values of the IV that are used to predict values in the DV. For example, in Chapter 8, the relationship between years spent in college (assume the individual graduated) and hourly wage was found to have a significant relationship. This chapter extends the discussion by looking at different values in years spent in college that can actually be used to predict hourly wage. For example, with an additional year of college education (a one-unit increase), how much of this unit will cause the hourly wage to rise? On a different matter, with an additional child born, how many parental responsibilities will a parent gain?

Just to reiterate, in correlation, the *DV* is better known as the *criterion* or *outcome* variable, and the *IV* is better known as the *predictor* variable and must be scaled with interval or ratio data. Overall, the *basic predictive functions of regression are introduced in this chapter.* Meyers et al. (2006) state that *when a single variable is used to predict another single variable, the procedure is called "simple linear regression"* (p. 127). Meyers and colleagues also state that the Pearson correlation between two variables can be used as a basis for predicting the values for one variable given knowledge of the values of the other. As a result, *linear regression amounts to an advanced version of the Pearson correlation coefficient.*

Chapter 8 discusses the correlation coefficient (which provides an overall picture of the linear relationship between two interval/ratio variables, represented by *r*). When r is squared, the r^2 *also provides an understanding of the strength of the relationship.* By examining the correlation coefficient (r) or the coefficient of determination (r^2), the researchers have evidence that the linear relationship produced by two or more variables probably was not due to chance or sampling error. This means that the result actually mirrors the population from which the sample was randomly drawn. Based on r^2, the researchers know that a certain portion of the variability of the DV can be explained.

Consider the question, *"What causes the explained portion of the variability?"* The quick response to the question is that one could use the *values (only the values, not another variable)* of a specific IV (e.g., $x_1, x_2, x_3, \ldots x_n$) to make a prediction about the effects it has on the DV. *Each x is an incremental value of the IV.* $X_1, X_2, X_3, \ldots X_n$ and not just the values of an IV. They can also be used to represent multiple predictor variables. In turn, *whether through correlation analyses, common sense, or other personal logic, researchers understand that regardless of the issue under investigation, many factors can affect or influence its outcome.*

As a reminder, in Chapter 8, the correlation coefficient for years spent in college and hourly wage was equal to 0.927 (r = .927). If this r is squared and the product is multiplied by 100%, its result of 85.93% becomes powerful information. The result of this multiplication is called the coefficient of determination, usually abbreviated as r-squared (r^2).

While years spent in college (IV) explains 85.93% of the variations in hourly wage (DV), the other 14.07% (100 − 85.93 = 14.07) could not be accounted for. The result from the subtraction shows that beyond years spent in college, researchers still do not know what else influenced people's ability to earn a highly competitive hourly wage. As a simple explanation, college alone cannot account for 100% of people's hourly wage. Researchers still need to find out what contributes to the remaining 14.07%. Statistically, people's ability to earn a highly competitive hourly wage can be explained by answering a very important question:

Beyond college degrees, what are the other variables that could be used as predictor variables to better understand highly competitive hourly wages?

Linear regression analysis is one of the mathematical probability statistical tools that could help answer questions of this nature. Researchers could use a set of questions, say ten IVs, to see how much each of the variables contribute to a highly competitive hourly wage, or they could simply examine the values of a single scale variable and see how much each value contributes to it. In the case of hourly wage and years spent in college, researchers can easily use the bachelor's, master's, and doctoral levels to see how each level of education contributes to higher wage earning.

Essentially, if statistical proof exists that years spent in college is an influential factor to hourly wage, then people might encourage their family members to go to college regardless of its difficulties. Meyers and colleagues (2006) explained that *simple linear regression is a procedure that uses a single variable to predict another single variable* just as in the case of hourly wage and years spent in college.

THE MEANING OF SIMPLE LINEAR REGRESSION

As stated earlier, regression analysis goes beyond correlation analysis. It is a belief among statistics teachers that if two variables are related, it is possible to make causal predictions because they provide better accuracy about the generalization of the variables under investigation (Myers et al., 2006; Nowaczyk, 1988; Science Direct, 2015). *Regression literally means going back or returning* (Weinbach & Grinnell, 2015). *One may wonder, going back to where? The simplest response is going back to the correlation variables.* It is a linear function that provides either a good or a poor description of the relationships regarding how *y* (the DV) relates to *x* (the IV) in a straight line (Agresti & Finlay, 2009). *It also measures a linear relationship between two interval/ratio variables in which the observations displayed in a scatter diagram can be approximated with a straight line* (Leon-Guerrero & Frankfort-Nachmias, 2012). Leon-Guerreros and Frankfort-Nachmias specifically state that "the line itself provides a predicted value of Y for any value of X" (p. 234).

In simple terms, researchers can take the results of the regression to predict the value of the DV. The underlying goal in regression analysis is to organize data and explain its effects on the variables. Suppose that in a research study, a significant relationship is observed between the DV (*y*) and IV (*x*) variables. If nothing is done to *x*, then nothing will happen to *y*. Take, for example, the study hours of college students. In regression analysis, the hypothesis is that knowledge gained is directly related to the time spent in study. In this case, knowledge (y) is a direct effect of study hours (x). We know that correlation analysis simply shows that there is a relationship between knowledge and study hours but nothing concerning other possible contributing factors. Regression takes us a step further by examining the effects of study hours. Therefore, someone who spent considerable time studying can say that *x* is a necessary phenomenon in understanding the empirical effects of the subject matter *y*.

The amount of effects, specifically the slope of the regression line (b), matters most in linear regression. Why? This is *because statistical analyses involving one or more forms of regression always include the correlation coefficient (r) and the coefficient of determination (r²) as there generally is no perfect correlation between the variables.*

THE MEANING OF PREDICTION IN HEALTH AND HUMAN SERVICES

Health and human services workers, such as social workers, nurses, physical therapists, and speech pathologists, as well as behaviorists like clinical psychologists and family therapists, often are called on to make informed guesses about causes and factors that are related to certain health conditions, behavioral health issues, or types of interventions. The following are several applicable statements in health and human services settings where linear regression can be helpful (Lee et al., 2016):

- Social workers may want to know how best to predict child maltreatment owing to chemical dependency (i.e., illegal drugs and hard liquor).
- Nurses may want to examine the causes and effects of medical noncompliance.
- Physical therapists may want to predict the effect of exercises for people who are involved in car accidents.
- Clinical psychologists may want to examine the effects of drugs prescribed by psychiatrists in treating children's ADHD.

Results produced by regression will enable individuals from many professions to make educated guesses regarding certain outcome (y) variables based on the value of a particular predictor (x) variable. Before looking at the computational formula for making predictions on these issues, let us look at the rules of statistics pertaining to linear regression.

STATISTICAL REQUIREMENTS/CONDITIONS FOR SIMPLE LINEAR REGRESSION

The following conditions are important when calculating simple linear regression (Hays, 1994, Meyers et al., 2006):

- Similar to other forms of statistical tests, simple linear regression involves the use of inferential statistics. Inferential statistics is the body of statistical computations relevant to extrapolating findings based on a sample to a larger population.
- A requisite is random sampling; however, in health and human services settings, there may be situations for which random sampling is impossible, especially when the number of clients is small. In situations like this, random assignment instead of random sampling may prove useful.
- The sampling distribution must be normally distributed under the areas of the normal curve.

- The DV and IVs must be continuous and interval or ratio level. In addition to interval or ratio data, the data must be *homoscedastic, which means that the degree of variation in the two variables being correlated is similar and does not vary widely.*

COMPUTATIONAL FORMULA FOR LINEAR REGRESSION

Making a prediction is not as hard and complex as described. The computational formula for making a prediction is simple and can be computed by

$$Y' = a + bX$$

where

Y' = Predicted regression coefficient (also called the predicted Y value from the particular X value);
a = Y intercept; it is the point where the regression line would intercept the y-axis and is better known as the constant;
b = Slope of the regression line, where the amount of change in Y is directly related to the amount of change in X (better known as the regression coefficient); and
X = Selected value of the predictor variable about which researchers want to make a prediction concerning the value of the DV or Y.

With all the statistical symbols used throughout the book to this point, the only one in this equation that you are familiar with is X. The symbols "a = constant or the Y intercept," "b = slope of the regression line," and "Y' = predicted regression coefficient" in the equation are new; therefore, let us see how they are calculated. The first symbol in the equation, the constant "a," is computed by

$$a = \bar{Y} - b(\bar{X})$$

where

$\bar{Y}$ = Mean of Y (arithmetic average for the dependent or criterion variable), and
$\bar{X}$ = Mean of X (arithmetic average for the independent or predictor variable).

Please note that the constant (a) cannot be computed without the slope (b) of the regression line. The computational formula for the slope of the regression is computed as

$$b = \frac{N(\Sigma XY) - (\Sigma X)(\Sigma Y)}{N(\Sigma X^2) - (\Sigma X)^2}$$

where
N = Total sample for the study project,

ΣXY = Sum of the multiplication between X and Y,
ΣX = Sum of the independent/predictor variable,
ΣY = Sum of the dependent/criterion variable,
ΣX^2 = Sum of the X squares, and
$(\Sigma X)^2$ = Squares the sum of X.

From algebra to advanced statistics, there are different formulas to calculate the slope. What is shown here is one of them. Please note that this formula is a partial segment of the Pearson correlation coefficient formula. It is computed by using the first half of the Pearson's r formula without the square root. Since the goal is to make predictions for the criterion variable (Y), the segment for the sum for Y squared and squaring the sum of Y is omitted. To help with anyone's recollection of the Pearson correlation coefficient, the formula is redisplayed here.

$$r = \frac{N(\Sigma XY) - (\Sigma X)(\Sigma Y)}{\sqrt{[N(\Sigma X^2) - (\Sigma X)^2][N(\Sigma Y^2) - (\Sigma Y)^2]}}$$

Now that the general statistical concepts and symbols for the meaning of linear regression are more familiar, let us apply this knowledge to situations related to health and human services.

Practice Example 1

In Chapter 8 (Table 8.1), a vignette was presented about an employment-related situation where the research study focused on hourly wage (Y) based on years spent in college (X), assuming that the participants graduated from school in a timely fashion. Now, let's examine how high school level graduates, bachelor level graduates, and master's level graduates can earn a competitive hourly wage based on the sample vignette. For easy viewing, Table 8.1 was copied and pasted below. For learning purposes, the new hypotheses are now changed as follows:

H_o = *Wage earnings for health and human services workers cannot be based on the years spent in college.*
H_a = *Wage earnings for health and human services workers are highly dependent on the years spent in college.*

By examining the formula for computing the predicted regression line (Y'), the slope (b) must be calculated first and then the constant (a). For the constant, once b is known, the $\bar{x}$ for the DV, which is the $\bar{Y}$ and the $\bar{x}$ for the IV, which is the $\bar{X}$ must be calculated too. Notice that the steps occur sequentially.

$$b = \frac{30(18{,}911) - (506)(1{,}037)}{30(8{,}810) - (506)^2}$$

$$= \frac{567{,}330 - 524{,}722}{264{,}300 - 256{,}036}$$

$$= \frac{42{,}608}{8{,}264}$$

$$b = 5.16$$

The result for b indicates that every unit of change in the IV (x axis) variable will have a 5.16 effect on the DV (y axis) variable. For a simpler explanation, presume that every person's hourly wage begins at zero (0). Each year a person completes one year of extra college study beyond high school, the probability that the person's hourly wage will increase is about $5.16 per hour. Thus, the minimum hourly wage for a typical 4-year college graduate is about $20.64 ($5.16 × 4 = 20.64).

Now that b is known, a can be calculated. Based on Table 8.2, $\bar{Y}$ is 34.57 and $\bar{X}$ is 16.87; the constant can be calculated by

$$a = 34.57 - 5.16(16.87)$$

$$= 34.57 - 87.05$$

$$= -52.48.$$

Do not be alarmed by the huge negative constant. The result simply indicates that the Y intercept will always start at −52.48 or that the hourly wage earning of everyone will always begin below zero before the employer factors level of education and other related factors into the hiring process.

When both the slope and the constant are known, researchers can use various years of schooling completed from Table 8.2 to make predictions about competitive hourly wage earning for the general public (see the first and second columns).

First, let's examine high school level graduates (12 years of schooling).

$$Y'_{12 \text{ or ID } 01} = -52.48 + 5.16(12)$$

$$= -52.48 + 61.92$$

$$= 9.44$$

TABLE 8.2 Expanding Table 8.1 Into Segments for the Pearson's r Calculation

ID	X	X²	Y	Y²	XY
01	12	144	15	225	180
02	16	256	20	400	320
03	18	324	32	1,024	576
04	21	441	60	3,600	1,260
05	14	196	17	289	238
06	18	324	35	1,225	630
07	20	400	62	3,844	1,240
08	21	441	65	4,225	1,365
09	18	324	35	1,225	630
10	19	361	30	900	570
11	12	122	14	196	168
12	14	196	18	324	252
13	18	324	40	1,600	720
14	16	256	25	625	400
15	21	441	72	5,184	1,512
16	12	144	14	196	168
17	13	169	17	289	221
18	16	256	26	676	416
19	18	324	38	1,444	684
20	21	441	55	3,025	1,155
21	13	169	15	225	195
22	16	256	29	841	464
23	18	324	35	1,225	630

24	21	441	56	3,136	1,176
25	12	144	14	196	168
26	16	256	33	1,089	528
27	15	225	30	900	450
28	18	324	38	1,444	684
29	18	324	42	1,764	756
30	21	441	55	3,025	1,155
N = 30	ΣX = 506	ΣX² = 8,810	ΣY = 1037	ΣY² = 44,361	ΣXY = 18,911
	$\bar{X}$ = 16.87		$\bar{Y}$ = 34.57		
	Variance = 9.499		Variance = 293.633		
	SD_x = 3.082		SD_y = 17.136		

For evidence-based practice, the result is used to predict the probability that any high school level graduate will be earning about $9.44 per hour for their starting wage.

Next, let's examine the probability of a 4-year college graduate (16 years of schooling).

$$Y'_{16 \text{ or ID } 02} = -52.48 + 5.16(16)$$

$$= -52.48 + 82.56$$

$$= 30.08$$

The evidence-based practice indicates that competitive wage earning for a 4-year college graduate is $30.08 per hour. More importantly, a 4-year college graduate can earn as much as 218.64% higher in hourly wage than a high school graduate (30.08 – 9.44. Divide the difference by 9.44 and then multiply by 100%, which will result in 218.64).

Finally, the master's level of education (18 years of schooling) can be predicted by

$$Y'_{18 \text{ or ID } 03} = -52.48 + 5.16(18)$$

$$= -52.48 + 92.88$$

$$= 40.4$$

Evidence-based practice predicts that having a master's-level education can start hourly wages at about $40.40 per hour. One can continue and make the same prediction for doctoral-level education with

21 years of schooling. All three predictions show that in evidence-based practice, the research hypothesis is supported, and the results are generalizable from the sample to the population.

Practice Example 2

For another evidence-based practice example, suppose that a clinical social worker is working with 20 clients with very low self-esteem. After several months of group counseling, the social worker decided to randomly select five members of the group to participate in socialization skills training with members of the larger community. Socialization skills training includes taking them to the shopping mall, helping them interact with public officials, and having them read a children's book to children at several elementary schools.

The clinical social worker used two instruments to measure the treatment effect. One is the self-esteem measure, and this measure is being treated as the criterion variable (Y). The other is the socialization skills training, and it is being treated as the predictor variable (X). Both used a metric scale of 1 to 5 with five items each. A higher score indicates higher self-esteem and higher socialization skills. The cutoff for the self-esteem and socialization skills are as follows:

22-25 = Very effective
18-21 = Effective
14-17 = Somewhat effective
13 and below = Not effective

Once the training program is completed, the social worker collected the final self-rated scores from the five participants and their scores are displayed in Table 10.1.

TABLE 10.1 Self-Rated Socialization Skills Training to Improve Self-Esteem

Participant	Socialization Skills (X)	Self-Esteem (Y)
01	15	19
02	12	16
03	8	14
04	20	23
05	18	21

Tasks to be completed:
1. Complete the remaining columns for both the correlation and regression analysis.
2. Calculate the Pearson correlation coefficient for the situation under investigation.
3. Calculate the slope and the constant for the regression line.
4. Make predictions for participants number 3 and 5.

5. How many participants self-rated that the socialization skills training was effective? How do you know?

Answers

1. Column expansion

TABLE 10.2 Expansion on Self-Rated Socialization Skills Training to Improve Self-Esteem

Participant	Socialization Skills (X)	X²	Self-Esteem (Y)	Y²	XY
01	15	225	19	361	285
02	12	144	16	256	192
03	8	64	14	196	112
04	20	400	23	529	460
05	18	324	21	441	378
	$\Sigma X = 73$ $\overline{X} = 14.6$	$\Sigma X^2 = 1{,}157$	$\Sigma Y = 93$ $\overline{Y} = 18.6$	$\Sigma Y^2 = 1{,}783$	$\Sigma XY = 1{,}427$

2. The Pearson correlation coefficient

$$r = \frac{5(1{,}427) - (73)(93)}{\sqrt{[5(1{,}157) - (73)^2][5(1{,}83) - (93)^2]}}$$

$$= \frac{7{,}135 - 6{,}789}{\sqrt{[5{,}785 - 5{,}329][8{,}915 - 8{,}649]}}$$

$$= \frac{346}{\sqrt{(456)(266)}}$$

$$= .993$$

3. Slope

$$b = \frac{5(1{,}427) - (73)(93)}{5(1{,}157) - (73)^2}$$

$$= \frac{7{,}135 - 6{,}789}{5{,}785 - 5{,}329}$$

$$= \frac{346}{456}$$

$$= .76$$

Constant

$$a = 18.6 - .76(14.6)$$

$$= 18.6 - 11.08$$

$$= 7.52$$

4. Making prediction

$$Y'_{03} = 7.52 + .76(8)$$

$$= 7.52 + 6.08$$

$$= 13.6$$

Evidence-based practice indicates that any client with a socialization skill score of 8 will have a maximum self-esteem score of only 13.6, which shows that the treatment is only somewhat effective. Continue the prediction with client number 5.

$$Y'_{05} = 7.5 + .76(18)$$

$$= 7.52 + 13.68$$

$$= 21.2$$

With a socialization skill of 18, clients with very low self-esteem within a treatment program will improve to 21.2, which shows that the treatment is effective.
5. Only clients number 4 and 5 show that the treatment is effective. None of the five clients rated the socialization skills training as very effective.

Other Statistical Symbols (Notations)

What has been discussed thus far has involved only simple linear regression. There are many statistical configurations regarding regression models and other regression coefficients. It was stated at the beginning of the chapter that the study of regression by itself is a difficult course and involves complex statistical computations. Because this is an introductory statistics book, the computations for other regression models and coefficients are not illustrated. Because regressions are hardly calculated manually nowadays, this section explains some of the common statistical configurations that appear in a computerized output. With the explanations that follow, even if one does not know how the symbols (notations) were computed, the author(s) of the report should still be able to explain these additional symbols or statistical notations with ease for evidence-based practices and research purposes (Lee et al., 2016).

- *R*. *R* is the same as *r* in Chapter 8, and it is the correlation coefficient (r) between the DV and IVs. The *SPSS* and other computer applications, as well as statistics textbooks, use the capital letter *R* to help author(s) of a report remember that this part of the correlation coefficient appears under regression, and it is used to show the relationship between the criterion and predictor variables. Please review Chapter 8 to determine the range of the strength of the relationship. *It is not used to stand for "regression coefficient."*

- R^2. Because R is the same as r, then one should know that is the same as the coefficient of determination (r^2). Therefore, R^2 *represents the percentage of variance in the DV that can be explained by one or more IVs*. Most statistics books suggest that .15 or higher represents a good amount of the variance explained between the criterion and predictor variables.

- Adjusted *R-squared*. $R^2_{Adjusted}$ is a more conservative measure than the standard R^2. *It is the adding or dropping of predictor variables from the regression model and still represents the percentage of the variance in the DV that can be explained by two or more IV (also called factors) as opposed to the sample size.* In using computerized applications to compute solutions, notice that each time a new predictor variable is entered into the regression model the adjusted R^2 always becomes smaller than the standard R^2.

- *Unstandardized regression coefficient* (B or b). The first coefficient labeled "*constant*" is the Y intercept (a) where X meets Y for the first time. The coefficient below the "*constant*" is the slope in the regression equation (b). Remember that the slope of the line refers to the proportion of change in the criterion variable (Y) for each unit of change in the predictor variable (X). *It is usually referred to as "raw" coefficients produced by regression analysis because it represents the relation between raw data, unstandardized variables.*

- *Standardized regression coefficient* (beta coefficients or beta weights, β). Lowercase beta (β) is also known as a partial correlation coefficient representing a linear correlation between the criterion and predictor variables while controlling for the effect of other predictor variables in the analysis. Please note that when writing a research report, the standardized coefficient (β) is more desirable than the unstandardized coefficient (b). However, the previous illustrations in this chapter were based on b instead of β. *They are calculated nearly the same way except when calculating β, it is treated as the standardized slope coefficient based on the z score.* Beta weights are used to estimate a regression analysis that has been standardized so that the variances of dependent and independent variables are 1, which indicates how many standard deviations a DV will change when the standard deviation in the predictor variable increases.

- *Standard error of the estimate*. This is broadly defined as the standard error of the estimate from the sample to the population. Typically, it is computed by dividing the sample standard deviation by the square root of *n* or its degrees of freedom. *However, be cautious that the coefficient is different from one regression model to the next.*

- *Statistical significance*. When there is only one criterion and one predictor variable, report the significant difference between the variables using the column that shows the t-statistic (Chapter 9). When there are two criteria and two or more predictor variables, explain the statistical significance using the *F* ratio (Chapter 11).

SPSS INSTRUCTIONS ON LRM

Recall that linear regression is used to estimate the coefficients of the linear equation involving one or more IVs that best predict the value of the dependent (outcome) variable. The first practice example in this chapter discussed the linear relationship between hourly wage (DV) and years spent in college (IV). Duplicating the manual calculation, SPSS is now being used to achieve a similar outcome. Again, regression is one of the extremely complex statistical equations. This section only provides instructions to achieve the LRM model. To compute the LRM linear regression, simply follow these steps:

- For practical purposes, open the SPSS file that you created for Chapter 8 or open another file of your own research project that contains interval- and ratio-level data.
- Pull down the *Analyze* ribbon. Move the cursor down to *Regression* and then move the cursor over to the *Linear*. Click it. Note that above the *Regression* ribbon, there are two similar functions labeled "*General Linear Model*" and "*Generalized Linear Model*." These two functions are used for the advanced regression model. Once you click *Linear*, this mini window will pop up. Note that the two variables that appear on the variable list were the ones the author of this book created for Chapter 8.

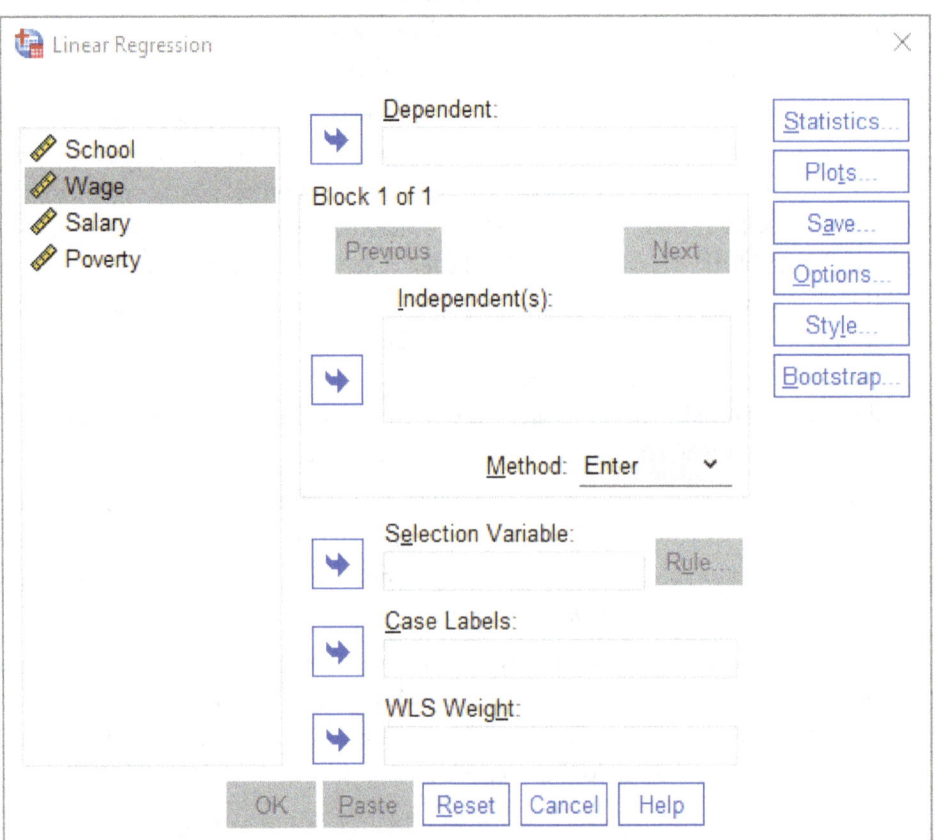

Image 10.1

- In Chapter 8, it was stated to use "*hourly wage*" as the dependent (outcome) variable. Select and hit the forward arrow (→) to move the variable "*Wage*" into it. Now, select and forward the "*years spent in college*" to the independent(s) mini window.
- *In your own research project, in case there are multiple independent (predictor) variables, one of the following methods must be chosen.* SPSS 27 (SPSS, 2020) provides the following instructions for the method selections:

    Enter (Regression). A procedure for variable selection in which all variables in a block are entered in a single step.

    Stepwise. At each step, the IV not in the equation that has the smallest probability of F is entered, if that probability is sufficiently small. Variables already in the regression equation are removed if their probability of F becomes sufficiently large. The method terminates when no more variables are eligible for inclusion or removal.

    Remove. A procedure for variable selection in which all variables in a block are removed in a single step.

    Backward Elimination. A variable selection procedure in which all variables are entered into the equation and then sequentially removed. The variable with the smallest partial correlation with the DV is considered first for removal. If it meets the criterion for elimination, it is removed. After the first variable is removed, the variable remaining in the equation with the smallest partial correlation is considered next. The procedure stops when there are no variables in the equation that satisfy the removal criteria.

    Forward Selection. A stepwise variable selection procedure in which variables are sequentially entered into the model. The first variable considered for entry into the equation is the one with the largest positive or negative correlation with the DV. This variable is entered into the equation only if it satisfies the criterion for entry. If the first variable is entered, the IV not in the equation that has the largest partial correlation is considered next. The procedure stops when there are no variables that meet the entry criterion.
- Click on *Statistics* to change the confidence interval and other options. For duplication with the manual calculation, change the confidence interval to 99%.
- On *Plot*, if so desired for a histogram or other type of graph, click and select the type of scatter plot for the result.
- Click on *Options*. Options are only useful when multiple predictor variables are entered into the model. When there is only one predictor variable, the option will not matter. On *Use of Probability of F*, enter the lowest and highest values you are willing to tolerate for the significant relationship.
- On *Selection Variable*, in case you want to put a limit on a particular variable—for example, limiting the computation on age and only including those between the ages of 18 to 65—then enter the variable and set the limitations. On *WLS Weight*, select the variable for a weighted least-squares analysis, which is beyond the scope of this course.
- Click *OK*. Momentarily, among the tables, the following two tables (Tables 10.3—10.4) will be included.

TABLE 10.3 **Model Summary**

Model	R	R-Squared	Adjusted R-Squared	Std. Error of the Estimate
1	.927[a]	.860	.855	6.527

a. Predictors: (Constant), Years spent in school
b. DV: Hourly wage

TABLE 10.4 **Coefficients**

Model		Unstandardized Coefficients		Standardized Coefficients	t	Sig.	99.0% Confidence Interval for B	
		B	Std. Error	Beta			Lower Bound	Upper Bound
1	(Constant)	−52.395	6.739		−7.775	.000	−71.016	−33.775
	Years spent in school	5.156	.393	.927	13.112	.000	4.069	6.242

DV: Hourly wage

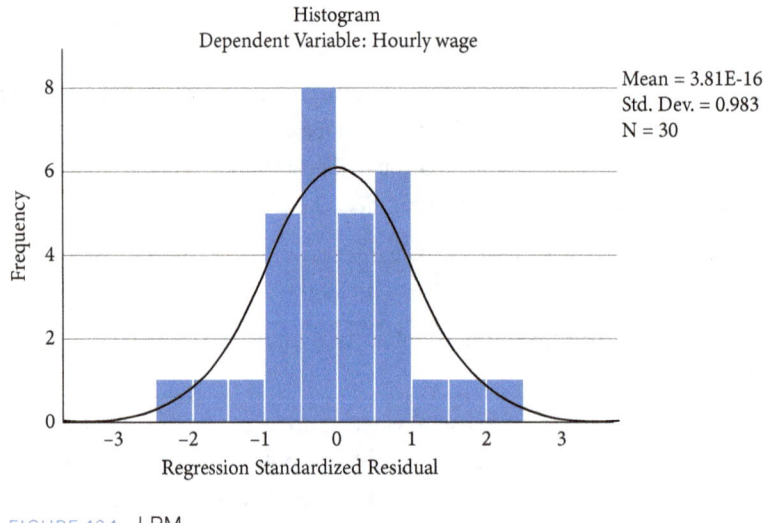

FIGURE 10.1 LRM

All coefficients on the manual calculation for hourly wage and years spent in college were reaffirmed by SPSS for the LRM. Table 10.3 shows that *R* and *R-squared are* the same as from the manual calculations for Chapter 8. Table 10.4 duplicates the constant (−53.395) and the slope for the regression line

(5.156) as in Practice Example 1. The t-statistic indicates a significant means difference between hourly wage and years spent in college ($t = 13.112$, $p < .000$). The histogram graph (Figure 10.1) also shows a uniform bell curve for hourly wage.

SUMMARY

This chapter introduced the basic form of regression analyses. Regression literally means going back or returning. One may wonder, going back to where? The simplest response is going back to the correlation variables. Regression is a statistical technique used to model and analyze the relationships between variables in how they are related together in a particular situation. Stat Analytica (2020) states that regression is one of the branches of the statistics subject that is essential for predicting the analytical data of finance, investments, and other disciplines. Stat Analytica states further that regression is also used to calculate the character and strength of the connection between the DVs with a single or more series of predicting variables.

From business management to engineering and pure social science research, regression is used to make predictions, help make a decision, understand demand and supply, understand the process of different variables that affect outcomes, and manage the issue under investigation. Overall, there are two basic kinds of regression. One is the simple linear regression, and the other is multiple linear regression. Simple linear regression is used to make a prediction or explain the result of the DV using a specific IV. Multiple linear regression, such as logistic regression, is used to analyze complex data where there are two or more IVs.

Simple linear regression means that a regression results from the actions taken to analyze outcomes from manipulating the value of the predictor variable (x) to predict the value of the DV (y). The underlying goal in linear regression analysis is to organize data and explain its effects on the variables. Suppose that in a research study, a significant relationship is observed between the dependent (y) and independent (X) variables. If nothing is done to X, then nothing will happen to Y. Take, for example, the study hours of college students. In regression analysis, the hypothesis is that knowledge gained is directly related to the time spent in study. In this case, knowledge (Y) is a direct effect of study hour (X). We know that correlation analysis simply shows that there is a relationship between knowledge and study hours but nothing concerning other possible contributing factors. Regression takes us a step further by examining the effects of study hours. Therefore, someone who spent considerable time studying can say that X is a necessary phenomenon in understanding the empirical effects of the subject matter Y

The next chapter introduces the analysis of variance and is the last chapter introducing the basic functions of inferential statistics. Once learners are knowledgeable about these and all the material presented in other chapters in this book, they will be well on their way to achieving competence in handling basic data analyses and interpretations.

Study Questions

Multiple Choice. The following study questions are helpful to understand linear regression

1. Which of the following statements is correct about making predictions?
    a. Y′ (Y prime) is the arithmetic average for the criterion variable.
    b. "b" is the constant where X and Y intercept.
    c. "a" is the slope of the regression line.
    d. None of them is correct.

2. Which of the following statements is/are true about the meaning of simple linear regression?
    a. It is used to make causal predictions between interval and ratio dependent and independent variables.
    b. It is used to make causal predictions between nominal and ordinal dependent and independent variables.
    c. It is used to compare the mean difference between nominal and interval/ratio dependent and independent variables.

3. In simple linear regression, which of the following statistical configurations reflect the amount of change from one unit to another?
    a. The predicted value
    b. The constant
    c. The slope
    d. The sample mean

4. Which of the following statistical assumptions is not very important for linear regression?
    a. Sample size
    b. Random sampling
    c. Normal distribution
    d. Interval- or ratio-level data

5. Why is regression also known as the advanced form of correlation?
    a. Because the correlation coefficient and coefficient of determination still play dominant roles
    b. Because of R^2
    c. Because of the adjusted R^2
    d. Because of the slope of the regression line

6. Which of the following statistical configurations is the conservative measure for regression?
    a. Slope "b"
    b. R-squared
    c. Adjusted R-squared
    d. Standardized regression coefficient

7. What is the difference between r and R?
   a. r is the correlation coefficient, while R is used to stand for "Regression."
   b. r is the correlation coefficient under Pearson, while R is the correlation coefficient under regression.
   c. R is the adjusted R-squared under regression.
   d. r is the standardized regression coefficient.

8. In regression analysis, the DV is called:
   a. the predictor variable.
   b. the y-axis.
   c. the regression coefficient.
   d. the criterion variable.

9. If r = 0.642. What is the value of R?
   a. .412
   b. 0.642
   c. Either one is correct.
   d. There is insufficient information.

10. Which of the following statements is suitable for regression analysis?
    a. Social workers may want to know how best to correlate gender with race.
    b. Nurses may want to know how to associate rural and urban health care with race.
    c. Physical therapists may want to predict the effect of exercises on people who were involved in car accidents.
    d. Professors may want to associate race and passing for students in a statistics class.

11. If given $\bar{X}$ = 28.21, $\bar{Y}$ = 14.60, b = .05, and X = 8. What is the constant for this situation?
    a. 16.01
    b. 13.19
    c. −3.60
    d. Need more information

12. In Question 11, what is the predicted value for the equation?
    a. 13.19
    b. 14.64
    c. 13.59
    d. There is insufficient information.

13. In Question 11, suppose that another person scored two points higher. What would you say about the regression line?
    a. The regression line would stay the same.
    b. The regression line would go up.

c. The regression line would go down.
d. Unable to predict.

14. Regression means going back. The term *going back* refers to which of the following?
    a. Going back to descriptive statistics
    b. Going back to chi-square
    c. Going back to t-test
    d. Going back to correlation

15. Which of the following statements is incorrect about regression assumptions?
    a. Regression is a part of descriptive statistics.
    b. Either random sampling or random assignment is required.
    c. The data set must be normally distributed.
    d. Required interval and ratio data for the predictor and criterion variables.

16. When controlling for one or more predictor variables, which of the following statistical figures is preferred?
    a. R^2
    b. $R^2_{Adjusted}$
    c. Unstandardized regression coefficient
    d. Standardized regression coefficient

Answers to Study Questions

QUESTION	ANSWER	QUESTION	ANSWER
1	d	9	b
2	a	10	c
3	c	11	b
4	a	12	c
5	a	13	b
6	c	14	d
7	b	15	a
8	d	16	d

CHAPTER 11

Inferential Statistics
One-Way ANOVA

OVERVIEW

This chapter discusses research situations where one interval or ratio dependent variable and three or more nominal independent (factor) variables are being tested. Some statistics books combined the t-tests (Chapter 9) and the contents of this chapter. A lot of times a research project is designed to include three or more groups or several factors. For example, a research project aims to reduce youthful delinquent behaviors. The project targets five population groups (K = 5). The groups are Asian American, African American, Latino, Native American, and White. The goal is to use life coaching methods to educate youths from these five groups. Presume that life coaching is defined as teaching techniques that can change the perception and direction of youth and keep them in continuous growth, development, and happiness. The measurement tool is based on a scale from 0 to 10 to evaluate the effectiveness of life coaching. In this particular example, the dependent and independent samples t-tests are no longer applicable. For situations like this scenario, the *one-way analysis of variance or simple ANOVA must be used.*

As stated in Chapter 9, when there are two or more interval or ratio DVs, the statistical analysis goes far beyond the scope of this book. It is called multiple analysis of variance (MANOVA). In either ANOVA or MANOVA, the statistical report and their meanings and interpretations are the same. Recall that the purpose of t-tests is to compare means (i.e., sample mean with population mean). In turn, with either ANOVA or MANOVA, the purpose is to compare means with multiple groups or factors (Mogull, 2004).

In ANOVA, *factor analysis* refers to a procedure used to study the relationship of two or more IVs to a DV. A single factor includes things such as the earnings of a group of people at a particular locale or the GPA of college students at different levels (i.e., freshman, sophomore, junior, and senior) within a college campus. *ANOVA calculates the between- and within-groups variances with the difference between the two variance estimates provided by Fisher's F distribution called the F-ratio. The term F-ratio or F-statistic is used interchangeably.* Meyers et al. (2006) state that "although the terminology differs somewhat, the conceptual underpinnings of the t-test and the ANOVA are the same. They are both computed as the ratio of the variability (or differences) of sample means to an estimate of error variance" (p. 282). Do not get lost or confused. *Note that without $\bar{x}$, it is impossible to calculate the SS^2 or variability among the scores.* In Chapter 4, variance is called the *sum of squares,* which is designated with SS^2. *As the term ANOVA implies, it does not partition deviations of scores. This means that it does not deviate each of the scores (x) from the sample mean ($\bar{x}$). Rather, it partitions variances by calculating SS^2 between groups and within groups.* This last sentence is quite confusing, and you will see why later in the chapter.

In simple display, the F-ratio is calculated by

$$F = \frac{Variance_{between\ groups}}{Variance_{within\ groups}}$$

Well, it is easier said than done. The F-ratio is more complex than how it is displayed here. Let's discuss it in more detail before the correct formula is fully displayed and the calculation is shown.

THE T- TEST AND F-RATIO

Typically, when using computer applications, such as SPSS and SAS, to compute solutions for the dependent samples and independent samples t-tests, both the *t* and *F* will be shown in the output. Without conscience, the researchers may opt to report either one of them. With the knowledge gained from the t-tests (see Chapter 9) and detailed knowledge from this chapter, one should be able to report findings correctly.

Meyers and colleagues (2006) pointed out that when only one IV with two correlated conditions (i.e., social workers' hourly wage in two nearby counties) exist, it is possible to use either a t-test or the F-statistic to compare the means. Essentially, the choice between the *t* and *F* ratios reflects the personal preference of the researchers if the IV has two correlated conditions. *A reason researchers do not want to use the t-test when there are three or more factors/conditions is because they must conduct multiple t-tests. When multiple t-tests are conducted, the odds of having a Type I error significantly increases.* Recall that Type I error is the chance of finding significance when there is none.

For example, usually, there are several different groups of people when examining income earnings at a particular locale. The F-ratio measures the difference of the group means versus the grand mean of scores for all subjects and compares it against the remaining error. This error is the difference between the actual scores and the means of all the groups. Thus, Fisher's F-ratio is a measure of the ratio of the systematic and unsystematic variances, and higher scores are considered better than lower scores (Meyers et al., 2006).

Statistical Assumptions

The first scenario presented earlier includes Asian American (K_1), African American (K_2), Latinos (K_3), Native American (K_4), and White (K_5). Because the groups are divided by racial background and cultural differences, they are treated as independent groups ($K_1 \neq K_2 \neq K_3 \neq K_4 \neq K_5$). *With this situation in mind, one should immediately notice that ANOVA is similar to the independent samples t-test. The ANOVA allows researchers to examine the means ($\bar{x}_s$) among three or more independent groups to determine whether any differences are statistically significant.* The capital letter K is usually used to denote a group. Because ANOVA is similar to the independent samples t-test, the same statistical assumptions are required, mainly interval or ratio data for the DV and nominal data for the IVs. Also, because the F-ratio reflects variations among the means of several groups, a larger sample size is required to complete the study. *Some social scientists suggest that a minimum sample of 50 subjects per group is necessary.*

King et al. (2011, p. 315) provided the following assumptions associated with ANOVA:

- The populations are normally distributed.
- The variances (SS^2) of several populations are the same (*homogeneity of variance*). For example, $SS^2_{\mu 1} = SS^2_{\mu 2} = SS^2_{\mu K}$. Mu ($\mu$) is the population variance.
- The selection of elements comprising any particular sample is independent of selection of elements of any other sample.
- Samples are drawn at random with replacement. Are the data normally distributed? Use the scatter diagram to display the obtained scores to visualize the distributions.
- Similar to the independent samples t-test, the DV must be measured at the interval/ratio level and the IV must be nominal.

In turn, the null and alternative hypothesis for any research study can be stated as

$H_0 = SS^2_1 = SS^2_2 = SS^2_3 \ldots = SS^2_K$ (K is the number of groups or factors).

$H_a = SS^2_1 \neq SS^2_2 \neq SS^3_3 \ldots = SS^2_K$.

Overall Meaning of the F-Ratio

King et al. (2011) stated that "the ANOVA technique allows us to simultaneously compare several means with the level of significance specified by the investigator" (p. 300). The result of the *F*-ratio essentially reflects variations among the means ($\bar{x}_s$) of several groups ($SS^2_{between}$) in relation to the variation within a group (SS^2_{within}). Because of this, the significance of ANOVA simply reveals whether at least one of the means is significantly different from the others. The significant difference in group means says nothing about which mean is different from which or the degree of difference. Once the null hypothesis has been rejected, and to find out which group is significantly different from the others, two additional tests must be performed. One is called the "posteriori test or posttest," a Latin word for "What comes later?" The other is called the "post hoc or post hoc comparison," which in Latin means "after this."

These two tests are designed to examine which means are significantly different from each other. The post hoc test will be discussed at the end of the chapter.

Before computing the F-statistic, it is important to understand two sources of variability that are always involved in the complex computational formula. These two sources, as explained next, are *variability between-groups means* and *variability within-groups means*. Each source involves complex partitioning of the variances.

TWO SOURCES OF VARIABILITY FOR ANOVA

It is well-known to statistics instructors and researchers alike that when using ANOVA, there are two sources of variability: (1) between-groups means ($MS_{Between}$) and (2) within-groups means (MS_{Within}). Each source of variability has a distinct meaning.

Variability for Between-Groups Means ($MS_{Between}$)

Variability between groups ($MS_{Between}$) refers to the variation among the variance of treatment conditions because of either treatment effect or an inherent chance of variation among the individuals in a research project. It is either the treatment effect or chance because each of the groups receives a different treatment or the groups are naturally different (i.e., cultural differences). The first case scenario discussed earlier states that the research team wants to use coaching methods as a teaching technique to reduce youthful gang activities. Variability between groups means is being used to examine whether the groups report different effects, or it could be a chance that all five groups report the same effect with the teaching technique.

Variability for Within-Groups Means (MS_{Within})

Variability within groups (MS_{Within}), on the other hand, is a little more complex than variability between-groups means. It is the variation of individual scores ($x_1, x_2, x_3, ... x_n$) around the sample mean ($\bar{x}$) as a direct reflection of chance rather than as caused by different types of treatment or groups. It is the variation between the sample mean and the scores owing to chance and chance alone because members of the group receive the same treatment. Researchers are highly conscientious that regardless of the situation under investigation, not every research subject will report the same effect. In case the subjects report the same effect, then there is no variability within the group means.

Yuen (2020) explained variability within and between groups as follows:

> *The within group variance is the difference among members in each of the groups (p. 367). The difference is just part of the naturally occurring difference and should have nothing to do with the independent variable or the interaction with other groups. The between group variance is the difference among individual groups. This difference may have something to do with the effect of the independent variable, the treatment effect* (p. 367).

Practice Example

This practice example presents an evidence-based practice using ANOVA. Suppose that a joint effort between a school district and a college professor decided to study the effects of life coaching methods for a group of junior high school students in an attempt to help the students avoid joining street gangs. The research hypothesis states that as youth become more aware of youthful life stressors and other associated life conditions, they will grow and develop their young life with happiness. After randomization, the subjects were categorized into five groups. The group assignment included Asian American (x_1), African American (x_2), Latino (x_3), Native American (x_4), and White (x_5).

There were 20 subjects in each group. After 6 months of participation in the life coaching methods, each of the subjects was administered a self-rated metric scale with a range from 0 to 10 (0 is for not helpful at all and 10 is extremely helpful). The self-rated scores are displayed in Table 11.1. Please use a 95% CI, two-tailed hypothesis to complete the hypothesis test. The null and alternative hypotheses are stated as follows:

H_0 : *The sample means are similar to the means in the population.*
H_a : *The sample means are significantly different from the means in the population.*

TABLE 11.1 **Helpfulness of Life Coaching Methods**

ID	Asian American	African American	Latino	Native American	White
01	9	10	7	6	4
02	8	10	8	7	3
03	10	8	9	8	3
04	9	9	7	8	4
05	8	9	6	7	4
06	8	9	7	6	2
07	9	10	6	5	3
08	10	8	6	5	4
09	10	9	7	4	5
10	8	9	6	7	7
11	9	9	5	8	5
12	9	10	5	7	5

(Continued)

TABLE 11.1 (Continued)

ID	Asian American	African American	Latino	Native American	White
13	10	10	6	7	4
14	8	9	7	6	2
15	10	8	7	4	3
16	10	9	8	8	2
17	9	10	5	7	1
18	9	9	6	8	1
19	10	9	7	6	5
20	8	10	4	5	3

STEPS IN CALCULATING THE F-RATIO

The steps illustrated next show how the F-ratio for the simple ANOVA is calculated (Figure 11.1). The steps involve in calculating the F-ratio are numbered from 1 to 4 and formulated as Formula 11.1(a) through 11.1(e). As is true of regression (Chapter 10), the F-ratio calculation is another complex procedure because the steps are used in both ANOVA and MANOVA. The MANOVA formula simply expands the ANOVA formula. Therefore, to better understand ANOVA's multiple functions, it is recommended that one take a course involving both the simple and advanced forms of ANOVA. *Please notice that the F-ratio (Step 4) is calculated by dividing the $MS_{between}$ by MS_{within}* (Aron et al., 2011).

Note that before getting to Step 4, the first three steps must be completed. First, let's understand how the sum of squares total (SS^2_{Total}) is calculated. It is calculated by adding the sums of squares (variances) between groups ($SS^2_{between}$) to the sums of squares (variances) within groups (SS^2_{within}). Recall that the term *sum of squares* was introduced in Chapter 4 and repeated in other chapters. For example, in Chapter 8, it was stated how the variations in the DV could be explained by a particular IV. When the term *sum of the squares* is used, either in this chapter or elsewhere, it always refers to the variability between the scores obtained from the research study and its sample mean. This variability is called the sum of the squared deviations of the score set and its sample mean. However, computing the sum of squares between and within groups for ANOVA is much more complex than the simple variance presented in Chapter 4.

The complexity of the F-ratio is partitioning $SS^2_{between}$ and SS^2_{within}. Recall in Chapter 4 that to obtain the variability for the mean MD and the SS^2, the $\bar{x}$ must first be known. For ANOVA, it is also necessary to compute the $\bar{x}$ for subjects in the study project. The only difference between measures of variability as presented in Chapter 4 and this chapter is that the term *variance* is changed to the *mean squares between groups* (MS$_{between}$) and the *mean squares within groups* (MS$_{within}$). Again, the reason for the term's change in definition is to avoid doing repeated t-tests. Recall that the t-test is used to test one or two sample means. The term *partition* is used to describe how to break down into subparts/subcomponents.

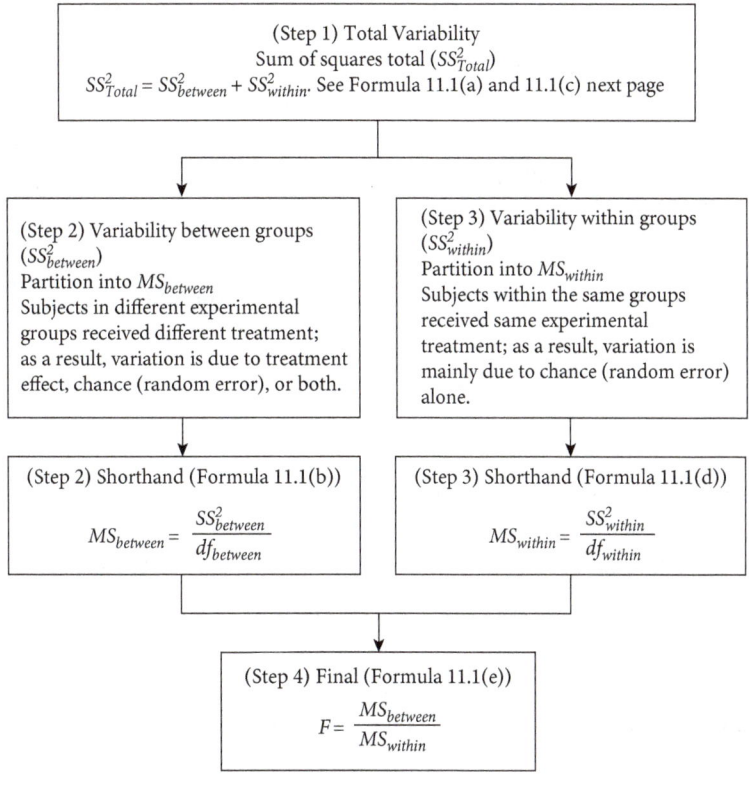

FIGURE 11.1 Partitioning the F-Ratio

Therefore, how does one partition the between-groups and within-groups variability? The abbreviated version for the sum of the squares between groups ($SS^2_{between}$) can be calculated by Formula 11.1(a).

Formula 11.1(a) Partitioning the Sum of Squares Between Groups ($SS^2_{between}$)

$$SS^2_{between} = \sum \frac{(\Sigma x_K)^2}{N_K} - \frac{(\Sigma x)^2_{Total}}{N_{Total}}$$

where
  $(\Sigma x_K)^2$ = Square the sum of the group (i.e., square the sum of the scores for the first group),
  N_K = Sample size of the group,
  $(\Sigma x)^2_{Total}$ = Square the sum of the total for all groups' scores, and
  n_{Total} = Total sample for the research project.

CHAPTER 11: INFERENTIAL STATISTICS: ONE-WAY ANOVA   217

In an expanded version, the variability between groups is calculated by

$$SS^2_{between} = \left[\frac{(\text{1st group scores total})^2}{\text{1st sample size}} + \ldots + \frac{(\text{last group scores total})^2}{\text{last sample size}}\right] - \frac{(\text{Overall scores total})^2}{\text{Overall sample size}}$$

This expanded version is much easier to understand than the abbreviated version. Note that this part of the partition is only for Step 1. One still needs to complete Steps 2 and 3 before the F-statistic can be calculated (step 4). *Once the sum of squares (SS^2) is calculated, the between-groups mean squares ($MS_{between}$) must still be calculated. The between-groups mean squares is calculated by taking the sizes of the groups into consideration by using Formula 11.1(b).*

Formula 11.1(b) The Mean Squares Between ($MS_{between}$) Calculation (See Step 2)

$$MS_{between} = \frac{SS^2_{between}}{df_{between}}$$

The degrees of freedom for the between-groups mean squares is defined as taking the total number of groups minus 1 ($df = K-1$).

Now that the variability between-groups formula is known, the variability within-groups formula can be calculated as well. The abbreviated version of the variability within groups (SS^2_{within}) is calculated by using Formula 11.1(c).

Formula 11.1(c) Partitioning the Sum of the Square Within Groups (SS^2_{within}) (See Step 3)

$$SS^2_{within} = \Sigma x^2_{Total} - \Sigma \frac{(\Sigma x_K)^2}{N_{Total}}$$

where

Σx^2_{Total} = Sum of squares of the scores for all groups, and

$(\Sigma x_K)^2$ = Square the sum of the group scores (i.e., square the sum of the scores of the first group).

In an expanded version, the variability within groups is calculated by

$$SS^2_{within} = \text{Sum of squared total} - \frac{(\text{1st group scores total})^2}{\text{1st sample size}} + \ldots + \frac{(\text{last group scores total})^2}{\text{last sample size}}$$

As indicated in Step 3, the within-groups mean squares (MS_{Within}) is calculated by using Formula 11.1(d).

Formula 11.1(d) Calculating the Mean Squares Within Groups (MS_{Within})

$$MS_{Within} = \frac{SS^2_{Within}}{df_{Within}}$$

The degrees of freedom for the within-groups mean squares is defined as taking the total number of subjects minus the number of groups ($df = N - K$).

Formula 11.1(e) The F-Ratio (See Step 4)

$$F = \frac{MS_{Between}}{MS_{Within}}$$

Calculating the Vignette

Table 11.2 shows the original scores for the life coaching methods vignette and the squared of their respective scores that are needed to complete the F-ratio calculation.

The two sources of variability can now be easily calculated by using the expanded versions of the formula by starting with the second step as displayed earlier.

$$SS^2_{Between} = \frac{(181)^2}{20} + \frac{(184)^2}{20} + \frac{(129)^2}{20} + \frac{(129)^2}{20} + \frac{(70)^2}{20} - \frac{(693)^2}{100}$$

$$= \frac{32{,}761}{20} + \frac{33{,}856}{20} + \frac{16{,}641}{20} + \frac{16{,}641}{20} + \frac{4{,}900}{20} - \frac{480{,}249}{100}$$

$$= 1{,}638.05 + 1{,}692.80 + 832.05 + 832.05 + 245 - 4{,}802.49$$

$$= 5{,}239.95 - 4{,}802.49$$

$$= 437.46$$

$$SS^2_{Within} = 5{,}365 - \frac{(181)^2}{20} + \frac{(184)^2}{20} + \frac{(129)^2}{20} + \frac{(129)^2}{20} + \frac{(70)^2}{20}$$

$$= 5{,}365 - \frac{32{,}761}{20} + \frac{33{,}856}{20} + \frac{16{,}641}{20} + \frac{16{,}641}{20} + \frac{4{,}900}{20}$$

$$= 5{,}365 - 1{,}638.05 + 1{,}692.80 + 832.05 + 832.05 + 245$$

$$= 5{,}365 - 5{,}239.95$$

$$= 125.05$$

TABLE 11.2 Helpfulness of Life Coaching Methods Scores and the Sum of the Squares

Asian American (x_1)	(x_1^2)	African American (x_2)	(x_2^2)	Latino (x_3)	(x_3^2)	Native American (x_4)	(x_4^2)	White (x_5)	(x_5^2)
9	81	10	100	7	49	6	36	4	16
8	64	10	100	8	64	7	49	3	9
10	100	8	64	9	81	8	64	3	9
9	81	9	81	7	49	8	64	4	16
8	64	9	81	6	36	7	49	4	16
8	64	9	81	7	49	6	36	2	4
9	81	10	100	6	36	5	25	3	9
10	100	8	64	6	36	5	25	4	16
10	100	9	81	7	49	4	16	5	25
8	64	9	81	6	36	7	49	7	49
9	81	9	81	5	25	8	64	5	25
9	81	10	100	5	25	7	49	5	25
10	100	10	100	6	36	7	49	4	16
8	64	9	81	7	49	6	36	2	4
10	100	8	64	7	49	4	16	3	9
10	100	9	81	8	64	8	64	2	4
9	81	10	100	5	25	7	49	1	1
9	81	9	81	6	36	8	64	1	1
10	100	9	81	7	49	6	36	5	25
8	64	10	100	4	16	5	25	3	9
Σx_1 = 181	Σx_1^2 = 1,651	Σx_2 = 184	Σx_2^2 = 1,702	Σx_3 = 129	Σx_3^2 = 859	Σx_4 = 129	Σx_4^2 = 865	Σx_5 = 70	Σx_5^2 = 288

$\Sigma x = 181 + 184 + 129 + 129 + 70 = 693$
$\Sigma x^2 = 1,651 + 1,702 + 859 + 865 + 288 = 5,365$
Total sample size (N_{Total}) = 100

Now that the $SS^2_{between}$ and SS^2_{within} are known, the next steps are calculating the $MS^2_{between}$ and MS^2_{within}. First, the degrees of freedom for between groups ($df_{Between}$) and within groups (df_{Within}) are needed.

$$df_{between} = 5 - 1 = 4$$

$$df_{within} = 100 - 5 = 95$$

The mean squares between ($MS_{between}$) and mean squares within (MS_{within}) (Step 2 and 3) can be easily calculated as

$$MS_{between} = \frac{437.46}{4}$$

= **109.365** (using three decimals to keep it consistent with SPSS),

$$MS_{Within} = \frac{125.05}{95}$$

= **1.316**

Lastly, the F-ratio can be calculated as

$$F = \frac{109.365}{1.316}$$

= **83.104** (owing to the rounding error, SPSS shows the more precise result of 83.084).

By referring to Appendix B ("Critical Values of F") using the preset alpha at a 95% CI, two-tailed, the critical value is 2.46. The critical value indicates that one will need to have a calculated value of 2.46 or greater to reject the null hypothesis. *The calculated value of 83.104 is many times greater than the required value; therefore, it is safe to reject the null hypothesis by saying that life coaching methods are extremely helpful to the five junior high student groups ($F = 83.104$, $df = 4, 95$, $p < .05$).* As usual, the notations inside the parenthesis are required by APA. Even if it is now known that life coaching methods are helpful, we still need to know whether the helpfulness occurs for all five groups or only some of the groups. Essentially, one still needs to know where the difference is.

TESTS OF STATISTICAL SIGNIFICANCE

As discussed earlier, when the F-ratio shows a significant difference, it does not indicate where the difference(s) occurs. Does the significant difference occur for all groups/factors? Or does it only occur for some of the groups? Of course, if H_0 is retained, then there is no need to do more tests. It is suggested that when a significant difference is detected, a post hoc test should be conducted to pinpoint the difference. There are about 14 post hoc tests. The three most common ones are Bonferroni, Scheffe, and Tukey. For demonstration purposes, the Scheffe post hoc test will be shown next using SPSS.

SPSS INSTRUCTIONS ON ANOVA

This last part of the SPSS instructions is used to replicate the manual calculations regarding the life coaching methods. First of all, learners need to know how to create a data file for Table 11.1. For detailed help with creating an SPSS data file, either refer to Chapter 3 or Appendix A. In Table 11.1, there are five groups. Each group consists of 20 participants for a total of 100 (N= 100). Although there are five columns shown on the table, there are only two variables. The first variable is race. Race has five groups or five factors. The second variable is the self-rated scores given by the research subjects. It is important that the data file be created correctly, or ANOVA will not compute it.

To create the data file for the vignette once the blank SPSS dialogue screen is opened, click on *Variable View* (bottom left of the screen). You may name the first variable "Race." Change the *Decimal* column to 0 and provide a title for the *Label* column. On *Values*, label 1 for Asian American, 2 for African American, 3 for Latino, 4 for Native American, and 5 for White. On *Measure*, select *Nominal*.

Move the cursor back to column 1, row 2. Give a name to the second variable. Perhaps name it "*Helpful.*" As usual, change the *Decimal* column to 0 and give a title to the variable under the *Label* column. Leave the *Values* column blank. On the *Measure* column, select *Scale*.

Save the file by giving it a name. Click *Data View* (bottom left of the screen) to return to the data file screen. Notice that the two variable names that were created under *Variable View* appear in columns 1 and 2. On Race, enter the values you have just created. Simply type 1 (Asian American) for the first 20, 2 for African American for the next 20, and so forth until all five groups are entered. Move the cursor to the second variable "*Helpful.*" Do the same for the scores. The first 20 scores (9, 8, 10, …8) are the self-rated scores given by the Asian American research participants. After the 20 scores are entered, move onto the second column of Table 11.1. For the African American participants, their scores begin with 10, 10, and end at 10. On your SPSS screen, the last score for African American should stop at row 40. Once done, continue on to Latinos. The Latino scores will stop at 60. Native Americans' scores will stop at 80. The White group scores begin at 81 and end at 100.

When the data entry is completed, save the SPSS data file and then follow the instructions that follow to replicate the manual calculations. The first page (first 22 scores) of the data set should look as shown in the following image.

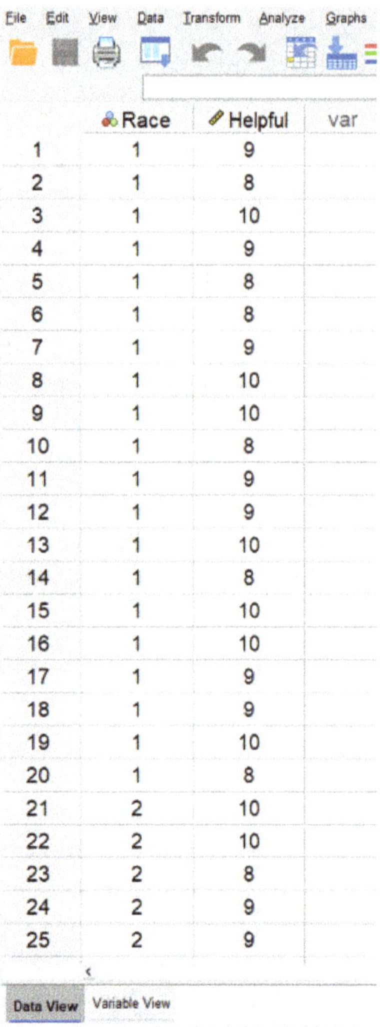

	Race	Helpful
1	1	9
2	1	8
3	1	10
4	1	9
5	1	8
6	1	8
7	1	9
8	1	10
9	1	10
10	1	8
11	1	9
12	1	9
13	1	10
14	1	8
15	1	10
16	1	10
17	1	9
18	1	9
19	1	10
20	1	8
21	2	10
22	2	10
23	2	8
24	2	9
25	2	9

Image 11.1

- Pull down the *Analyze* ribbon. Move the cursor down to *Compare Means* and then move the cursor over to the *One-Way ANOVA*. Click it. Notice that it is the last item on the list. The following mini window will pop up.

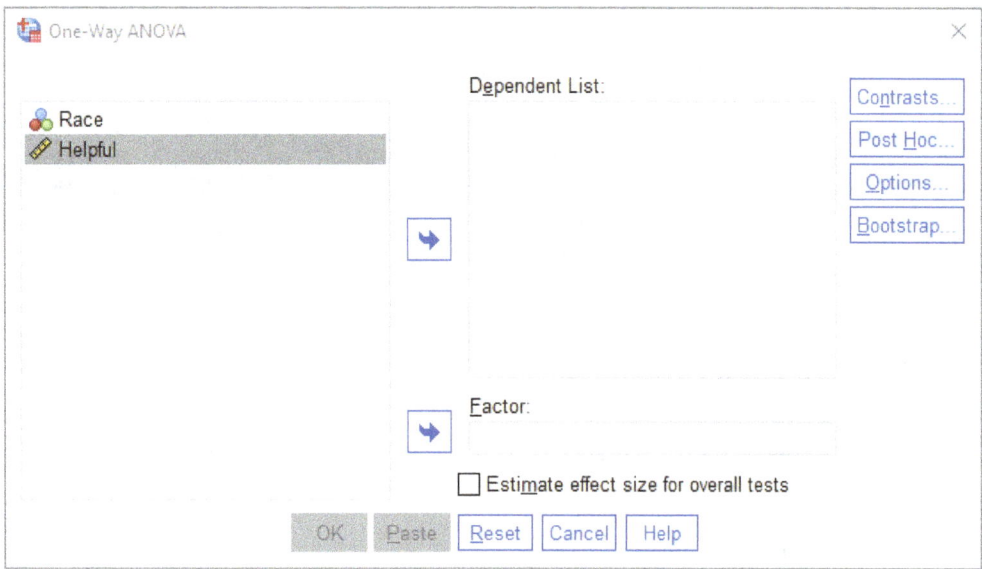

- Your variable list should look similar to this screen. Select *Helpful* and hit the forward arrow (→) to move it to the *Dependent List*. Recall that for t-test and ANOVA, the DV must be interval or ratio scale. This is the reason why the self-rated effectiveness of the new antidepressant drug is being treated as the DV. Select and forward (→) Race to *Factor*. Factor or condition is the IV. Similar to the t-test, ANOVA must use nominal data for *Factor*. Races for the vignette are nominal data.

- Next, click *Post Hoc* and select *Scheffe*. Change the p value (significance level) to your personal preference. On *Option*, select *Other* option if so preferred.

- Hit *OK*. Momentarily, the following three tables (Tables 11.3–11.5) will pop up.

TABLE 11.3 **ANOVA for the Helpfulness of Life Coaching Methods**

	Sum of Squares	df	Mean Square	F	Sig.
Between Groups	437.460	4	109.365	83.084	.000
Within Groups	125.050	95	1.316		
Total	562.510	99			

Similar to the manual calculation, SPSS also provides the variability between groups ($SS^2_{Between}$) at 437.460 and the variability within groups (SS^2_{Within}) at 125.05 with 4 and 95 degrees of freedom, respectively. By dividing the between-groups mean squares of 109.365 with the within-groups mean squares of 1.316, the F-statistic is equaled to 83.084 (owing to a rounding error, a hand calculator will provide the result of 83.104). The mean difference is significant at the .000 level.

TABLE 11.4 Mean Difference Among the Groups

(I) Group of Participants	(J) Group of Participants	Mean Difference (I-J)	Sig.
Asian Americans	African Americans	−.150	.996
	Latino	2.600*	.000
	Native Americans	2.600*	.000
	White	5.550*	.000
African Americans	Asian Americans	.150	.996
	Latinos	2.750*	.000
	Native Americans	2.750*	.000
	White	5.700*	.000
Latinos	Asian Americans	−2.600*	.000
	African Americans	−2.750*	.000
	Native Americans	.000	1.000
	White	2.950*	.000
Native Americans	Asian Americans	−2.600*	.000
	African Americans	−2.750*	.000
	Latinos	.000	1.000
	White	2.950*	.000
White	Asian Americans	−5.550*	.000
	African Americans	−5.700*	.000
	Latinos	−2.950*	.000
	White	−2.950*	.000

*The mean difference is significant at the .01 level.

TABLE 11.5 The Mean Scores for All Five Groups (From Lowest to Highest)

Native Americans	20	3.50		
Latinos	20		6.45	
White	20		6.45	
Asian Americans	20			9.05
African Americans	20			9.20

The result for the Scheffe post hoc test is shown in Table 11.4. The test shows that the means for all five groups are significantly different from each other. The reason is that the mean for each group is large enough to be statistically different as shown in Table 11.5. The African American group has the highest mean at 9.20 followed by Asian Americans at 9.05. The Native American group has the lowest mean at 3.50. If all five groups showed a similar mean, then the H_0 would have been retained and the Scheffe post hoc test would not be necessary.

SUMMARY

This is the last chapter that formally introduced the basic tools of quantitative data analysis. When only one IV with two correlated conditions (i.e., social workers' hourly wage in two nearby counties) exist, it is possible to use either a t-test or the F-statistic to compare the means. Essentially, the choice between the *t* and *F* ratios reflects the personal preference of the researchers if the IV has two correlated conditions. A reason researchers do not want to use the t-test when there are three or more factors/conditions is because they must conduct multiple t-tests. When multiple t-tests are conducted, the odds of having a Type I error significantly increases. Recall that Type I error is the chance of finding significance when there is none.

When there are several different groups of people or factors, Fisher's F-ratio is used. The F-ratio is used to measure the differences of the group means versus the grand mean of scores for all subjects and compares it against the remaining error. This error is the difference between the actual scores and the means of all the groups. Thus, Fisher's F-ratio is a measure of the ratio of the systematic and unsystematic variances, and higher scores are considered better than lower scores.

The result of the F-ratio essentially reflects variations among the means ($\bar{x}_s$) of several groups ($SS^2_{between}$) in relation to the variation within a group (SS^2_{within}). Because of this, the significance of ANOVA simply reveals whether at least one of the means is significantly different from the others. The significant difference in group means says nothing about which mean is different from which or the degree of difference. Once the null hypothesis has been rejected, and to find out which group is significantly different from the others, two additional tests must be performed. One is called the "posteriori test or posttest," a Latin word for "What comes later?" The other is called the "post hoc or post hoc comparison," which in Latin means "after this." These two tests are designed to examine which means are significantly different from each other.

When computing the F-ratio, it is important to pay attention to the two sources of variability. The sources are variability between groups and variability within groups. Variability between-group means ($MS_{between}$) refers to the variation among the variance of treatment conditions owing to either treatment effect or an inherent chance of variation among the individuals in a research project. It is either the treatment effect or chance because each of the groups receives a different treatment or the groups are naturally different (i.e., cultural differences). Variability within-group means (MS_{within}), on the other hand, is a little more complex than variability between-groups means. It is the variation of individual scores ($x_1, x_2, x_3, ... x_n$) around the sample mean ($\bar{x}$) as a direct reflection of chance rather than as caused by different types of treatment or groups. It is the variation between the sample mean and the scores owing to chance and chance alone because members of the group receive the same treatment.

Study Questions

Multiple Choice. The study questions should help learners to understand ANOVA in various ways

1. What is the difference between the t-test and the F-test?
    a. The t-test is used when the IV has multiple categories.
    b. The IV for the t-test is limited to two value categories, while the F-test focuses on three or more value categories.
    c. The DV for the t-test can have two or more interval/ratio variables, while the F-test is limited to one interval/ratio variable.

2. What is the level of measurement you must have for the DV when using the F-test?
    a. Nominal
    b. Ordinal
    c. Interval/ratio

3. What is the main purpose of the F-test?
    a. It examines the variation among the means of several groups in relation to the variation within a group.
    b. It examines the extent to which samples are similar or different within a group.
    c. It examines the correlation between the sample means and population means.

4. The two main sources of variability for the F-test include
    a. between-groups means and sum of all squared scores.
    b. within-groups means and the population mean.

    c. between-groups means and within-groups means.
    d. between sum of square deviation and within sum of square deviation.

5. What is variability for within-group means?
   a. It is the variation among the means of treatment conditions owing to either treatment effect or an inherent chance of variation among the individuals.
   b. It is the variation of individual scores around the sample mean as a direct reflection of chance rather than as caused by different treatment types.
   c. It is the variation for the sum of all squared scores.

6. What is variability for between-groups means?
   a. It is the variation among the means of treatment conditions owing to either treatment effect or an inherent chance of variation among the individuals.
   b. It is the variation of individual scores around the sample mean as a direct reflection of chance rather than as caused by different treatment types.
   c. It is the variation for the sum of all squared scores.

7. The term *partition* describes which of the following steps for ANOVA?
   a. How to break down the sum of squares into subparts.
   b. How to calculate the within-groups variability.
   c. How to calculate the between-groups variability.
   d. How to calculate the F-test.

8. Which of the following statements is suitable for ANOVA?
   a. One wants to examine the level of clients' satisfaction in four different social services departments.
   b. One wants to examine the association of racial identity for groups within four college campuses.
   c. One wants to examine the marital status of clients served in four different social services departments.

9. If it is given that $F = 17.21$, $df = 4, 9$, $p > .07$, what would you say about the H_0?
   a. H_0 is retained.
   b. H_0 is rejected.
   c. Either retained or rejected is correct.
   d. There is insufficient information.

10. When comparing the ANOVA with the t-tests, ANOVA is similar to
    a. one sample t-test.
    b. independent samples t-test.
    c. dependent samples t-test.

11. According to the author of this book, it is highly recommended that the sample size for ANOVA should be
    a. at least 30 per group.
    b. at least 50 per group.
    c. at least 500 per group.
    d. at least 1,000 per group.

12. Which of the following is correct about calculating the F-ratio?
    a. Divide the mean square for between groups by the mean square for within groups.
    b. Divide the sum of square for between groups by the sum of square for within groups.
    c. Divide the sum of square for between groups by its degrees of freedom.
    d. Divide the sum of square for within groups by its degrees of freedom.

13. Which of the following statements is a reason for calculating the degrees of freedom for ANOVA?
    a. To allow one group's scores and one participant's score to vary.
    b. To allow two people's scores and two participants' scores to vary.
    c. To allow a row and a column for the expanded scores to vary.

14. If $K = 3$, $n = 247$, then the degrees of freedom for within groups in this scenario is equal to
    a. 3.
    b. 2.
    c. 246.
    d. 245.
    e. 244.

15. For Question 14, the degrees of freedom between groups for the scenario is equal to
    a. 3.
    b. 2.
    c. 246.
    d. 245.
    e. 244.

16. When there are three or more groups for the IV, what is the reason for not conducting a multiple independent samples t-test?
    a. The F-ratio is easier to calculate.
    b. The researcher should have considered the dependent samples instead of the independent samples t-test.
    c. Repeated t-tests will increase Type I error.
    d. Repeated t-tests will increase Type II error.

17. Post hoc test in Latin means
    a. what comes before this.

b. what comes after this.
   c. what comes later.
18. Which of the following group of post hoc tests is commonly used by social sciences researchers?
   a. Bonferroni, Scheffe, and Tukey
   b. Sidak, Scheffe, and Tukey
   c. Duncan, Scheffe, and Tukey

Answers to Study Questions

QUESTION	ANSWER	QUESTION	ANSWER
1	b	10	b
2	c	11	b
3	a	12	a
4	c	13	a
5	b	14	e
6	a	15	b
7	a	16	c
8	a	17	b
9	a	18	a

CHAPTER 12

A Snapshot of Qualitative Research

OVERVIEW

Chapters 1 to 11 presented basic quantitative research and its respective data analysis using various statistical tools and functions. In these chapters, three important procedures were discussed. The first was how to use numeric variables (quantitative) to report attributes and parameters, such as mental illness situations, stressful life events, and residents' attitudes toward social workers and nurses. Second, by conducting hypothesis tests, it was described how to understand and estimate the breadth and depth of the attributes. The results of hypothesis tests enable researchers and practitioners to explain the relationships, associations, and mean(s) differences—as well as make predictions—between the data set of the sample group and the population where the sample was drawn. Third, it was demonstrated from Chapters 4 to 11 how to use one of the well-known statistical software applications known as SPSS to compute solutions for the analysis.

This chapter introduces a parallel way of understanding attributes and parameters in the form of words (qualitative). Nowadays, mixed methods, which combines quantitative and qualitative research, are becoming popular in social sciences research. For this reason, many research projects combine quantitative and qualitative research methods. To help make mixed-methods research data easier to report and understand to readers, this chapter provides a quick highlight of the meaning of qualitative research, data gathering procedures, and its data reporting procedures (Creswell, 2009). Because of the length of the chapter, other important qualitative methods, such as case studies, will not be introduced.

By no means will the knowledge gained from this chapter be sufficient to understand qualitative research. *Please understand that qualitative research by itself is another complex research course that must be taken separately.* Rather, this chapter offers a snapshot of qualitative research and data analysis.

WHAT IS QUALITATIVE RESEARCH?

As human societies become more globalized every day, the traditional way of just doing quantitative research is no longer perceived as "that's it." In the past couple of decades, qualitative research methods have been combined with quantitative methods in many aspects of research. For example, when modern medical scientists examine the causes of COVID-19, they are no longer just exploring the plausible biomedical, physiological, and environmental factors that caused coronavirus; they may also want to understand the social and behavioral impacts on individuals. For example, researchers from John Hopkins University (2020) with preliminary data have already found that Blacks in the United States suffer 6 times more deaths from COVID-19 than any other group. Similarly, when social workers investigate the causes of child abuse and neglect, they look for social and economic reasons, as well as bruises, signs of malnourishment, and behaviors of both the parents/caretakers and children.

When assessing situations in past social work practices, such as alleged child sexual abuse and post-traumatic stress disorders of veterans, the biopsychosocial assessment must use both quantitative and qualitative methods. Quantitative data must include questions like the age of the victim and perpetrator, educational background of the perpetrator, and family size (both the perpetrator's parents and their own family). For the qualitative data, questions must include things like what causes a person to sexually assault a child or why does a veteran easily lose their temper?

For any type of evidence-based situation, no matter how well the researchers manipulate numbers, the results produced from those numerical scores may be insufficient to fully understand the causes of the situation. For example, to better understand the effect of COVID-19 on individuals and families or the behavior of delinquent children, *collecting additional data in the form of words (qualitative) can be insightful*. In scientific terminology, even though qualitative findings are not generalizable, the methods allow researchers and practitioners the flexibility to incorporate observations and use subjectivity to generate deeper understandings of human experiences. This is in contrast to quantitative research methods for which researchers and practitioners are not expected to deeply examine human experiences because of the generalization requirements of the findings. In addition, because researchers always caution their audience of the overgeneralization of numerical findings, supplemental qualitative data can help alleviate such concerns. *Essentially, in quantitative research generalizing beyond the results provided by the numbers runs high risks on the probability of committing not just random errors but also unintentional errors. In turn, the reliability and validity of the evidence are at a high stake.*

So, how does one prepare to collect qualitative data? The answer to this question is data collection procedures. For either quantitative or qualitative research, data collection procedures typically involve operationalizing the data collection protocols (such as open- and close-ended questionnaires) and when, where, and on whom to administer the questionnaire. Then, the process is followed by indicating the mechanism for data recording and protecting the social and psychological well-being of the participants, commonly referenced as *human subjects* or *research subjects*.

Different from quantitative data collection, where the questionnaires can be face-to-face, self-administered, posted online, or mailed, qualitative data are most often collected by face-to-face interviews. Face-to-face interviews heavily rely on two important concepts: (1) fieldwork and (2) field notes.

DATA COLLECTION JUSTIFICATIONS

Typical questions to think about for qualitative researchers are the following: *"How can we access the research subjects?" "How do we record and transcribe the data?" "How do we prepare the data for analysis?"*

Many qualitative research textbooks will state that information from *qualitative data is not generalizable from the sample to the population parameters. Qualitative information from one sample to the next or to the population may or may not be reliable.* Because of reliability concerns, the information is not considered valid either. Why? Because in qualitative research, a single word or concept can have many meanings, but in quantitative research, one knows that 2 + 2 is equal to 4. When it is not equated to 4, the researchers have justifications for the unequal outcome. *Therefore, in social sciences research, and especially quantitative research, reliability and validity go hand in hand.* In fact, reliability must precede validity. What this means is that reliability can occur by itself, but validity cannot occur without reliability.

Reliability is the consistency of a measuring instrument. In research methods textbooks, the authors usually mention three types of reliability: (1) test-retest reliability, which refers to the consistency of the measure over time; (2) inter-rater reliability, which is the consistency of the measure among different researchers or groups; and (3) internal consistency, which is when researchers examine the consistency of the items in the measuring instrument (Rubin & Babbie, 2017; Yuen, 2020).

Validity, on the other hand, is *the extent to which the scores from the measuring instrument represent the variable the researchers intended to investigate.* The judgment is always based on how well the reliability coefficients that have already been examined represent the situation under investigation. *Even when the measuring instrument shows strong coefficients, mainly test-retest, inter-rater, and internal consistency, the researchers can only consider the measure as reliable but not valid.* To consider the measuring instrument valid, the researchers must conduct additional tests. There are four types of validity: (1) face validity, which is the extent to which the measurement instrument method appears *"on its face"* to measure the issue under investigation; (2) content validity, which is the extent to which the items of the measure cover the issue of interest; (3) criterion validity, which is the extent to which the scores given by the testing subjects are correlated with one another; and (4) discriminant validity, which is the extent to which the scores responded to by the research subjects are not correlated with other issues similar to the issue under investigation. For example, when measuring generalized depression, the scores should only represent the symptoms for depression (unclassified type) and not for anxiety or manic episodes (Rubin & Babbie, 2017; Yuen, 2020).

Because of the sequential reliability and validity issues previously discussed, there are no scientific assumptions or statistical rules regarding qualitative data collection procedures and its data analysis guidelines. Although there are no specific guidelines when it comes to the preparation and use of qualitative research methods, there are two common concepts known as fieldwork and field notes that qualitative researchers abide by.

FIELDWORK VERSUS FIELD NOTES

Fieldwork

Fieldwork is a classical anthropological method researchers use to collect data while at the site(s) of interest. With fieldwork, researchers have a specific site of interest they want to study (e.g., a specific school); they want to examine a phenomenon in its natural environment (e.g., people crossing the street); they want to study how cultural traditions of a specific ethnic minority group can be infused with micro-social practices. Fieldwork has its own research design, recruitment strategies, and data collection protocols. *The data collection protocols must include the protection of human subjects from unnecessary social and psychological harm.* This means that participants must not experience anything harmful during their time in the study.

In accessing the fieldwork site, researchers are actively involved in the preparation and execution of the research project. Most qualitative researchers are not only actively involved in the preparation of the research project and recruitment of respondents but also engaged in the interviewing phase. For this reason, qualitative researchers must clearly operationalize where to conduct the research, when the data collection begins and ends, how to protect the prospective respondents, and how to collect and protect the data. Data obtained from fieldwork and other qualitative methods are called *field notes* (Glaser & Straus, 1967).

Field Notes

Field notes are like memos or texts to oneself, the research assistants (if any), and the recorded words/responses given by the respondents during the interviews (Glaser & Straus, 1967). It is extremely important that anything the respondents say be precisely recorded. Treat the field notes exactly as one would the numeric data collected from quantitative research. There should not be any alteration or summarization to the field notes. *Why?* Because the "text" recorded and transcribed from the interviews, as well as participant observations, become the "results" for the research project.

In quantitative research, numeric variables are used to understand issues encountered by people behind the scenes. In qualitative research, words are used to understand the richness of the human experience. The only difference between the two methods is that words tend to change meanings, while numbers, after being collected, are *constant* or *stay static*. The meaning of text then becomes the extent to which researchers are able to infer and analyze meanings on social issues. *Field notes can be recorded in two ways.* The first is recorded word for word as precisely as possible. Why? This is because some of these notes (texts) will end up in the final report as direct quotes. The accuracy of information explained in the final report depends largely on the precision of the researcher/practitioner in narrating the field notes. Because of this, qualitative researchers always carry electronic recording devices or notepads. The second way to record field notes is a personal reaction to the interactions the researchers have with the respondents. These notes may only be used to help the researcher remember what transpired during the interview. However, none of these personal summaries or narrative notes should appear in the final report. *Keep in mind that personal opinions and reactions do not constitute "findings" for the research study.* These personal notes can only be used to support the final discussions for the research project.

QUESTIONNAIRE CONSTRUCTION

Despite the differences between quantitative and qualitative methods, the studies that employ them either separately or in combination (i.e., mixed methods) follow the same research patterns. As stated earlier, in modern days, mixed methods are commonly used. A mixed method means that the researcher combines quantitative and qualitative research methods. For example, the researcher may structure two thirds of the questionnaires using a quantitative method and the remaining one third of the questionnaires using a qualitative design or vice versa. Just be mindful that the nature of data collection or research design does not dictate whether it is quantitative or qualitative.

In the quantitative design, questionnaires are structured using mostly close-ended questions while the qualitative design mainly uses open-ended questions. However, some questions will always elicit numerical responses, regardless of how they are asked (e.g., *How many people are in your family*?). Sometimes, the qualitative research design does not have preformatted questions. In this case, the researcher will explore the situation more in-depth with the respondent while conducting fieldwork. Just as in all forms of human inquiry, the researcher must make sure that proper human subject protection is sought and approved accordingly. Even if a structured questionnaire is used in fieldwork, subjects involved in the study still must be fully protected from social and psychological harm. This leads directly to various issues pertaining to data recording. Data recording is the structure of a database, which contains the entire data file (Rubin & Babbie, 2017).

In quantitative data analysis, the reliability and validity of research findings are based on sampling, particularly probability sampling and the accuracy of the measuring instruments. Whether one is conducting quantitative or qualitative research, poorly developed measurements will lead not only to unreliable evidence but also to no validity, while well-developed instruments lead to stronger reliability and validity. The quality of the data set depends largely on the clarity of the questions.

Quality refers to the "get to the point but with nonoffending, double-barrel, or prejudicial" questions. *Clarity* is making the questions clear and easy to understand. Suppose that a researcher asks, "What do you think about civil disobedient persons, and what should be done about them?" Or, "At what age did you become aware that your family doesn't like you and why?" These two sample questions are poorly constructed. Let us look at the first question. There are several problems with it. First, it is extremely vague. Even highly educated people will ask, *"What do you mean by civil disobedience?"* Next, it is a double-barrel question. The respondent does not know which part of the question the researcher wants to be answered first. Third, the question is poorly structured. It is a confusing question. And lastly, it is a prejudicial question. The researcher is asking about the punishment that should be given to this group of people. Remember that with both quantitative and qualitative questions, researchers should try to obtain an in-depth and objective understanding of the issue rather than seek conclusions about morality.

QUALITATIVE DATA RECORDING

Another point about reliability and validity issues with qualitative data is the consistency of notetaking (field notes). *The more consistent the field notes are, the easier researchers will be able to identify behavioral patterns between and among the respondents.* As stated, notetaking can occur using electronic devices or can be handwritten. The philosophical roots of qualitative inquiry mandate that the respondent's answers to any question be recorded and transcribed as fully as possible (Monette et al., 2005; Rubin & Babbie, 2017). Some qualitative scientists even suggest that notetaking should occur in stages. The stages mean that at the initial interaction, the researcher only takes minimal notes at the start of the interview or the first interview. The researcher then writes notes in more detail in the following hour or during subsequent interviews. Afterward, the researcher can ask themselves a reflective question, such as, *"Do I need to do anything else before I proceed with my research questions?"* Bogdan and Biklen (as cited by Monette et al., 2005) provide five categories for observation and recording of individuals or groups before the interview/observation begins. Some of the categories can be recorded after the meeting. The five categories are briefly highlighted next:

I. *The Setting.* First, describe the field setting. Field notes should contain some description of the general physical and social setting being observed. The following are sample questions about the setting:
   1. Is the meeting place a home, an apartment, a community-based agency, or a governmental agency?
   2. Is it an individual interview, group interview, community forum, or political forum?

II. *The People and the Geographical Setting.* Field notes should include a physical and social description of the main characters that are the focus of the observation. Examples include the following:
   1. *Who is being* observed/interviewed?
   2. How many people?
   3. How are they dressed?
   4. What are their ages, genders, and socioeconomic characteristics?
   5. What are the cultural backgrounds of the respondents?

III. *Individual Actions and Activities.* Monette and Sullivan explain that the central observations in most studies are the behaviors of people in the setting. Possible questions in this part of the record may include:
   1. How do they relate to one another?
   2. Who talks to whom and in what fashion?
   3. What sequences of behaviors occur?

IV. *Group Behavior.* In some cases, the behavior of groups is important information. Example questions include the following:
   1. How long does a group of people remain on the scene?

2. How does one group relate to another? Monette and Sullivan also state that what should be recorded here describes the social structure of the setting, statuses, and roles of people occupying the various relationships between or among them.

V. *Meaning and Perspectives.* Finally, field researchers must be sensitive to the subjective meaning that people give to themselves and their behaviors; thus, field notes should contain observations about these meanings and what words or behaviors are evidence of those meanings. Bogdan and Biklen (as cited by Monette et al., 2005) explain that *perspective* refers to the general ways of thinking that people exhibit, evidence of which should appear in the field notes.

Researchers can consider these general observations as records for themselves before and after the interviews. Similar to quantitative data analysis, these five categories will be *background information* about the participants/respondents, which is normally gathered before other variables are described. Before discussing different ways of doing qualitative data analysis, let's discuss the meaning of narrative data first.

NARRATIVE DATA

Researchers, when narrating an area under investigation (research), could be telling a real-life story from which the data are structured. The narrative could take the form of an essay, but the form can vary greatly depending on the situation or case. For example, narrative writing in college education is a form by which students try to prove a point, state an argument, or address an important issue. *When combining narrative writing with narrative data analyses, it is a simplified concept that takes many shapes and forms of qualitative data analysis.* The academic rigors are no different than completing quantitative data entry for both descriptive and inferential statistics.

Narrative data analysis is one of many techniques that researchers can use to analyze and evaluate qualitative data. Beyond the interviewing data, the data sources can be clients' logs, participants' verbal responses to a set of open-ended questions, a transcript from a community gathering, diaries from a person's life story, text from a published source (such as books or journal articles), and images about societal problems from mainstream media sources. Therefore, qualitative data sources could come from a community, many people, several individuals, just a single person, or the Internet.

The remaining sections of this chapter discuss four steps that can be used for qualitative data analyses. Some of these steps overlap, so one may want to switch back and forth between them. Before discussing the specific steps, let us discuss two of the concepts often used by qualitative researchers—*research findings* and *data interpretations*.

TYPES OF QUALITATIVE DATA ANALYSIS

Qualitative data analysis usually involves a combination of one of these four types: (1) discovering patterns, (2) content analysis, (3) semiotics, and (4) conversation analysis (Rubin & Babbie, 2017).

When analyzing qualitative data, similar to quantitative data analysis, the researchers must clearly understand the differences between *research findings* and *data interpretation*. Research findings refer to the examination and statistical tabulations of raw scores (i.e., words or numbers) and display of important results that pertain to the research purposes or hypotheses. Data interpretation goes beyond tabulating raw scores and displaying results. Data interpretation is the description and explanation of research findings that reflect three major components:

1. significant findings that support or do not support the research objectives,
2. significant findings that either confirm or do not confirm the literature pertaining to the issue under investigation, and
3. personal reactions or opinions about either significant or nonsignificant research findings.

Being able to understand research findings and data interpretation will help researchers properly present both quantitative and qualitative data and clearly explain findings to the audience.

As a result, when analyzing qualitative data, Rubin and Babbie (2014) provide the following linkages between research theory and analysis. Always consider the linkages as proper steps in completing qualitative data analysis. At the end of each step, an example is given on how narrative data analysis can assist the researcher(s) with better understanding the processes involved.

Discovering Patterns

The first type is discovering patterns. As cited by Rubin and Babbie (2014), in 1995, Lofland and Lofland suggested six different ways of looking for patterns in a particular research topic. Lofland and Lofland's six different ways are briefly summarized next:

1. *Similar to quantitative research, the first step in research findings is frequency count.* Even without numerical scores, frequency count in qualitative data is gathering key concepts (common terms) provided by the interviewees. This process is also called *enumeration*. Enumeration is the process of quantifying data (both quantitative and qualitative). In qualitative research, researchers might count the number of times a word appears in a document, or they might count the number of times a code is applied to the data. For example, when interviewing homeless veterans, researchers might count how many times words such as *depression*, *unable to sleep*, and *loneliness* are mentioned. In this example, the researchers could assign "DEP" for depression, "USL" for unable to sleep, and "L" for loneliness. Suppose there is a huge client log. The researchers can count (enumerate) the number of times each code occurs by putting these codes in the log.
2. *The second step is looking at the magnitude of the data set. Magnitude* is the degree of severity of the problem or the strength of the relationship between two concepts. For example, a homeless person may describe the relationship between loneliness (X) and self-worth (Y) or the number

of times sleeplessness (Z) occurs at night. By using self-worth (Y) as the main focus or title of the problem, the researchers could diagram the relationship between X and Y as in Table 12.1.

TABLE 12.1 Example of Data Analysis Using the Magnitude Concept

The Problem (Self-Worth or Y)	Form of Relationship
Isolation	X is a kind of Z (loneliness is related to sleeplessness). Sleeplessness relates to social isolation.
Withdrawal	Isolation causes clients to withdraw from society because of a feeling of worthlessness.

3. *Structures.* Structures are the different types of issues under the same topic and the relationship between the issues. A homeless person may talk about being a veteran, and because of the stress from serving in the military, the person becomes a substance abuser. In turn, the person is rejected by their family.
4. *Process.* Process involves ordering categories of issues confronted by subjects under investigation/research by time and shows the characteristics or subcategories that are associated with the stages of life development. The researchers could consider process as the "phases or stages of the occurring problem." For example, the homeless veteran may rationalize that the reason they became homeless is substance abuse. When the veteran started to use and abuse drugs and alcohol, a mental illness syndrome began to develop. The homeless veteran then became confrontational with family members, which was when family members began to reject them. It may not be true, but that is how the respondent/interviewee views and explains their reasons for becoming homeless. To put this situation into phases, the researchers could diagram the homeless veteran's situation as follows:
    a. Phase 1: Life situation before joining the military
    b. Phase 2: Life situation in the military
    c. Phase 3: Life situation after the military
    d. Phase 4: Life situation as a homeless person
    e. Phase 5: Wishing outcome for the immediate future
5. *Causes.* These are how the respondents "*state*" or "*believe*" what the causes of the problem are. Be mindful that in qualitative research, the term *cause* does not imply causation or effect. It applies to only how the respondent believes or states it. In statistical analysis, particularly quantitative analysis, the term *cause* or *regress* usually means going back or returning. Cause is different from process. In going back for quantitative research, researchers must be able to identify the real factor(s) that cause the problem. Essentially, the variable(s) that correlates strongest to the problem will then be investigated further by completing various forms of regression analyses. For example, when examining what causes veterans to become homeless, it was found that chemical dependency is the primary factor. Although, it was found that chemical dependency

correlated strongest to homelessness, the term chemical dependency is too broad. Because of this reason, the researchers must narrow it down to the actual type of chemical. Is the effect from hard liquor, illegal drugs, or both? In the real world, it will be both. In this sense, qualitative study will enable researchers to further explore what veterans believe the causes are.

6. *Consequences.* Finally, consequences refer to the magnitude or costs of the issue. Is this how the issue under investigation affects individuals, families, and society in the short and long term? The following is a sample narrative of a mentally ill client's log relating to medical noncompliance:[1]

> *The client rapidly shifts his moods, which has been observable in the office, exhibiting odd behaviors (intense stares, hysterical laughing bouts, tilting head, and freezing self in position) that differ from week to week, visual hallucinations (seeing three ghosts), distressing nightmares that biological mother has died, internal preoccupations of stimulation, poor verbal reciprocation, and thought poverty. The symptoms listed continue to affect the client to a significant degree, which requires caregivers to prompt the client physically and verbally to attune reality on a daily basis.*

It is not necessary when analyzing qualitative data to observe evidence that is related to all six issues. For example, when studying spirituality, it will be difficult to rank order which spiritual component is more important to the individuals, families, or community. One may argue that hiking to the mountain alone is the most spiritual, while another may argue that going to a church, temple, or mosque is the most spiritual.

Content Analysis

Content analysis is a type of qualitative data analysis in which researchers summarize any form of archival content, usually written words, by counting various aspects of the content. For example, a researcher may look at three social work research journals and three psychology research journals that were published in the past 3 years. The goal is to search for three key concepts—*depression*, *veterans*, and *post-traumatic stress disorder.* The goal is to do a frequency count on how many times each of the three concepts appear in each of the journals in the past 3 years. After the frequency count is completed, the researcher can report the individual counts, as well as the total counts for those three words/concepts.

This type of words count enables a more objective evaluation than comparing content based on the understanding of the audience. The results of content analysis are numbers and percentages. Content analysis is based on the grounded theory (Glaser & Strauss, 1967) that enables a researcher to transform qualitative material into quantitative data. Rubin and Babbie (2014) state that this method can be applied to virtually any form of communication, not just available records. It consists primarily of coding and tabulating the occurrences of certain forms of content that are being communicated: "Content analysis is essentially a coding operation. Communication whether oral, written, or other—is coded or classified according to some conceptual framework" (Rubin & Babbie, 2014, p. 454).

---

1 Reprinted from Jenny Chang (MFT, 2012). Dignity Health, Sacramento, California, USA.

Rubin and Babbie (2014) further state that *when coding content analysis, there are two choices: manifest content and latent content.* Manifest content applies more of a quantitative approach by focusing on a specific form of communication (i.e., journal article, book, magazine, newspaper) to determine the extent to which the issue is accounted for. For example, if a researcher wants to know how much attention people and politicians pay to the needs of homeless veterans, they could select the last 12 or 60 issues of the local newspaper. The researcher then systematically sorts through the pages of the newspaper and documents the number of times the selected newspaper mentions "homeless veterans."

Latent content applies specifically to a qualitative approach. Latent researchers still have to select a specific form of communication but only analyze the meaning of the communication. For the situation with the homeless veterans, instead of counting the number of times the local newspaper mentions homeless veterans, the researcher will examine how the local reporters discussed the situations of homeless veterans. Essentially, in manifest content, researchers do the frequency count on the occurrences of the term *homeless veterans*. In latent content, the researchers account for the extended coverage of homeless veterans or explain the meaning of the homeless veterans as discussed or interpreted by local reporters.

When providing reasons for research situations, there are two methods of reasoning or logic. One is the *deductive* method and the other is the *inductive* method. Deductive reasoning works from the more broad or general down to the specific (Rubin & Babbie, 2017). Usually, researchers will start with a theory about the research topic. It is then narrowed down into specific hypotheses. Once the hypotheses are formulated, the researchers move on to collect data, including observations. Finally, based on the collected data, the hypotheses are either retained or rejected. Inductive reasoning works the other way, moving from specific observations to broader generalizations and theories (Rubin & Babbie, 2017).

Qualitative data analysis is typically based on the inductive method. More importantly, most exploratory research studies (whether quantitative or qualitative) fall under this categorization. The reason is that researchers examine a few cases to apply their findings from this small observation to the larger population, or the researchers hope to generate a plausible theory from these small observations. Furthermore, one of the main goals for qualitative researchers is to develop a theoretical framework from the observations so perhaps formal hypotheses can be generated from the sample to the population from which the sample was drawn.

For example, Anders and Dinis (2009), in a latent content analysis on workplace challenges in institutions of higher education, reported one of their findings was related to ideological change. They stated that managers like "Eleanor, for instance, noted the manager has to be 'aware of the labor laws…and you have to learn to manage within a union set-up. She thought the workplace was dealing with more rules, regulations, and laws. Marie said the workplace has become more 'unionized, more litigious, more complicated'" (p. 288).

Semiotics

The third type of qualitative data analysis is *semiotics*. Semiotics is defined as the science of signs and has to do with symbols and meanings (Rubin & Babbie, 2014). This is how researchers link words in the data set with language and cultural symbols of the respondents to find meanings. For example, while interviewing groups of people, the interviewers constantly notice that women do not shake hands with men. By exploring with the group, the interviewers learn that avoidance of shaking hands with a female is a sign of cultural respect. In a different example, while interviewing female subjects in a rural community, the interviewees kept avoiding eye contact. The researcher later learned that indirect eye contact is a sign of being ashamed. Table 12.2 provides an example of semiotic data analysis.

TABLE 12.2 Example of Data Analysis Using the Semiotic Concept

Sign	Meaning
Two fingers up in a V	Victorious
Handshake	Greetings or congratulations
Hands to mouth	Eat or ready to eat
Scream	Fear, anger, frustration
Turn back to interview	Avoidance

Conversation Analysis

The last form of qualitative data analysis is the *conversation* method. In semiotics, signs, symbols, and cultural concepts were used to translate meaning. In conversation analysis, *terms*, *words*, or *perspectives* are used to uncover the inherent assumptions and structures in social life through extreme scrutiny of the way humans converse with one another. Conversation analysis usually happens when qualitative researchers pick up someone else's concept, perspective, or theory and try to interpret its meaning. Conversation analysis happens a lot in social sciences research.

For example, one could pick up the term *ecological perspective* and try to insert one's own interpretations of the meaning of the person in the environment. Not only that, Rubin and Babbie (2014) also state that in conversation analysis, researchers also try to uncover words like "uhs, ers, and poor grammar." Therefore, in a statistics course, when someone says, "I ain't like statistics," the researchers will try to interpret the term "ain't" using conversation analysis by trying to interpret its meaning as: "I do not like statistics," "I am not like statistics," "I hate statistics," or "I cannot like statistics." The researcher will try every possible way to understand the term "ain't." Similarly, when someone says, I want that "application" in this technological and gadget age, the researcher will have to try to understand whether the person is referring to a computer program or a paper application form.

Computer Applications and Online Resources

Even without displaying an actual example, as demonstrated in Chapters 4–11 with SPSS, the mechanisms discussed throughout this chapter should give you some good ideas about gathering and displaying qualitative data via a computer. The following are several computerized programs, some of which are available free online:

MAXQDA: qualitative data analysis software for Windows
ATLAS.ti: qualitative data analysis software
QDA Miner Lite: free qualitative data analysis software
NVivo: research software for analysis and insight
QDAP (Qualitative Data Analysis Program): of the University Center for Social and Urban Research at the University of Pittsburgh, Pennsylvania.

Other referenced sources that one may obtain to help with qualitative data analysis include *Analyzing Social Settings: A Guide to Qualitative Observation and Analysis* (Lofland et al., 2006) and *Social Work Research and Evaluation: Quantitative and Qualitative Approaches* (Grinnell, 2000). In addition, the following free reference sources are available online:

- *Qualitative Data Analysis*, http://www.sagepub.com/upm-data/43454_10.pdf
- *Qualitative Data Analysis*, http://www.southalabama.edu/coe/bset/johnson/lectures/lec17.pdf
- *Analyzing Qualitative Data*, http://learningstore.uwex.edu/assets/pdfs/g3658-12.pdf
- *Qualitative Data Analysis*, ftp://ftp.qualisresearch.com/pub/qda.pdf
- *Steps in Qualitative Data Analysis*, http://www.slideshare.net/guest7f1ad678/qualitative-data-analysis-steps

SUMMARY

This chapter provides a brief discussion on the meaning of qualitative research and data summary tools that beginning researchers may apply to field research. In scientific terminology, even though qualitative findings are not generalizable, the methods allow researchers and practitioners the flexibility to incorporate observations and use subjectivity to generate deeper understandings of human experiences.

Qualitative research involves two very important concepts. The concepts are *fieldwork* and *field notes*. Fieldwork is a classical anthropological method the researcher uses to collect data while at the site(s) of interest. With fieldwork, researchers have a specific site of interest they want to study (e.g., a specific school). They want to examine a phenomenon in its natural environment (e.g., people crossing the street), and they want to study how cultural traditions of a specific ethnic minority group can be infused with micro-social practices. Fieldwork has its own research design, recruitment strategies, and data collection protocols. *The data collection protocols must include the protection of human subjects from unnecessary social and psychological harm.* This means that participants must not experience anything harmful during their time in the study.

Field notes are like memos or texts to oneself and the research assistants (if any), and the recorded words/responses given by the respondents during the interviews. It is extremely important that anything the respondents say be precisely recorded. Treat the field notes exactly as one would the numeric data collected from quantitative research. There should not be any alteration or summarization to the field notes. Why? Because the "text" recorded and transcribed from the interviews, as well as participant observations, become the "results" for the research project.

Qualitative data analysis usually involves a combination of one of four types: (1) discovering patterns, (2) content analysis, (3) semiotics, and (4) conversation analysis. To fully understand all aspects of qualitative research, one must take a course specifically designed for that purpose.

Study Questions

Multiple Choice. These study questions should enable learners to better prepare for qualitative research

1. In a research study, when words are used to gather data and are then categorized, the method for this data collection is called

    a. qualitative research.
    b. quantitative research.
    c. mixed-methods research.
    d. all of the above.

2. Which of the following is not a good reason to include qualitative research with quantitative research? Qualitative research

    a. provides rich information for understanding human conditions.
    b. allows the flexibility to incorporate subjective meanings and interpretations to the issue under investigation.
    c. makes findings more generalizable.

3. According to the author of this book, research findings from which of the following research methodologies makes it more generalizable?

    a. Qualitative research
    b. Quantitative research
    c. Mixed-methods research
    d. All of the above

4. When using qualitative research, one must abide by the same set of statistical assumptions as in quantitative research.

    a. True
    b. False
    c. Either one is correct

5. The mechanism that qualitative researchers use to keep fieldwork information for themselves while collecting data is called
    a. fieldwork record.
    b. record process.
    c. field notes.
    d. all of the above.

6. According to the author of this book, in modern days, the type of research method that is more popular among various research groups is
    a. qualitative research.
    b. quantitative research.
    c. mixed-methods research.
    d. all of the above.

7. In qualitative research inquiry, when the researchers state that they will "get to the point in a nonoffending and nonprejudicial view," this type of statement reflects
    a. commitments made by the research group to get to the bottom of the issue under investigation/
    b. commitments made by the research group to make the research questions clear and easily understandable for the issue under investigation.
    c. commitments made by the research group to obtain quality data for the issue under investigation.

8. Which of the following reflects a doubled-barrel question for qualitative research?
    a. How is your day?
    b. Have you been outside your country of birth, and what do you feel about it?
    c. Why did you decide to attend college?
    d. How do you feel about the campus environment?

9. When a researcher is taking field notes about meanings of words spoken/explained by the research subjects, this part of the recording is called
    a. the setting.
    b. the people and the geographical setting.
    c. group behavior.
    d. meaning and perspectives.

10. When a researcher is taking field notes about how members of the research participants are related to one another and their interactions and roles, this part of the recording is called
    a. the setting.
    b. the people and the geographical setting.
    c. individual actions and activities.
    d. group behavior.

11. When a researcher is taking field notes about who is being interviewed and the socioeconomic background of the research subjects, this part of the recording is called
    a. the setting.
    b. the people and the geographical setting.
    c. individual actions and activities.
    d. group behavior.

12. When a researcher is taking field notes about the behaviors of the people in the setting—for example, who talks to whom and in what fashion—this part of the recording is called
    a. the setting.
    b. the people and the geographical setting.
    c. individual actions and activities.
    d. group behavior.

13. In either qualitative or quantitative data analysis, one may speak/write "enumeration." Enumeration is used to describe
    a. the type of statistics.
    b. the length of the data set.
    c. the quantification of the data set.
    d. the magnitude of the data set.

14. In qualitative data analysis, when a researcher is trying to discover the patterns of the data set by ordering categories of issues confronted by subjects under investigation, the mechanism being used by the researcher is called
    a. frequencies.
    b. structures.
    c. processes.
    d. consequences.

15. In qualitative data analysis, a researcher selects a specific form of communication and analyzes the meaning of the communication without specifying a time line for the communication. The mechanism applied by the researcher is called
    a. communication interpretation.
    b. latent content.
    c. manifest content.

16. The type of quantitative data analysis that is based on signs and symbols of a particular group's culture and traditions is called
    a. discovering patterns.
    b. content analysis.
    c. semiotics.
    d. conversation analysis.

Answers to Study Questions

QUESTION	ANSWER	QUESTION	ANSWER
1	a	9	d
2	c	10	d
3	b	11	b
4	b	12	c
5	c	13	c
6	c	14	c
7	c	15	b
8	b	16	c

APPENDIX A

SPSS Instructions

OVERVIEW

Detailed instructions were provided for each area of descriptive and inferential statistics throughout the book. For example, if a learner wants to know how to do data entry and complete frequencies, then the learner should turn to Chapter 3, measures of central tendency in Chapter 4, and so on. Appendix A only provides a quick highlight on other important steps about preparing data for statistical analysis and the utilization of SPSS.

PREPARING THE DATA FOR ANALYSIS

Statisticians and researchers find that when it comes to preparing data for analyses, even with various forms of computer applications, there is no simple way to organize, display, and analyze raw scores. Although each researcher individually makes decisions according to personal habits, styles, and objectives, those decisions must comply with the laws or guidelines of statistics. The following are suggested steps for consideration when analyzing quantitative data.

SUGGESTED STEPS IN PREPARING THE OBTAINED SCORES FOR ANALYSIS

Before analyzing any data set, there are many steps that good researchers should take into consideration. The following are the suggested steps:

- *The research data.* Before working on data entry, look through the research questionnaires and the raw scores obtained. Take note of areas with discrepancies or inconsistencies or areas requiring new variables. Sometimes, one or more variables emerge during the data collection process that was not a part of the original questionnaire. This problem arises because participants have unexpected reactions to questions and their responses may differ from the precoded values.

- *While doing data entry.* The information returned by the research subjects (participants) should be coded or assigned ID numbers. Use a codebook/code sheet. Even with the assistance of software applications, a coding sheet/coding scheme is needed to help track both the variable and the values of the variables being entered. The coding sheet will make data analyses much easier. Take note that humans do not have the memory of a computer application.

- *After data entry is complete.* Once data entry is completed, use frequency distributions as shown in Table A.1 to *check for typographical errors.* Incorrect data may have been mistakenly entered into the data file, perhaps an illegal character or an incorrect response. Careful researchers edit typos and correct missing data before proceeding to data analyses and interpretations.

- *Data recoding.* For inference, the original categories, or values of one or more of the variables (both dependent and independent) may need to be recoded. For example, the researcher may need to recode several racial backgrounds into a new category, such as a main minority group. Alternatively, one may need to recode ordinal data into nominal. *Sometimes, recoding can help make data meet specific statistical assumptions.* For practical purposes, the variable "*Class*" in Table 3.1 will be shown later in the appendix.

- *Clearly understand the level of measurement for each of the research questions, as well as the hypotheses.* For this author, levels of measurement are as important as religious texts like the Bible, the Koran, Buddha, and shamanistic rituals. If the levels of measurement used for a research study are misunderstood or incorrectly used, research findings and data interpretations can easily be compromised.

- Clearly *understand measures of central tendency.* Measures of central tendency help us to understand the overall distribution of the scores, find outliers, and even make educated guesses about *homogeneity of variance.*

- Lastly, but most importantly, *understand the tail of the hypothesis test and its statistical significance.* DO NOT rely solely on what is given by a software application. For example, a correlation coefficient of .752 produced based on a sample size of 30 is not as strong as a correlation coefficient of .340 produced from a sample size of 300. Chapter 8 noted that with a large sample size, just a very small correlation coefficient is sufficient to reject the H_o. Also, whenever possible, change the preset α (p value) level listed by the computer program.

INTRODUCTION AND DATA ENTRY USING SPSS

The term *Statistical Package for the Social Sciences* (SPSS) is featured throughout the book. SPSS is a popular software package for statistical analysis and data management applications. However, it is advisable that students or practitioners do not use the so-called student version of SPSS. The basic student version has many limitations in usage. As stated by SPSS (2020), its graphic environment is powerful.

The descriptive menus (ribbon) have simple dialog boxes that are useful for most facets of statistical computation. Once the data entry is completed, most other tasks are accomplished simply by pointing and clicking the mouse.

In basic statistical computations, especially activities that are relevant to the contents of this book, two types of files are introduced: (1) a *data or system file* and (2) an *output file*. The *data file* is where variable names are created, the title of a variable is created, the value of the variable is entered, the correct levels of measurement for the variables are selected, and data are entered into the system. *Data file* simply refers to the common concept of data entry. The *output file* is where information ready for analysis is computed and stored. In addition, the output file contains outcome information based on descriptive and inferential statistics and information that is ready to be printed. To put it simply, the *output file* is the result of the statistical computations.

Data Entry Using SPSS

Once SPSS is started, either a blank screen or a question mark appears asking which file is to be opened. If the user is unsure, click to return to a blank screen. The blank screen is where the user can create a personal data file or open other files on the computer. *Take note that all imported files must be cleaned to meet SPSS data file requirements.* To create a new data file or clean up an imported file, simply follow these steps:

- Each variable in the questionnaire must be given a name or be defined. For example, if a research study uses 50 questions, then 50 variable names must be given. To define a name for each of the variables, look at the bottom left of the screen (see Figure A.1) where two keywords are visible. These two keywords are *Data View* and *Variable View*. *Variable View* is where several tasks must be completed, specifically *Name*, *Type*, *Label*, *Value*, and *Measure*.

- *"Name" is the name given to the variable.* SPSS prefers that each name is eight characters or less and the name does not have to make sense. While creating a name for the variable, do not use these special characters: period (.), semicolon (;), question mark(?), front slash (/), backslash (\), underscore (_), space bar, and dollar sign ($). These special characters are reserved for internal usage. In brief, when the term "Variable name contains an illegal character" pops up after pressing the "Enter" key, give a different name to the variable.

- *"Type" is where to select whether the variable is numeric, string, or others (such as dollar ($) sign).* It is also the location where you can change the width and decimals for the variable. For example, gender will not have a decimal, but school GPA must use decimals. Typically, numeric is the preferred mode for data entry. But in some cases, other types may have to be used.

- *"Label" is the title of the variable.* When a research project uses numerous variables, it is a best practice to type the title as clearly as possible. It is strongly recommended that the title not be longer than two lines. Also, it is NOT recommended that the title be entered exactly as how the question was phrased.

- *"Values" is the responses/answers precoded for the variable (see Figure A.2).* If the question has precoded answers, such as 1 for female and 2 for male or 1 for no anxiety at all to 5 for extremely high anxiety, then the precoded categories or values must be entered. Open-ended questions, such as how old someone is without precoded age categories, can be left as "None."

- *"Measure" is the scale used for each of the questions.* Nominal and ordinal scales must be individually checked, or SPSS will treat the variable as an unknown scale. Scale is used for interval and ratio variables.

With the aforementioned instructions, one can easily create an SPSS data file for Table 3.1. *To create a data file for Table 3.1, do the following*:

- Once SPSS is opened, click *Variable View* (bottom left screen).

- Put the cursor on column 1 row 1 and then type "*Gender.*" Since Table 3.1 is in alphanumeric form, move the cursor to the *Decimal* column. Click on the right-hand corner of that row; click the downward arrow to change 2 to 0.

- Move the cursor to the *Label* column. Type "*Gender of the student respondents.*"

- Once finished with the title of the variable, move the cursor to the *Values* columns. As stated earlier, *Values* are the precoded answers/responses to a question. Click the right-hand corner on that bubble. A new mini window that looks like the one in Figure A.2 will pop up.

FIGURE A.1 Blank SPSS Screen

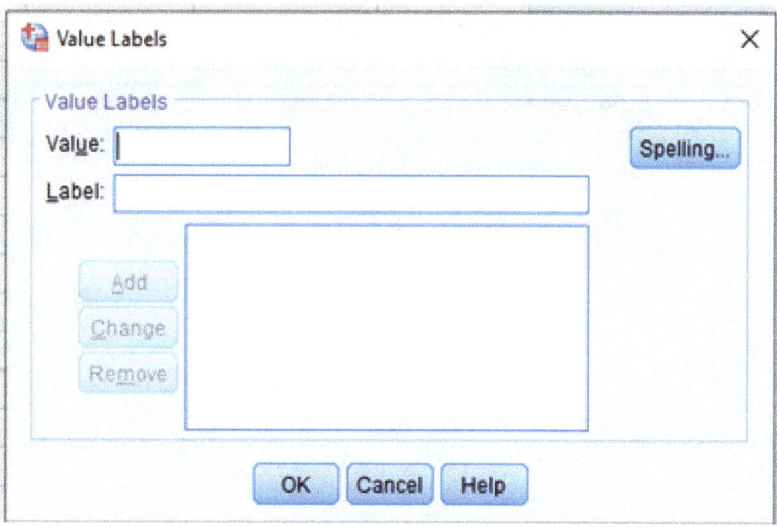

FIGURE A.2 The Value Label Column

- Put the cursor on *Value* and then type "*1.*" Move the cursor to *Label* and then type "*Female.*" Press *Enter*. Note that when 1 = "Female" is entered onto the mini window, the cursor immediately moves back to *Value*. Now, type "*2.*" Move the cursor to *Label* and type "*Male.*" Press *Enter*. Click *OK*. Note that only the word "Female" is visible.

- The next three columns are *other options*. Select them based on the research criteria. On *Missing*, many researchers enter 999 for the missing scores. On *Align*, choose how you want your scores to appear on the left, right, or center.

- Move the cursor to the *Measure* column. Click on the right-hand corner. Select *Nominal*.

- Move the cursor to column 1 row 2. Repeat the same process for age, class, anxiety, and self-care. On *Values for Age*, leave it as *None*, and on *Measure* select *Scale*. On Class, use 1 = Freshman, 2 = Sophomore, 3 = Junior, 4 = Senior. On Anxiety, list 1 = No anxiety at all, 2 = Little anxiety, 3 = Some anxiety, 4 = High anxiety, and 5 = Extremely high anxiety. On *Measure* select *Ordinal*. On *Self-Care* repeat the same process as you entered for Age. Leave *Value* as *None* and select *Scale* for *Measure*.

- After the five variables are constructed, select *Data View*. Your window now should look like Figure A.3.

- Note that "*Gender*" now appears with three balloons of different colors. The colors of the balloons indicate that they are in different categories. "*Age*" and "*Self-Care*" show a ruler, which indicates interval-level data. "*Class*" and "*Anxiety*" show bars of different colors (from low to high) to indicate rank order.

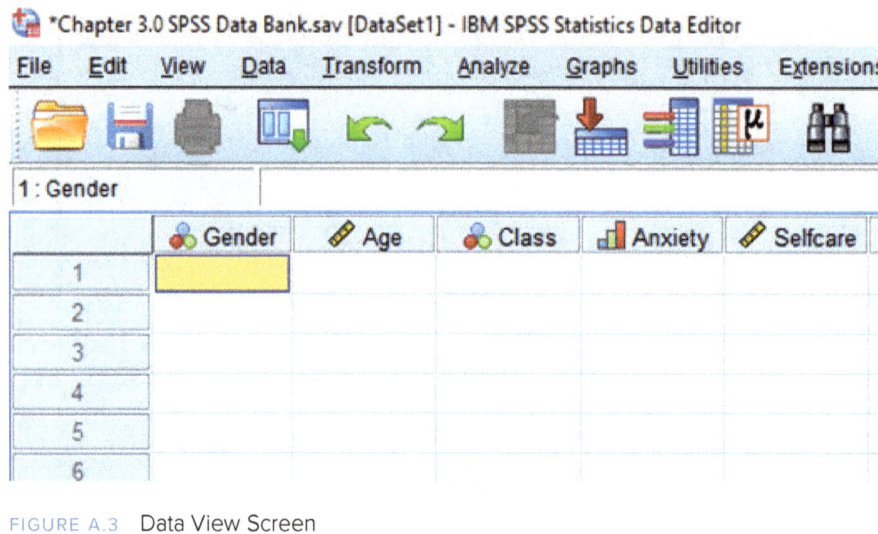

FIGURE A.3   Data View Screen

- Now enter the scores on Table 3.1 to their respective variables. After the data entry is completed, the data spreadsheet will look like Figure A.4.
- The data file is now created. Both descriptive and inferential statistics can now be computed from the data file.

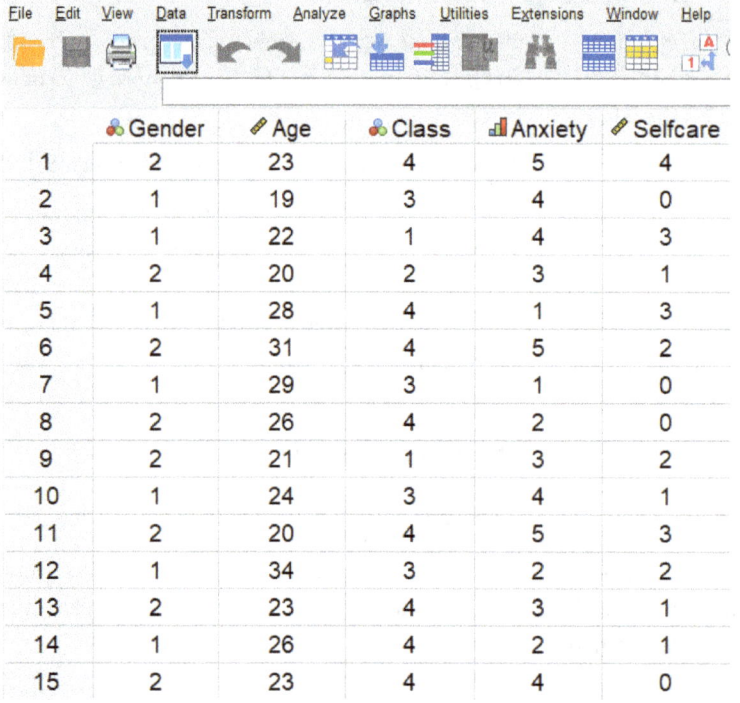

FIGURE A.4   Chapter Data Bank

Saving Data

Saving an SPSS file is no different from saving word-processing documents. In fact, there are several ways to save your files (both data and output). Like most programs, SPSS automatically saves the file as a default file every 10 or so minutes. However, it is better to manually save your data file using a recognizable file name. Without this, SPSS will assign a random name and save it in the most recent file location.

To save work, follow these brief steps. Pull down the *File* Menu from the left-hand side of the screen. Select *Save As* and then the *Look In* field at the top of the window. Find the location where the file is to be saved and then type a suitable file name. Also, remember whether the file is saved as *DATA*, *SYNTAX*, *OUTPUT*, or *SCRIPT*. Syntax is an alternative way of computing solutions by avoiding point-and-click operations. Thus, to avoid point-and-click moves, consider using Syntax. Script is relatively new to SPSS.

Now that data entry using *Variable View* **and** *Data View* **has** been covered, let us move to an explanation of the basics of *descriptive and inferential statistics* using SPSS. But first, frequency distributions using SPSS are introduced.

Practice Example

To get the first practical experience on SPSS with the data file you have just created, take the following steps. For practical purposes, let's create a frequency table for the "*Anxiety*" variable.

- Click the *Analyze* ribbon in the middle of the top menu. Move the cursor down to *Descriptive Statistics* and select *Frequencies*. A mini window will pop up. To change the variable *Label* to *Name* as it appears in the following image, click the right mouse. Another mini window will pop up. Select the first bubble on the list.

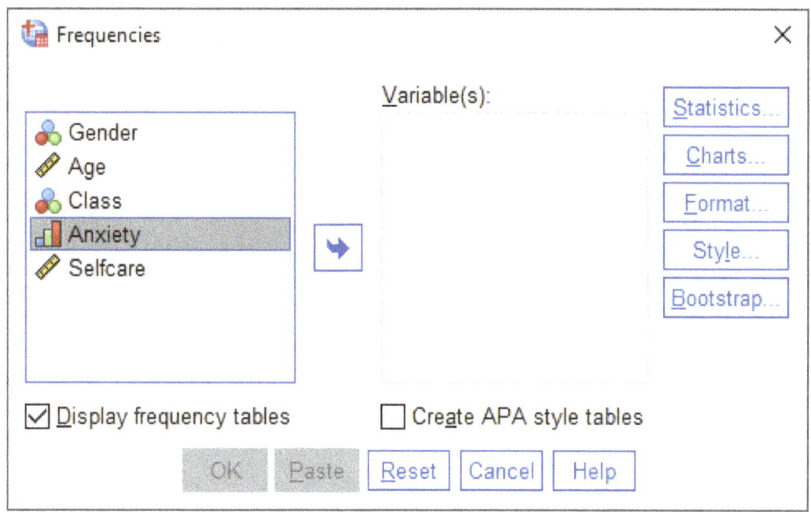

Image A.1

  o Select *Anxiety*. Hit the forward arrow (→) in the middle. The variable "*Anxiety*" is moved to the functional mini window. Click *OK*. Momentarily, the output file will display the completed frequency count that looks like Table A.1

TABLE A.1 The Students' Anxiety Level

		Frequency	Percent	Valid Percent	Cumulative Percent
Valid	No anxiety at all	2	13.3	13.3	13.3
	Little anxiety	3	20.0	20.0	33.3
	Some anxiety	3	20.0	20.0	53.3
	High anxiety	4	26.7	26.7	80.0
	Extremely high anxiety	3	20.0	20.0	100.0
	Total	15	100.0	100.0	

As stated earlier, when there are no missing scores, the *Percent* and *Valid Percent* look the same. When there are missing scores, the *Valid Percent* will always be higher than *Percent*. *Cumulative Percent* is the addition of the percentages from one row to the next.

Now, let's try to create a bar graph for the variable gender. To get the same bar graph as in Figure A.5, take the following steps:

- Click *Graphs*, move the cursor down to *Legacy Dialogs*, and select *Bar*. This mini window will pop up. On the *Bar Graph*, select *Simple*. Click *Define* at the bottom of the mini window.
  - On the new mini window, highlight *Gender*. Move it to *Category Axis*. Hit *OK*. Momentarily, the same graph as Figure A.5 appears. To design any part of the graph, double-click the graph, and various design functions will pop up. Once you are finished constructing the graph, X it out. All the new designs are now displayed in the original graph.

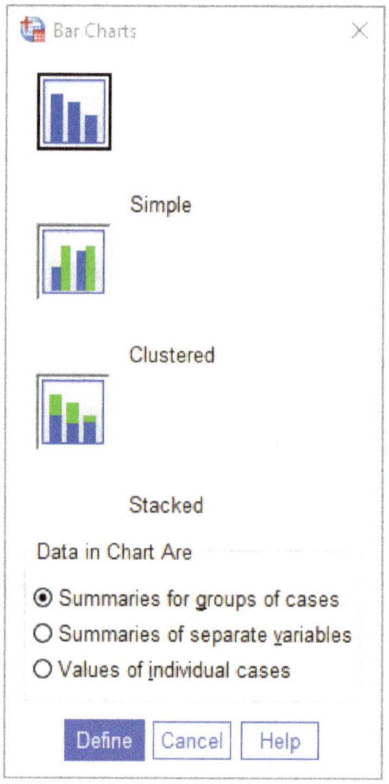

Image A.2

Computing Descriptive Statistics

As explained in this appendix, once a data file has been created, the first step is to examine the frequency distributions of the variables. If the data set contains only nominal and ordinal levels of measurement and the user does not want to generalize the findings, then the display and discussion of frequency tables are sufficient. If the user has interval- or ratio-level data, then going beyond frequency tables is important. Whenever the data set contains interval- or ratio-level data, it is crucial to compute measures

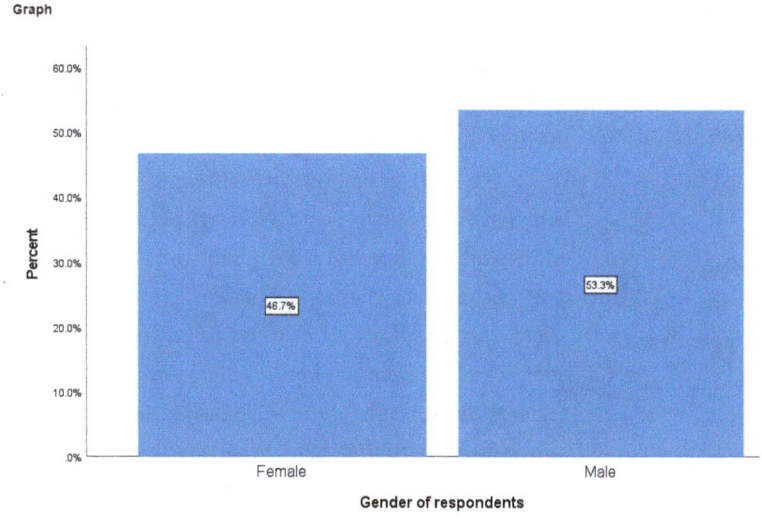

FIGURE A.5   Bar Graph for Gender

of central tendency and variability. To compute measures of central tendency and measures of variability for the variable of interest, follow these steps:

- Pull down the *Analyze* ribbon, move the cursor to *Descriptive Statistics*, and select *Frequencies*.
- Notice that two small windows appear. The window on the left lists all variables from the data file. The one on the right is currently blank. Using the cursor, select the variable being examined and then click the forward arrow in the middle between the two windows. The variable will automatically move into the window on the right. The user can select one or multiple variables and forward it/them to the functional mini desktop.
- Click *Statistics* (top-right corner of the screen), and then under *Central Tendency*, check *Mean, Median*, and *Mode*. On *Dispersion*, check *Std. deviation* and *Variance* (see Chapters 3 and 4).
- Click *Continue*. Additional available options will appear at the top right of the screen. Select the options that best fit the research objectives.
- Click *OK*.
- The results for the descriptive statistics (i.e., measures of central tendency and variability) for the variable being examined will appear on a nice-looking table.

Computing Inferential Statistics

Computing inferential statistics is no different than computing descriptive statistics. The only difference is that *cross-tabulation and chi-square* are located inside *Descriptive Statistics*. Once the *Analyze* ribbon is pulled down, move the cursor to *Descriptive Statistics* and then choose *Crosstabs*. If it is a *nonparametric statistic* (beyond the scope of this book), then on the *Analyze* ribbon, choose *Nonparametric*

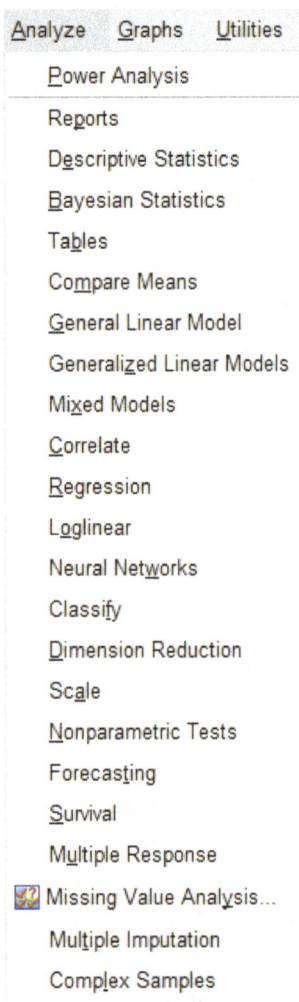

FIGURE A.6 Analyze Ribbon Showing Both Descriptive and Inferential Statistics

Tests, move the cursor over to *Legacy Dialogs*, and then choose *Chi-Square*.

For all other inferential statistics, such as correlation (Chapter 8), detailed instructions were provided at the end of the chapter. Figure A.6 shows the *Analyze* ribbon with different types of inferential statistics. When in doubt about the proper usage of particular inferential statistics, additional instructions are available on the *Help* ribbon listed under each of the inferential tests. For example, to get help with correlation, select *Correlate*, move the cursor to *Bivariate* (the focus of this book), and then select *Help* (see Figure A.7). Please note, do not choose the *Help* menu at the top right of the SPSS desktop screen. *The Help menu listed under each inferential test will in fact show the learners/practitioners not just how to complete the test but also how to write a correct report.*

FIGURE A.7 Sample Help for Correlation Analysis

When completing a descriptive or inferential statistic, the variables under investigation may need to be recoded. The following are quick instructions on recoding for any particular variable.

Recoding a Variable

Throughout the book, the issue of recoding several categories or values has not been introduced. The following are instructions on how to use SPSS to complete such a task. For practical purposes, let's assume that a researcher wants to recode the variable on class standing from "Class" (Table 3.1) into a simple new category, "*College Student*."

- Select *Variable View* (bottom left corner of the screen).

- Put the cursor on the column and row where you want the variable "*College Student*" to appear. Let us say the new name is "*Student*."

- Move the cursor to the location where you want the new name to appear and then type "*Student*."

- Knowing that college students do not have decimal places, move the cursor to *Column*. Change the *Decimals* column to 0. Next, move the cursor to the *Label* column and type "*College Student.*"

- In the *Values* column, type "*1*" on *Value* and *College Student* in the *Label* rectangle. Then, type "*2*" and label the category again as *College Student*. Repeat the same process until all four categories are entered. Recall that the variable "*Class*" on Table 3.1 listed "*freshman, sophomore, junior, and senior.*"

- On *Measure*, select *Nominal*.

- When done, click *Data View* (bottom left) to return to the data spreadsheet.

- Notice that the entire column on the newly created variable name "*Student*" is blank with only a dot, dot, dot throughout.

- Pull down *Transform* on the main ribbon. Then, move the cursor to recode it into a different variable. It is always advisable to recode the values or categories into a different variable. This way, the original data remain intact.

- Select the variable *Class and* then click the forward arrow in the middle of the two mini desktop windows. The variable should automatically move to the new mini window on the right, as shown in Figure A.8. In *Name*, type the newly created variable "*Student*" and on *Label*, type "*College Student.*"

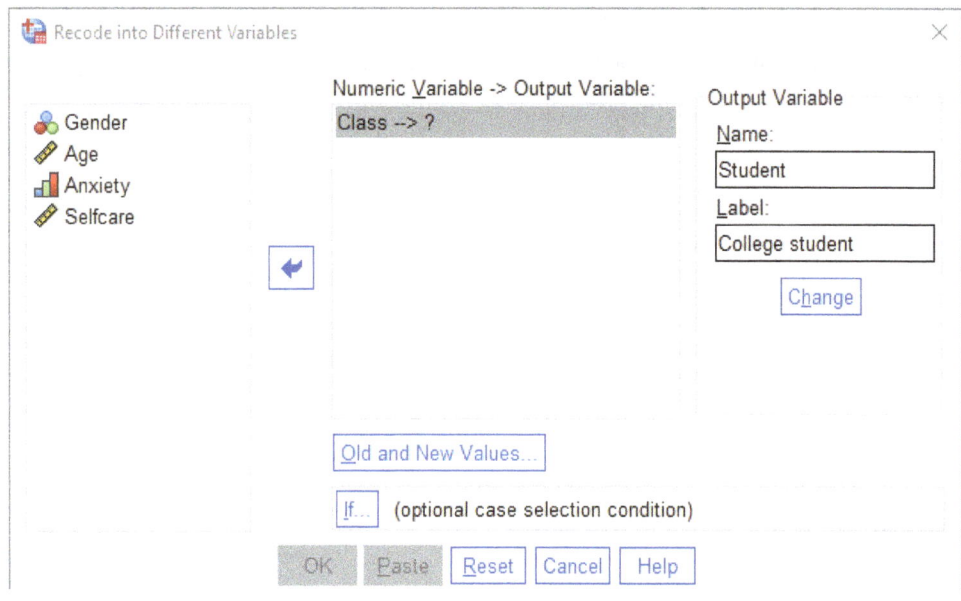

FIGURE A.8 Recode Variable

- Click *Old and New Values.*
- Notice that two mini windows appear. The window on the left is labeled *Old Value*, and the one on the right is labeled *New Value*. Type "1" (Freshman) on the *Old Value*, then "1" (College Student). Click the word *Add* in the middle of the screen. Move the cursor to *Old Value*, enter "2" (Sophomore), and then "1" (College Student). Next, type "3" (Junior) and "1" (College Student); finally, type "4" (Senior) and "1" (College Student) on *Old Value* and *New Value*, respectively. The result should look like Figure A.9. The objective is to change the participants' current class standing to college students.

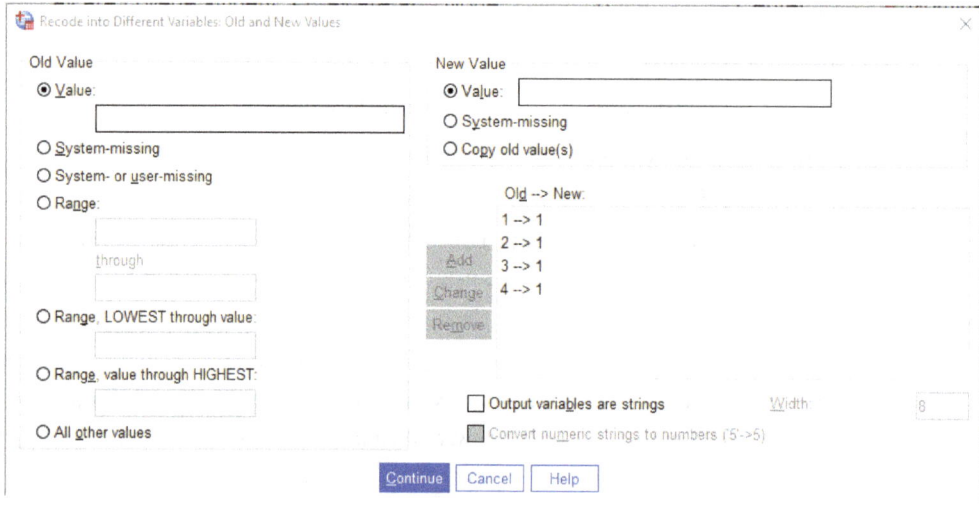

FIGURE A.9 Recode Old and New Variables

- Click *Continue*. Notice that SPSS is still not allowing the user to complete the task.
- To complete the task, click *Change* (top-right corner of the mini desktop). SPSS will ask whether this is what the user wants. Click *OK* and then click *Continue* (bottom of the mini desktop).
- Notice that the *Output* file says that the *Recode has been executed*. Close the *Output* file and then click *Data View* to return to the *Data* file (system file). Notice that the newly created values now appear under the variable *Student* (Figure A.10).

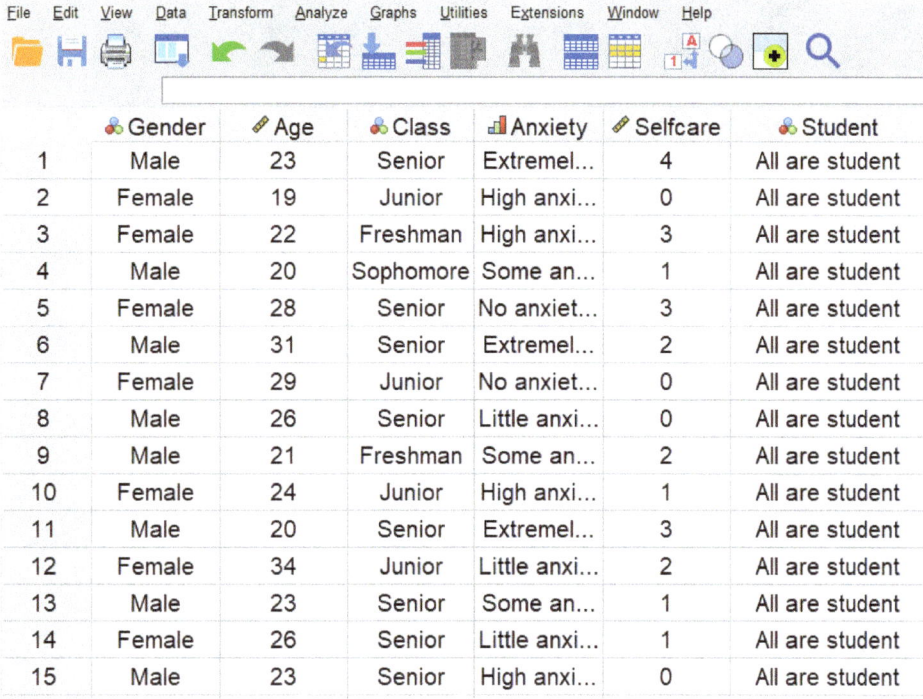

FIGURE A.10 Sample Recode Is Successful

- Essentially, recoding reduces several values to a smaller, more desirable outcome. Although the term *dichotomous* was not discussed throughout the book, recoding a long list of values, such as income, into two categories serves the same purpose.

APPENDIX B

Critical Values of F

CRITICAL VALUES OF F (α = .05) IN STANDARD TYPE, α = .01 IN BOLDFACE

Please note that the critical values of F in Appendix B only show the values for the 95% and 99% confidence intervals (α = .05 and .01), respectively. If a different level of confidence interval is desirable, then it is strongly suggested that the user uses one of the widely available *critical values of F calculators* available freely on the Internet. *Whether one uses the free calculator on the Internet or a table with the critical value of F, the critical value will always be the same.* The following are links to some of the available free websites:

- https://www.socscistatistics.com/tests/criticalvalues/default.aspx
- https://www.danielsoper.com/statcalc/calculator.aspx?id=4
- https://mathcracker.com/f-critical-values
- http://statcalculators.com/critical-f-value-calculator/
- https://stattrek.com/online-calculator/f-distribution.aspx
- https://www.easycalculation.com/statistics/f-critical-value.php

n_2	\multicolumn{12}{c}{n_1 Degrees of Freedom (for Numerator Mean Square)}
	1	2	3	4	5	6	7	8	9	10	11	12
1	161	200	216	225	230	234	237	239	241	242	243	244
	4,052	**4,999**	**5,403**	**5,625**	**5,764**	**5.859**	**5,928**	**5,981**	**6,022**	**6,056**	**6,082**	**6,106**
2	18.51	19.00	19.16	19.25	19.30	19.33	19.36	19.37	19.38	19.39	19.40	19.41
	98.49	**99.00**	**99.17**	**99.25**	**99.30**	**99.33**	**99.34**	**99.36**	**99.38**	**99.40**	**99.41**	**99.42**
3	10.13	9.55	9.28	9.12	9.01	8.94	8.88	8.84	8.81	8.78	8.76	8.74
	34.12	**30.82**	**29.46**	**28.71**	**28.24**	**27.91**	**27.67**	**27.49**	**27.34**	**27.23**	**27.13**	**27.05**
4	7.71	6.94	6.59	6.39	6.26	6.16	6.09	6.04	6.00	5.96	5.93	5.91
	21.20	**18.00**	**16.69**	**15.98**	**15.52**	**15.21**	**14.98**	**14.80**	**14.66**	**14.54**	**14.45**	**14.37**
5	6.61	5.79	5.41	5.19	5.05	4.95	4.88	4.82	4.78	4.74	4.70	4.68
	16.26	**13.27**	**12.06**	**11.39**	**10.97**	**10.67**	**10.45**	**10.27**	**10.15**	**10.05**	**9.96**	**9.89**
6	5.99	5.14	4.76	4.53	4.39	4.28	4.21	4.15	**4.10**	4.06	4.03	4.00
	13.74	**10.92**	**9.78**	**9.15**	**8.75**	**8.47**	**8.26**	**8.10**	**7.98**	**7.87**	**7.79**	**7.72**
7	5.59	**4.74**	4.35	4.12	3.97	3.87	3.79	3.73	3.68	3.63	3.60	3.57
	12.25	**9.55**	**8.45**	**7.85**	**7.46**	**7.19**	**7.00**	**6.84**	**6.71**	**6.62**	**6.54**	**6.47**
8	5.32	4,46	4.07	3.84	3.69	3.58	3.50	3.44	3.39	3.34	3.31	3.28
	11.26	**8.65**	**7.59**	**7.01**	**6.63**	**6.37**	**6.19**	**6.03**	**5.91**	**5.82**	**5.74**	**5.67**
9	5.12	4.26	3.86	3.63	3.48	3.37	3.29	3.23	3.18	3.13	3.10	3.07
	10.56	**8.02**	**6.99**	**6.42**	**6.06**	**5.80**	**5.62**	**5.47**	**5.35**	**5.26**	**5.18**	**5.11**
10	4.96	4.10	3.71	3.48	3.33	3.22	3.14	3.07	3.02	2.97	2.94	2.91
	10.04	**7.56**	**6.55**	**5.99**	**5.64**	**5.39**	**5.21**	**5.06**	**4.95**	**4.85**	**4.78**	**4.71**
11	4.84	3.98	3.59	3.36	3.20	3.09	3.01	2.95	2.90	2.86	2.82	2.79
	9.65	**7.20**	**6.22**	**5.67**	**5.32**	**5.07**	**4.88**	**4.74**	**4.63**	**4.54**	**4.46**	**4.40**
12	4.75	3.88	3.49	3.26	3.11	3.00	2.92	2.85	2.80	2.76	2.72	2.69
	9.33	**6.93**	**5.95**	**5.41**	**5.06**	**4.82**	**4.65**	**4.50**	**4.39**	**4.30**	**4.22**	**4.16**
13	4.67	3.80	3.41	3.18	3.02	2.92	2.84	2.77	2.72	2.67	2.63	2.60
	9.07	**6.70**	**5.74**	**5.20**	**4.86**	**4.62**	**4.44**	**4.30**	**4.19**	**4.10**	**4.02**	**3.96**

n_1 Degrees of Freedom (for Numerator Mean Square)											
14	**16**	**20**	**24**	**30**	**40**	**50**	**75**	**100**	**200**	**500**	**∞**
245	246	247	248	259	251	252	253	253	254	254	254
6,142	**6,169**	**6,208**	**6,234**	**6,258**	**6,286**	**6,302**	**6,323**	**6,334**	**6,352**	**6,361**	**6,366**
19.42	19.43	19.44	19.45	19.46	19.47	19.47	19.48	19.49	19.49	19.50	19.50
99.43	**99.44**	**99.45**	**99.46**	**99.47**	**99.48**	**99.48**	**99.49**	**99.49**	**99.49**	**99.50**	**99.50**
8.71	8.69	8.66	8.64	8.62	8.60	8.58	8.57	8.56	8.54	8.54	8.53
26.92	**26.83**	**26.69**	**26.60**	**26.50**	**26.41**	**26.35**	**26.27**	**26.23**	**26.18**	**26.14**	**26.12**
5.87	5.84	5.80	5.77	5.74	5.71	5.70	5.68	5.66	5.65	5.64	5.63
14.24	**14.15**	**14.02**	**13.93**	**13.83**	**13.74**	**13.69**	**13.61**	**13.57**	**1332**	**13.48**	**13.46**
4.64	4.60	4.56	4.53	4.50	**4.46**	4.44	4.42	4.40	4.38	4.37	4.36
9.77	**9.68**	**9.55**	**9.47**	**9.38**	**9.29**	**9.24**	**9.17**	**9.13**	**9.07**	**9.04**	**9.02**
3.96	3.92	3.87	3.84	3.81	3.77	3.75	3.72	3.71	3.69	3.68	3.67
7.60	**732**	**7.39**	**7.31**	**7.23**	**7.14**	**7.09**	**7.02**	**6.99**	**6.94**	**6.90**	**6.88**
3.52	3.49	3.44	3.41	3.38	3,34	3.32	3.29	3.28	3.25	3.24	3.23
6.35	**6.27**	**6.15**	**6.07**	**5.98**	**5.90**	**5.85**	**5.78**	**5.75**	**5.70**	**5.67**	**5.65**
3.23	3.20	3.15	3.12	3.08	3.05	3.03	3.00	2.98	2.96	2.94	2.93
5.56	**5.48**	**5.36**	**5.28**	**5.20**	**5.11**	**5.06**	**5.00**	**4.96**	**4.91**	**4.88**	**4.86**
3.02	2.98	2.93	2.90	2.86	2.82	2.80	2.77	236	2.73	2.72	2.71
5.00	**4.92**	**4.80**	**4.73**	**4.64**	**4.56**	**4.51**	**4.45**	**4.41**	**4.36**	**4.33**	**4.31**
2.86	2.82	2.77	2.74	2.70	2.67	2.64	2.61	2.59	2.56	2.55	2.54
4.60	**4.52**	**4.41**	**4.33**	**4.25**	**4.17**	**4.12**	**4.05**	**4.01**	**3.96**	**3.93**	**3.91**
2.74	2.70	2.65	2.61	2.57	2.53	2.50	2.47	2.45	2.42	2.41	2.40
4.29	**4.21**	**4.10**	**4.02**	**3.94**	**3.86**	**3.80**	**3.74**	**3.70**	**3.66**	**3.62**	**3.60**
2.64	2.60	2.54	2.50	2.46	2.42	2.40	2.36	2.35	2.32	2.31	2.30
4.05	**3.98**	**3.86**	**3.78**	**3.70**	**3.61**	**3.56**	**3.49**	**3.46**	**3.41**	**3.38**	**3.36**
2.55	2.51	2.46	2.42	2.38	2.34	2.32	2.28	2.26	2.24	2.22	2.21
3.85	**3.78**	**3.67**	**3.59**	**3.51**	**3.42**	**3.37**	**3.30**	**3.27**	**3.21**	**3.18**	**3.16**

n_2	\multicolumn{12}{c}{n_1 Degrees of Freedom (for Numerator Mean Square)}
	1	2	3	4	5	6	7	8	9	10	11	12
14	4.60	3.74	3.34	3.11	2.96	2.85	2.77	2.70	2.65	2.60	2.56	2.53
	8.86	**6.51**	**5.56**	**5.03**	**4.69**	**4.46**	**4.28**	**4.14**	**4.03**	**3.94**	**3.86**	**3.80**
15	4.54	3.68	3.29	3.06	2.90	2.79	2.70	2.64	2.59	2.55	2.51	2.48
	8.68	**6.36**	**5.42**	**4.89**	**4.56**	**4.32**	**4.14**	**4.00**	**3.89**	**3.80**	**3.73**	**3.67**
16	4.49	3.63	3.24	3.01	2.85	2.74	2.66	2.59	2.54	2.49	2.45	2.42
	8.53	**6.23**	**5.29**	**4.77**	**4.44**	**4.20**	**4.03**	**3.89**	**3.78**	**3.69**	**3.61**	**3.55**
17	4.45	3.59	3.20	2.96	2.81	2.70	2.62	2.55	2.50	2.45	2.41	2.38
	8.40	**6.11**	**5.18**	**4.67**	**4.34**	**4.10**	**3.93**	**3.79**	**3.68**	**3.59**	**3.52**	**3.45**
18	4.41	3.55	3.16	2.93	2.77	2.66	2.58	2.51	2.46	2.41	2.37	2.34
	8.28	**6.01**	**5.09**	**4.58**	**4.25**	**4.01**	**3.85**	**3.71**	**3.60**	**3.51**	**3.44**	**3.37**
19	4.38	3.52	3.13	2.90	2.74	2.63	2.55	2.48	2.43	2.38	2.34	2.31
	8.18	**5.93**	**5.01**	**4.50**	**4.17**	**3.94**	**3.77**	**3.63**	**3.52**	**3.43**	**3.36**	**3.30**
20	4.35	3.49	3.10	2.87	2.71	2.60	2.52	2.45	2.40	2.35	2.31	2.28
	8.10	**5.85**	**4.94**	**4.43**	**4.10**	**3.87**	**3.71**	**3.56**	**3.45**	**3.37**	**3.30**	**3.23**
21	4.32	3.47	3.07	2.84	2.68	2.57	2.49	2,42	2.37	2.32	2.28	2.25
	8.02	**5.78**	**4.87**	**4.37**	**4.04**	**3.81**	**3.65**	**3.51**	**3.40**	**3.31**	**3.24**	**3.17**
22	4.30	**3.44**	3.05	2.82	2.66	2.55	2.47	2.40	2.35	2.30	2.26	2.23
	7.9	**5.72**	**4.82**	**4.31**	**3.99**	**3.76**	**3.59**	**3.45**	**3.35**	**3.26**	**3.18**	**3.12**
23	4.28	3.42	3.03	2.80	2.64	2.53	2.45	2.38	2.32	2.28	2.24	2.20
	7.88	**5.66**	**4.76**	**4.26**	**3.94**	**3.71**	**3.54**	**3.41**	**3.30**	**3.21**	**3.14**	**3.07**
24	4.26	3.40	3.01	2.78	2.62	2.51	2.43	2.36	2.30	2.26	2.22	2.18
	7.82	**5.61**	**4.72**	**4.22**	**3.90**	**3.67**	**3.50**	**3.36**	**3.25**	**3.17**	**3.09**	**3.03**
25	4.24	3.38	2.99	2.76	2.60	2.49	2.41	2.34	2.28	2.24	2.20	2.16
	7.77	**5.57**	**4.68**	**4.18**	**3.86**	**3.63**	**3.46**	**3.32**	**3.21**	**3.13**	**3.05**	**2.99**
26	4.22	3.37	2.98	2.74	2.59	2.47	2.39	2.32	2.27	2.22	2.18	2.15
	7.72	**5.53**	**4.64**	**4.14**	**3.82**	**3.59**	**3.42**	**3.29**	**3.17**	**3.09**	**3.02**	**2.96**

n_1 Degrees of Freedom (for Numerator Mean Square)											
14	**16**	**20**	**24**	**30**	**40**	**50**	**75**	**100**	**200**	**500**	**∞**
2.48	2.44	2.39	2.35	2.31	2.27	2.24	2.21	2.19	2.16	2.14	2.13
3.70	**3.62**	**3.51**	**3.43**	**3.34**	**3.26**	**3.21**	**3.14**	**3.11**	**3.06**	**3.02**	**3.00**
2.43	2.39	2.33	2.29	2.25	2.21	2.18	2.15	2.12	2.10	2.08	2.07
3.56	**3.48**	**3.36**	**3.29**	**3.20**	3.12	**3.07**	**3.00**	**2.97**	**2.92**	**2.89**	**2.87**
2.37	2.33	2.28	2.24	2.20	2.16	2.13	2.09	2.07	2.04	2.02	2.01
3.45	**3.37**	**3.25**	**3.18**	**3.10**	**3.01**	**2.96**	**2.89**	**2.86**	**2.80**	**2.77**	**2.75**
2.33	2.29	2.23	2.19	2.15	2.11	2.08	2.04	2.02	1.99	1.97	1.96
3.35	**3.27**	**3.16**	**3.08**	**3.00**	**2.92**	**2.86**	**2.79**	**2.76**	**2.70**	**2.67**	**2.65**
2.29	2.25	2.19	2.15	2.11	2.07	2.04	2.00	1.98	1.95	1.93	1.92
3.27	**3.19**	**3.07**	**3.00**	**2.91**	**2.83**	**2.78**	**2.71**	**2.68**	**2.62**	**2.59**	**2.57**
2.26	2.21	2.15	2.11	2.07	2.02	2.00	1.96	1.94	1.91	1.90	1.88
3.19	**3.12**	**3.00**	**2.92**	**2.84**	**2.76**	**2.70**	**2.63**	**2.60**	**2.54**	**2.51**	**2.49**
2.23	2.18	2.12	2.08	2.04	1.99	1.96	1.92	1.90	1.87	1.85	1.84
3.13	**3.05**	**2.94**	**2.86**	**2.77**	**2.69**	**2.63**	**2.56**	**2.53**	**2.47**	**2.44**	**2.42**
2.20	2.15	2.09	2.05	2.00	1.96	1.93	1.89	1.87	1.84	1.82	1.81
3.07	**2.99**	**2.88**	**2.80**	**2.72**	**2.63**	**2.58**	**2.51**	**2.47**	**2.42**	**2.38**	**2.36**
2.18	2.13	2.07	2.03	1.98	1.93	1.91	1.87	1.84	1.81	1.80	1.78
3.02	**2.94**	**2.83**	**2.75**	**2.67**	**2.58**	**2.53**	**2.46**	**2.42**	**2.37**	**2.33**	**2.31**
2.14	2.10	2.04	2.00	1.96	1.91	1.88	1.84	1.82	1.79	1.77	1.76
2.97	**2.89**	**2.78**	**2.70**	**2.62**	**2.53**	**2.48**	**2.41**	**2.37**	**2.32**	**2.28**	**2.26**
2.13	2.09	2.02	1.98	1.94	1.89	1.86	1.82	1.80	1.76	1.74	1.73
2.93	**2.85**	**2.74**	**2.66**	**2.58**	**2.49**	**2.44**	**2.36**	**2.33**	**2.27**	**2.23**	**2.21**
2.11	2.06	2.00	1.96	1.92	1.87	1.84	1.80	1.77	1.74	1.72	1.71
2.89	**2.81**	**2.70**	**2.62**	**2.54**	**2.45**	**2.40**	**2.32**	**2.29**	**2.23**	**2.19**	**2.17**
2.10	2.05	1.99	1.95	1.90	1.85	1.82	1.78	1.76	1.72	1.70	1.69
2.86	**2.77**	**2.66**	**2.58**	**2.50**	**2.41**	**2.36**	**2.28**	**2.25**	**2.19**	**2.15**	**2.13**

APPENDIX B: CRITICAL VALUES OF F

n_2	\multicolumn{12}{c}{n_1 Degrees of Freedom (for Numerator Mean Square)}
	1	2	3	4	5	6	7	8	9	10	11	12
27	4.21	3.35	2.96	2.73	2.57	2.46	2.37	2.30	2.25	2.20	2.16	2.13
	7.68	**5.49**	**4.60**	**4.11**	**3.79**	**3.56**	**3.39**	**3.26**	**3.14**	**3.06**	**2.98**	**2.93**
28	4.20	3.34	2.95	2.71	2.56	2.44	2.36	2.29	2.24	2.19	2.15	2.12
	7.64	**5.45**	**4.57**	**4.07**	**3.76**	**3.53**	**3.36**	**3.23**	**3.11**	**3.03**	**2.95**	**2.90**
29	4.18	3.33	2.93	2.70	2.54	2.43	2.35	2.28	2.22	2.18	2.14	2.10
	7.60	**5.42**	**4.54**	**4.04**	**3.73**	**3.50**	3.33	**3.20**	**3.08**	**3.00**	**2.92**	**2.87**
30	4.17	3.32	2.92	2.69	2.53	2.42	2.34	2.27	2.21	2.16	2.12	2.09
	7.56	**5.39**	**4.51**	**4.02**	**3.70**	**3.47**	**3.30**	**3.17**	**3.06**	**2.98**	**2.90**	2.84
32	4.15	3.30	2.90	2.67	2.51	2,40	2.32	2.25	2.19	2.14	2.10	2.07
	7.50	**5.34**	**4.46**	**3.97**	**3.66**	**3.42**	**3.25**	**3.12**	**3.01**	**2.94**	**2.86**	**2.80**
34	4.13	3.28	2.88	2.65	2.49	2.38	2.30	2.23	2.17	2.12	2.08	2.05
	7.44	**5.29**	**4.42**	**3.93**	**3.61**	**3.38**	**3.21**	**3.08**	**2.97**	**2.89**	**2.82**	**2.76**
36	4.11	3.26	2.86	2.63	2.48	2.36	2.28	2.21	2.15	2.10	2.06	2.03
	7.39	**5.25**	**4.38**	**3.89**	**3.58**	**3.35**	**3.18**	**3.04**	**3.04**	**2.86**	**2.78**	**2.72**
38	4.10	3.25	2.85	2.62	2.46	2.35	2.26	2.19	2.14	2.09	2.05	2.02
	7.35	**5.21**	**4.34**	**3.86**	**3.54**	**3.32**	**3.15**	**3.02**	**2.91**	**2.82**	**2.75**	**2.69**
40	4.08	3.23	2.84	2.61	2.45	2.34	2.25	2.18	2.12	2.07	2.04	2.00
	7.31	**5.18**	**4.31**	**3.83**	**3.51**	**3.29**	**3.12**	**2.99**	**2.88**	**2.80**	**2.73**	**2.66**
42	4.07	3.22	2.83	2.59	2.44	2,32	2.24	2.17	2.11	2.06	2.02	1.99
	7.27	**5.15**	**4.29**	**3.80**	**3.49**	**3.26**	**3.10**	**2.96**	**2.86**	**2.77**	**2.70**	2.64
44	4.06	3.21	2.82	2.58	2.43	2.31	2.23	2.16	2.10	2.05	2.01	1.98
	7.24	5.12	4.26	3.78	3.46	3.24	3.07	2.94	2.84	2.75	2.68	2.62
46	4.05	3.20	2.81	2.57	2.42	2.30	2.22	2.14	2.09	2.04	2.00	1.97
	7.21	5.10	4.24	3.76	3.44	3.22	3.05	2.92	2.82	2.73	2.66	2.60
48	4.04	3.19	2.80	2.56	2.41	2.30	2.21	2.14	2.08	2.03	1.99	1.96
	7.19	**5.08**	**4.22**	**3.74**	**3.42**	**3.20**	**3.04**	**2.90**	**2.80**	**2.71**	**2.64**	**2.58**

n_1 Degrees of Freedom (for Numerator Mean Square)											
14	16	20	24	30	40	50	75	100	200	500	∞
2.08	2.03	1.97	1.93	1.88	1.84	1.80	1.76	1.74	1.71	1.68	1.67
2.83	**2.74**	**2.63**	**2.55**	**2.47**	**2.38**	**2.33**	**2.25**	**2.21**	**2.16**	**2.12**	**2.10**
2.06	2.02	1.96	1.91	1.87	1.81	1.78	1.75	1.72	1.69	1.67	1.65
2.80	**2.71**	**2.60**	**2.52**	**2.44**	**2.35**	**2.30**	**2.22**	**2.18**	**2.13**	**2.09**	**2.06**
2.05	2.00	1.94	1.90	1.85	1.80	1.77	1.73	1.71	1.68	1.65	1.64
2.77	**2.68**	**2.57**	**2.49**	**2.41**	**2.32**	**2.27**	**2.19**	**2.15**	**2.10**	**2.06**	**2.03**
2.04	1.99	1.93	1.89	1.84	1.79	1.76	1.72	1.69	1.66	1.64	1.62
2.74	**2.66**	**2.55**	**2.47**	**2.38**	**2.29**	**2.24**	**2.16**	**2.13**	**2.07**	**2.03**	**2.01**
2.02	1.97	1.91	1.86	1.82	1.76	1.74	1.69	1.67	1.64	1.61	1.59
2.70	**2.62**	**2.51**	**2.42**	**2.34**	**2.25**	**2.20**	**2.12**	**2.08**	**2.02**	**1.98**	**1.96**
2.00	1.95	1.89	1.84	1.80	1.74	1.71	1.67	1.64	1.61	1.59	1,57
2.66	**2.58**	**2.47**	**2.38**	**2.30**	**2.21**	**2.15**	**2.08**	**2.04**	**1.98**	**1.94**	**1.91**
1.98	1.93	1.87	1.82	1.78	1.72	1.69	1.65	1.62	1.59	1.56	1.55
2.62	**2.54**	**2.43**	**2.35**	**2.26**	**2.17**	**2.12**	**2.04**	**2.00**	**1.94**	**1.90**	**1.87**
1.96	1.92	1.85	1.80	1.76	1.71	1.67	1.63	1.60	1.57	1.54	1.53
2.59	**2.51**	**2.40**	**2.32**	**2.22**	**2.14**	**2.08**	**2.00**	**1.97**	**1.90**	**1.86**	**1.84**
1.95	1.90	1.84	1.79	1.74	1.69	1.66	1.61	1.59	1.55	1.53	1.51
2.56	**2.49**	**2.37**	**2.29**	**2.20**	**2.11**	**2.05**	**1.97**	**1.94**	**1.88**	**1.84**	**1.81**
1.91	1.89	1.82	1.78	1.73	1.68	1.64	1.60	1.57	1.54	1,51	1.49
2.54	**2.46**	**2.35**	**2.26**	**2.17**	**2.08**	**2.02**	**1.94**	**1.91**	**1.85**	**1.80**	**1.78**
1.92	1.88	1.81	1.76	1.72	1.66	1.63	1.58	1.56	1.52	1.50	1.48
2.52	**2.44**	**2.32**	**2.24**	**2.15**	**2.06**	**2.00**	**1.92**	**1.88**	**1.82**	**1.78**	**1.75**
1.91	1.87	1.80	1.75	1.71	1.65	1.62	1.57	1.54	1.51	1.48	1.46
2.50	**2.42**	**2.30**	**2.22**	**2.13**	**2.04**	**1.98**	**1.90**	**1.86**	**1.80**	**1.76**	**1.72**
1.90	1.86	1.79	1.74	1.70	1.64	1.61	1.56	1.53	1.50	1.47	1.45
2.48	**2.40**	**2.28**	**2.20**	**2.11**	**2.02**	**1.96**	**1.88**	**1.84**	**1.78**	**1.73**	**1.70**

n_2	n_1 Degrees of Freedom (for Numerator Mean Square)											
	1	2	3	4	5	6	7	8	9	10	11	12
50	4.03	3.18	2.79	2.56	2.40	2.29	2.20	2.13	2.07	2.02	1.98	1.95
	7.17	5.06	4.20	3.72	3.41	3.18	3.02	2.88	2.78	2.70	2.62	2.56
55	4.02	3.17	2.78	2.54	2.38	2.27	2.18	2.11	2.05	2.00	1.97	1.93
	7.12	5.01	4.16	3.68	3.37	3.15	2.98	2.85	2.75	2.66	2.59	2.53
60	4.00	3.15	2.76	2.52	2.37	2.25	2.17	2.10	2.04	1.99	1.95	1.92
	7.08	4.98	4.13	3.65	3.34	3.12	2.95	2.82	2.72	2.63	2.56	2.50
65	3.99	3.14	2.75	2.51	2.36	2.24	2.15	2.08	2.02	1.98	1.94	1.90
	7.04	4.95	4.10	3.62	3.31	3.09	2.93	2.79	2.70	2.61	2.54	2.47
70	3.98	3.13	2.74	2.50	2.35	2.23	2.14	2.07	2.01	1.97	1.93	1.89
	7.01	4.92	4.08	3.60	3.29	3.07	2.91	2.77	2.67	2.59	2.51	2.45
80	3.96	3.11	2.77	2.48	2.33	2.21	2.12	2.05	1.99	1.95	1.91	1.88
	6.96	4.88	4.04	3.56	3.25	3.04	2.87	2.74	2.64	2.55	2.48	2.41
100	3.94	3.09	2.70	2.46	2.30	2.19	2.10	2.03	1.97	1.92	1.88	1.85
	6.90	4.82	3.98	3.51	3.20	2.99	2.82	2.69	2.59	2.51	2.43	2.36
125	3.92	3.07	2.68	2.44	2.29	2.17	2.08	2.01	1.95	1.90	1.86	1.83
	6.84	4.78	3.94	3.47	3.17	2.95	2.79	2.65	2.56	2.47	2.40	2.33
150	3.91	3.06	2.57	2.43	2.27	2.16	2.07	2.00	1.94	1.89	1.85	1.82
	6.81	4.75	3.91	3.44	3.14	2.92	2.76	2.62	2.53	2.44	2.37	2.30
200	3.89	3.04	2.65	2.41	2.26	2.14	2.05	1.98	1.92	1.87	1.83	1.80
	6.76	4.71	3.88	3.41	3.11	2.90	2.73	2.60	2.50	2.41	2.34	2.28
400	3.86	3.02	2.62	2.39	2.23	2.12	2.03	1.96	1.90	1.85	1.81	1.78
	6.70	4.66	3.83	3.36	3.06	2.85	2.69	2.55	2.46	2.37	2.29	2.23
1000	3.85	3.00	2.61	2.38	2.22	2.10	2.02	1.95	1.89	1.84	1.80	1.76
	6.66	4.62	3.80	3.34	3.04	2.82	2.66	2.53	2.43	2.34	2.26	2.20
∞	3.84	2.99	2.60	2.37	2.21	2.09	2.01	1.94	1.88	1.83	1.79	1.75
	6.64	4.60	3.78	3.32	3.02	2.80	2.64	2.51	2.41	2.32	2.24	2.18

n_1 Degrees of Freedom (for Numerator Mean Square)											
14	16	20	24	30	40	50	75	100	200	500	∞
1.90	1.85	1.78	1.74	1.69	1.63	1.60	1.55	1.52	1.48	1.46	1.44
2.46	**2.39**	**2.26**	**2.18**	**2.10**	**2.00**	**1.94**	**1.86**	**1.82**	**1.76**	**1.71**	**1.68**
1.88	1.83	1.76	1.72	1.67	1.61	1.58	1.52	1.50	1.46	1.43	1.41
2.43	**2.35**	**2.23**	**2.15**	**2.06**	**1.96**	**1.90**	**1.82**	**1.78**	**1.71**	**1.66**	**1.64**
1.86	1.81	1.75	1.70	1.65	1.59	1.56	1.50	1.48	1.44	1.41	1.39
2.40	**2.32**	**2.20**	**2.12**	**2.03**	**1.93**	**1.87**	**1.79**	**1.74**	**1.68**	**1.63**	**1.60**
1.84	1.80	1.73	1.68	1.63	1.57	1.54	1.49	1.46	1.42	1.39	1.37
2.37	**2.30**	**2.18**	**2.09**	**2.00**	**1.90**	**1.84**	**1.76**	**1.71**	**1.64**	**1.60**	**1.56**
1.84	1.79	1.72	1.67	1.62	1.56	1.53	1.47	1.45	1.40	1.37	1.35
2.35	**2.28**	**2.15**	**2.07**	**1.98**	**1.88**	**1.82**	**1.74**	**1.69**	**1.62**	**1.56**	**1.53**
1.82	1.77	1.70	1.65	1.60	1.54	1.51	1.45	**1.42**	1.38	1.35	1.32
2.32	**2.24**	**2.11**	**2.03**	**1.94**	**1.84**	**1.78**	**1.70**	**1.65**	**1.57**	**1.52**	**1.49**
1.79	1.75	1.68	1.63	1.57	1.51	1.48	1.42	1.39	1.34	1.30	1.28
2.26	**2.19**	**2.06**	**1.98**	**1.89**	**1.79**	**1.73**	**1.64**	**1.59**	**1.51**	**1.46**	**1.43**
1.77	1.72	1.65	1.60	**1.55**	1.49	1.45	1.39	1.36	1.31	1.27	1.25
2.23	**2.15**	**2.03**	**1.94**	**1.85**	**1.75**	**1.68**	**1.59**	**1.54**	**1.46**	**1.40**	**1.37**
1.76	1.71	1.64	1.59	1.54	1.47	1.44	1.37	1.34	1.29	1.25	1.22
2.20	**2.12**	**2.00**	**1.91**	**1.83**	**1.72**	**1.66**	**1.56**	**1.51**	**1.43**	**1.37**	**1.33**
1.74	**1.69**	1.62	1.57	1.52	1.45	1.42	1.35	1.32	1.26	1.22	1.19
2.17	**2.09**	**1.97**	**1.88**	**1.79**	**1.69**	**1.62**	**1.53**	**1.48**	**1.39**	**1.33**	**1.28**
1.72	1.67	1.60	1.54	1.49	1.42	1.38	1.32	1.28	1.22	1.16	1.13
2.12	**2.04**	**1.92**	**1.84**	**1.74**	**1.65**	**1.57**	**1.47**	**1.42**	**1.32**	**1.24**	**1.19**
1.70	1.65	1.58	1.53	1.47	1.41	1.36	1.30	1.26	1.19	1.13	1.08
2.09	**2.01**	**1.89**	**1.81**	**1.71**	**1.61**	**1.54**	**1.44**	**1.38**	**1.28**	**1.19**	**1.11**
1.69	1.64	1.57	1.52	1.46	1.40	**1.35**	**1.28**	1.24	**1.17**	**1.11**	**1.00**
2.07	**1.99**	**1.87**	**1.79**	**1.69**	**1.59**	**1.52**	**1.41**	**1.36**	**1.25**	**1.15**	**1.00**

Joan Welkowitz, Barry H. Cohen, and R. Brooke Lea, "Critical Values of F," *Introductory Statistics for the Behavioral Sciences*. Copyright © 2012 by John Wiley & Sons, Inc.

APPENDIX C

Basic Foundations of Statistical Analysis

Numbers of Variables	Level of Measurement	Study Purpose	Proper Statistics
1	Nominal	Any	Percent, valid percent, cumulative percent, graph
1	Ordinal	Any	Same as nominal
1	Interval or ratio	Any *Convert to standard score or compare to population parameter*	Same as nominal plus mean, median, mode, range, quartile, variance, and standard deviation Z score
2	Nominal	Relationship or association	Pearson chi-square (λ^2)
2	Ordinal	Relationship or association Strength of association	Pearson chi-square, Gamma or Kendall's Tau Phi and Cramer's V or Lambda
2	One nominal, one interval	Relationship or association	Eta and McNemar
2	Interval or ratio	Relationship or association Make prediction Cause and effect Strength or magnitude of relationship	Parametric: Pearson correlation. Also called the *Product Moment Correlation Coefficient (Pearson's r)* Nonparametric: Kendall's Tau or Spearman Rho *Remember that Kendall's Tau coefficients is the smallest followed by Spearman and Pearson* Linear regression models

			Regression models (beyond the scope of this book)
			Coefficient of determination (r^2)
2 or more with control variable(s)	Interval or ratio	Relationship or association	Partial correlation
2	The dependent variable (DV) is interval/ratio The independent variable (IV) is nominal and limited to two groups/categories *Notice that when the IV has more than two groups/categories, t-tests do not apply because of an increase in Type I error*	Compare mean(s) also called the means tests. Called the means tests (plural) because there are three distinctive types Significant difference in the magnitude between group 1 and group 2	Compare one group mean with a hypothesized mean or known mean: *One sample t-test* Compare means of two related groups, matched pairs, or correlated: *dependent samples t-test* Compare means of two unrelated, unmatched pairs or not correlated: *independent samples t-test* Effect size. *Most often used is the Cohen's d*
2	The DV is interval/ratio. The DV is limited to 1 The IV. There are multiple groups/categories	Compare means	When DV = 1 and IV ≥3, use analysis of variance or F ratio. When DV ≥2 and IV have multiple groups/categories, use multiple analysis of variance (MANOVA). MANOVA is beyond the scope of this book
≥3	Multivariate analysis	Need to take an advanced statistics course	

References

Agresti, A. (2018). *Statistical methods for the social sciences* (5th ed.). Pearson.

Agresti, A., & Finlay, B. (2009). *Statistical methods for the social sciences* (4th ed.). Pearson Prentice Hall.

American Psychological Association. (2020). *Publication manual of the American Psychological Association.* (7th ed.).

Anders, K. L., & Dinis, M. C. (2009). Workplace challenges in institutions of higher education: Perceptions of administrators. *The International Journal of Interdisciplinary Social Sciences, 4*(5), 283–294.

Aron, A., Coups, E. J., & Aron, E. N. (2011). *Statistics for the behavioral and social sciences: A brief course* (5th ed.). Pearson.

Barry, H. C., Lea, R. B., & Weiner, I. B. (2004). *Essentials of statistics for the social and behavioral sciences.* Wiley.

Batchelor, A. (2019). *Statistics in social work: An introduction to practical application.* Columbia University Press.

Bradford, A. (2017, August). *What is science?* Live Science. https://www.livescience.com/20896-science-scientific-method.html

Coolidge, F. L. (2013). *Statistics: A gentle introduction* (3rd ed.). SAGE Publications.

Council on Social Work Education. (2021). *2015 Educational Policy and Accreditation Standards (EPAS).* https://cswe.org/Accreditation/Standards-and-Policies/2015-EPAS.

Creswell, J. (2009). *Research design: Qualitative, quantitative, and mixed methods approaches.* SAGE Publications.

Digital E-Learning (May 27, 2018). *Descriptive vs inferential statistics.* https://www.youtube.com/watch?v=rPrXbbFo2-E

Engel, R. J., & Schutt, R. K. (2013). *The practice of research in social work* (3rd ed.). SAGE Publications.

Field, A. (2009). *Discovering statistics using SPSS.* SAGE Publications.

Finley, R. (1999). *Survey monkey.* SurveyMonkey.com.

Freeman, D., Pisani, R., & Purves, R. (1978). *Statistics.* Norton.

Frost, J. (n.d.). *Making statistics intuitive.* https://statisticsbyjim.com/basics/measures-central-tendency-mean-median-mode/

Geher, G., & Hall, S. (2014). *Straightforward statistics: Understanding the tools of research.* Oxford University Press.

Glaser, B. G., & Strauss, A. L. (1967). *The discovery of grounded theory: Strategies for qualitative research.* Aldine.

Grinnell, R. M. (2000). *Social work research and evaluation: Quantitative and qualitative approaches* (6th ed.). Cengage Learning.

Hays, W. (1994). *Statistics* (5th ed.). Harcourt Brace College.

IBM (2020). *SPSS software: Predictive analytics software and solutions.* https://www.ibm.com/products/spss-statistics.

IBM. (n.d.). *Learn how to get the most out of your research and analysis.* https://www.ibm.com/analytics/spss-statistics-software.

IBM. (n.d.). *IBM SPSS statistics help and support.* https://www.ibm.com/products/spss-statistics/support

John Hopkins University (April 20, 2020). *Coronavirus in African Americans and other people of color.* https://www.hopkinsmedicine.org/health/conditions-and-diseases/coronavirus/covid19-racial-disparities

King, B. M., Rosopa, P. J., & Minium, E. J. (2011). *Statistical reasoning in the behavioral sciences.* Wiley.

Lee, S. (2020). *From Earth to elite: The memoir of Dr. Serge Lee.* Austin McCauley Publishers Ltd.

Lee, S., Dinis, M. D., Lowe, L., & Anders, K. (2016). *Statistics for international social work and other behavioral sciences.* Oxford University Press.

Leon-Guerrero, A., & Frankfort-Nachmias. (2012). *Essentials of social statistics for a diverse society.* SAGE Publications.

Lofland, J., Anderson, L., & Lofland, L. H. (2006). *Analyzing social settings: A guide to qualitative observation and analysis* (4th ed.). Cengage Learning.

McDaniel, B. (April 19, 2016). *Null hypothesis, p value and statistical significance.* https://www.youtube.com/watch?v=YSwmpAmLV2s

Meyers, L. S., Gamst, G., & Guarino, A. J. (2006). *Applied multivariate research: Design and interpretation.* SAGE Publications.

Mogull, R. G. (2004). *Second semester applied statistics.* Kendall/Hunt.

Monette, D. R., Sullivan, T. J., & DeJong, C. R. (2005). *Applied social research: A tool for human services.* Brooks/Cole-Thompson Learning.

Montcalm, D., & Royse, D. (2002). *Data analysis for social workers.* Pearson Education.

Nowaczyk, R. H. (1988). *Statistics for Behavioral Research.* Harcourt College Publication.

Rubin, A. (2013). *Statistics for evidence-based practice and evaluation* (3rd ed.). Brooks/ Cole.

Rubin, A., & Babbie, E. (2014). *Essential research methods for social workers* (3rd ed.). Brooks/Cole.

Rubin, A., & Babbie, E. R. (2017). *Empowering series: Research methods for social workers* (9th ed.). Cengage.

SAS. (n.d.). *Statistical analysis: Look around you, statistics are everywhere.* https://www.sas.com/en_us/insights/analytics/statistical-analysis.html

Science Direct. (2015). *Inferential statistics.* https://www.sciencedirect.com/topics/medicine-and-dentistry/inferential-statistics

Stat Analytica. (n.d.). *What is regression in statistics: Types of regression.* https://statanalytica.com/blog/what-is-regression-in-statistics/

Tokunaga, H. T. (2018). *Fundamental statistics for the social and behavioral sciences.* SAGE Publications.

Trochim, W. M. K. (2020, March). *Descriptive statistics.* https://conjointly.com/kb/descriptive-statistics/

Weinbach, R. W., & Grinnell, R. M. (2015). *Statistics for social workers* (9th ed.). Pearson.

Welkowitz, J. Cohen, B. H., & Ewen, R. B. (2006). *Introductory statistics for the behavioral sciences* (6th ed.). Wiley.

Welkowitz, J., Cohen, B. H., & Lea, B. R. (2012). *Introductory statistics for the behavioral sciences* (7th ed.). Wiley.

Wesleyan University. (2021). *Applied Data Analysis. Chi-square test of independence.* https://adata.site.wesleyan.edu/schedule/chi-square-and-correlation/

Witte, R. (1993). *Statistics* (4th ed.). Harcourt Brace Jovanovich College.

Yuen, F. K. O. (2020). *Conceptual and practical research and statistics for social workers.* Cognella Academic Publishing.

Zeitlin, W., & Auerbach, C. (2019). *Basic statistics for the behavioral and social sciences using r.* Oxford University Press.

Index

A
adjusted *R-squared*, 203
algebraic function solving for x, 86
algebraic operations, 175
algorithm, 9, 36, 191
alpha (a), 103
alternative hypothesis, 98–99, 116, 152–153
American Psychological Association (APA), 33, 35, 37, 50, 60, 63, 67, 104, 109, 173
American Psychological Association (APA) notations, 104, 123, 147, 180, 221
analysis of variance (ANOVA), 166, 211–212
    evidence-based practice using, 215–216
    SPSS instructions for, 222–225
    statistical assumptions, 213
    variability for between-groups means ($MS_{Between}$), 214
    variability for within-groups means (MS_{Within}), 214
anonymity, 7
array, 52

B
bar graphs (bar charts), 37
Beck's Depression Inventory-II (BDI-II), 2
bivariate analysis, 5, 12, 115

C
categorical data, 3
categorical variables, 20
categories, 19
cause or regress, 239–240
central limit theorem, 95
child abuse, 21
clarity, 235
coefficient of determination (r^2), 148, 154, 158, 192, 203
coefficient of variation (CV), 60–61
Cohen's d, 181–183
    effect size, 182
condition, 94
confidence intervals (CI), 50, 77–79, 87, 93
    construction of, 101–105
    definition, 102
    elements, 79
    level of significance or rejection level, 102
    relationship between self-care and longevity, 104
    using z score, 105–107
confidentiality, 8
confounding variable, 21
consequences, 240
constant or stay static, 234
constant or the Y intercept. *See* linear regression models (LRM); simple linear regression
content analysis, 240–241
content validity, 233
contingency table, 116
    constructing, 118–119
continuous variables, 19–20
conversation analysis, 242
correlation
    coefficient range, 142–143

critical values of r, 147, 149
definition, 137
graphical display of direction of, 139–141
in social work and behavioral settings, 143–144
Kendall's tau b, 138, 154–155
negative, 141
not causation, 143
partial correlation coefficient, 154–156
Pearson correlation coefficient, 137–138, 141–142, 144–147
positive, 141
Spearman's rho, 138, 144
spurious association, 143
strengths and variations of relationship between interval- or ratio-level variables, 137
zero, near-zero, 141

Council on Social Work Education (CSWE), 1
Cramer's V, 126–127
criterion or outcome variable, 192. *See also* dependent variables (DVs)
criterion validity, 233
critical values, 81, 104
of chi-square, 122–123, 128
of F-ratio, 263–271
of r, 147, 149, 150
of t-distribution, 170–172, 180
of z score, 87
cross-tabulation, 115–116, 118
corresponding percentages, 119
Grand Total, 119
Marginal Columns Total, 119
Marginal Rows Total, 119
curvilinear correlation, 138

D

data
interval variable (interval data), 25–26
nominal variable (nominal data), 23–24
ordinal variable (ordinal data), 24–25
qualitative, 22–23
quantitative, 22
ratio variable (ratio data), 26–27
reduction, 4
set, 4, 9
summary, 4

data entry using SPSS, 40
creating SPSS data file, 41–42
label of a variable, 41, 251
measurement of a variable, 41, 252
name of a variable, 41, 251
type of a variable, 41, 251
values of a variable, 41, 252

declarative predictive statement, 99
deductive reasoning, 241
definition variance, 58
degrees of freedom, 128
for dependent samples t-test, 180
for independent samples t-test, 176
of t-distribution, 170
de Moivre, Abraham, 75, 77
dependent samples t-test, 176–180
dependent variables (DVs), 20, 93
descriptive statistics, 4–5, 10, 12, 17, 73
bar graphs, 37
frequency count, 35–37
frequency polygon (line graph), 39
graphs, 37
histogram graphs, 38
measures of central tendency, 4–5, 49–53, 73
pie, 37–38
design flaws, 109
dichotomous study, 125
dichotomy, 115
directional (one-tailed or one-sided) hypothesis, 100–101
discriminant validity, 233
distribution, 98
population, 94
population parameters, 94
sample, 94
sampling distribution of the mean, 95–96
set, 52
shape of, 98
standard error of the mean, 96

E

Educational Policy and Accreditation Standards (EPAS), 1, 3
enumeration, 238
equal variances, 167, 174
errors in hypothesis testing
    design flaws, 109
    rival hypotheses, 109
    sampling error, 109
    Type I error, 108
    Type II error, 108
estimated standard deviation. *See* t-tests
ethical issues in social science research, 7–9
    anonymity, 7
    confidentiality, 8
    informed consent, 7
    reliability, 8–9
    sensitive information, 8
    validity, 8–9
evidence-based practice, 6
Excel, 12, 33

F

face validity, 233
field notes, 234–235
50th percentile, 52
fieldwork, 234
F ratio, 204, 212
    calculating, 216–221
    critical values of, 263–271
    formula for, 219
    meaning of, 213–214
    posteriori test or posttest, 213
    post hoc or post hoc comparison, 213
    sources of variability, 214
    statistical assumptions, 213
frequency count, 35–37
    or variable anxiety, 36
frequency distributions
    bar graphs (bar charts), 37
    frequencies, 33–35
    frequency count and percentage, 36–37
    frequency polygons (line graphs or line charts), 39
    graphs, 37
    histograms, 38
    pie graphs (pie charts), 37–38
frequency polygons, 39

G

Gamma, 127
generalization, 93, 232
Gosse, William S., 168
graphs, 37
group, 94

H

histograms, 38
homogeneity of variance, 167
human subjects or research subjects, 232
hypothesis, 9, 97–98
    alternative, 98–99
    directional (one-tailed or one-sided), 100–101
    direction of, 99–101
    nondirectional (two-tailed), 101
    null, 98–99
hypothesis testing, 5, 74, 97–98
    alternative hypothesis and null hypothesis, 98
    crosstab, 116
    errors, 107–108
    level of measurement of variable, 97
    method of sampling or sampling design, 97
    one-tailed hypothesis test, 106–107
    possible outcomes associated with, 108
    sample size and tests, 98
    shape of distribution, 98
    statistical tests, interpreting, 104–105
    two-tailed hypothesis test, 105–106

I

independent samples t-test, 173–176
independent variables (IVs), 20, 93, 97, 99, 137, 192–193
inductive reasoning, 241

inferential statistics, 4–6, 10, 17, 26
    bivariate analysis, 115, 137
information, 9
informed consent, 7
internal consistency, 233
interquartile range (IQR), 55
inter-rater reliability, 233
interval variable (interval data), 25–26

K

Kendall's tau b, 138, 154–155
    using SPSS, 156–159
kurtosis, 76

L

Lambda, 127
latent content, 241
left-side directional hypothesis, 100
level of confidence (p value), 102–104
levels of measurement, 23–27
    interval variable, 25–26
    nominal variable, 23–24
    ordinal variable, 24–25
    ratio variable, 26–27
linear or product-moment correlation coefficient, 138
linear regression model (LRM), 191. See also simple linear regression
    slope of regression line, 195
    SPSS instructions on, 204–207
line graphs or line charts, 39

M

magnitude, 238–239
manifest content, 241
mean, 49–51, 75
    on outliers, 53–54
    properties of, 56–57
    random sampling distribution of, 95
    sampling distribution of, 95–96
    trimmed, 51
mean deviation (MD), 56–58

mean differences, 98
means test, 166
measures of central tendency, 4–5, 49–53, 73
measures of strength of association, 125–128
measures of variability or dispersion, 4–5, 49
median, 49, 52, 75
    rules for finding, 55
    statistical rules, 52
mediator variable, 21, 27
mode, 49, 52–53, 75
moderator variable, 21, 27
multiple analysis of variance (MANOVA), 166, 211
multivariate analysis, 5
mu (m) sign, 168

N

narrative data, 237
nominal/conceptual definition, 11
nominal variable (nominal data), 12, 23–24
nondirectional (two-tailed) hypothesis, 101
non-numerical meanings, 18–19
nonparametric statistics, 154
nonrandom (nonprobability) sampling, 97
normal curves, 73–75. See z score
    1/6 rule, 77
    areas under, 77–79
    background of, 75
    bilaterally symmetric, 73, 88
    confidence intervals, 87
    ideal, 75
    kurtosis, 76
    negative skewed, 74
    positive skewed, 74
    properties of, 73–74, 76–77
    real, 75
    shape of, 73, 75–76
    SPSS computation for, 84
    symmetry, 76
    with SD, 76
normal distribution, 75. See normal curves
normality, 138

null hypothesis, 98–99, 116, 151–152
    statements using, 99
numerical meanings, 18

O

observed frequencies, 118
1/6 rule, 77
1/8 rule, 77
one-sample *t*-statistic, 172–173
one-sample t-test, 168–169
one-tailed hypothesis test, 106–107
one-way analysis of variance (ANOVA). *See* analysis of variance (ANOVA)
open- and close-ended questionnaires, 232, 235, 237
ordinal variable (ordinal data), 24–25
outcome or criterion variable, 20
outlier bias, 51

P

parameters, 5
partial correlation coefficient, 154–156
Pearson chi-square (χ^2) test of independence, 116–117
    calculating, 117, 121–122
    contingency table, 116, 118–119
    critical values, 122–123, 128
    degrees of freedom, 122–123
    dichotomous study, 125
    example, 117–118
    expected frequencies, 121–122
    formula for statistic, 120–121
    grand total, 122
    interpreting results, 122–125
    marginal columns total, 120–121
    marginal rows total, 120–121
    measures of association using Cramer's V, 126–127
    observed frequencies, 118, 120, 122
Pearson correlation coefficient (r), 137–138, 141–142, 192
    critical values, 148–150
    formula for, 144–147
    magnitude for, 149
    unbiased formula, 150–154
percentage formula, 36
percentile conversion, statistical rule for, 80
Phi (ϕ), 125–126
philosophical roots, 236
pie graphs (pie charts), 37–38
population, 5, 94
population distribution, 94
population parameter, 168
population parameters, 94
predictor variable, 20
principal investigator (PI), 7
private matters, 3
probability, 75, 94
    nonprobability sampling, 97
    of an event, 95
    of COVID-19 family members as research subjects, 95
    sample, 94
    sampling error, 109
problem identification, 11
process, 239
public matters, 3
p value. *See* level of confidence (p value)

Q

qualitative data, 21–23
qualitative data analysis, 238–243
    computerized programs, 243
    content analysis, 240–241
    conversation analysis, 242
    reference sources for, 243
    semiotics, 241–242
    ways of looking for patterns in, 238–240
qualitative research, 2, 231–232
    data collection justifications, 233
    field notes, 234–235
    fieldwork, 234
    narrative data, 237
    questionnaire construction, 235

recording, 236–237
    reliability and validity issues, 233, 236
quality, 235
Qualtrics, 12, 33
quantifiable data, 2–3
quantitative data, 21–22
quantitative research, 2
quartile, 52
quartile range, 55
questionnaires, 235

R

random sampling distribution of mean, 95
range, 54
    interquartile, 55
    quartile, 55
rank correlation coefficient. See Kendall's tau b; Spearman's rho
rank-ordered variables, 19
ratio variable (ratio data), 26–27
regression coefficient, 201–202
    adjusted R square, 203
    standard error of estimate, 203
    standardized regression coefficient, 203
    unstandardized regression coefficient, 203
rejection or extreme regions, 78
reliability, 8–9
research cycle, 10–12
    methodology, 11
    operationalization, 11
    problem identification, 11
    statistical analysis, 12
research data, 9
research methodology, 9
research methods-statistics relationship, 9–10
research subject, 18
right-side directional hypothesis, 101
rival hypotheses, 109

S

safekeeping procedures, 8
sample, 94
sample mean, 168
sample population, 94
sample statistics or sample data, 5–6
sampling distribution
    of means, 95–96
sampling error, 109
Scheffe post hoc test, 221, 225
scientific knowledge, 6
semiotics, 241–242
sensitive information, 8
sigma (S), 18, 36, 58
simple linear regression, 191
    adjusted R-$squared$, 203
    computational formula for, 195–202
    meaning of, 193–194
    predictions, 194
    regression coefficient, 201–202
    slope of regression line, 195
    standard error (SE), 203
    standardized regression coefficient (beta coefficients or beta weights, b), 203
    statistical requirements/conditions, 194–195
    statistical symbols (notations), 202–203
    unstandardized regression coefficient, 203
simple random sampling, 94, 97
slope of regression line, 195
social sciences research, 7–9, 17, 22–23, 191, 207, 233, 242
social work profession, 1
Spearman's rho, 138, 144
    using SPSS, 156–159
SPSS. See Statistical Package for the Social Sciences (SPSS)
spurious association, 143
standard deviation (SD), 50, 59–60, 74, 96, 169
    distance between sample mean and, 78
    normal curves with, 76
standard error (SE), 168, 203
    of a sampling distribution, 79
    of mean, 96
    of standard deviation, 167

standardized regression coefficient (beta coefficients or beta weights, b), 203
standard score. *See* z score
Statgraphics, 12
static statistics, 2
statiscally dependent, 116
statiscally independent, 116
statistical analysis, 12, 273–274
statistical concepts, 2–3
statistical data, 3
statistical outlier, 53–54
Statistical Package for the Social Sciences (SPSS), 12, 39
    analysis of variance (ANOVA), 222–225
    basic statistical computations, 39–40
    calculation of measures of central tendency and variability, 61–67
    chi-square computation, 128–133
    computation of normal Curve, 85
    construction of confidence interval, 109–110
    data entry, 40–42, 250–254
    Data File, 42
    descriptive statistics computation, 256–257
    inferential statistics computation, 257
    likelihood of commiting crime, computation of, 64–67
    linear regression model (LRM), 204–207
    Pearson's r computation, 156–159
    practical experience, 43–44
    practical experience on, 255–256
    p value computation, 104
    recoding a variable, 258–261
    saving data, 255
    steps for scores for analysis, 249–250
    t-test computation, 183–186
    two-tailed nondirectional hypotheses, 101
    Variable View, 40–42
Statistical Software Suite (SAS), 12
statistical tests, 6
    interpreting, 104–105
statistics, 9–10
structured questionnaire, 235
structures, 239

sum of square (SS^2). *See* variance (SS2)
SurveyMonkey, 8

T

test of association. *See* Pearson chi-square (χ^2) test of independence
test of significance. *See* hypothesis testing
test-retest reliability, 233
tests of statistical significance, 221
tests of statistics, 6
third quartile (Q_3), 55
trimmed mean, 51
t-statistic, 166, 167, 170, 174, 180
t-tests, 166–167
    Cohen's d, 181–183
    correlation coefficient of effect size, 181–183
    critical value of, 171–172
    dependent and independent samples, 168
    dependent samples t-test, 176–180
    formula for correlation coefficient of effect size, 181–183
    homogeneity of variance, 174
    hypothesized population mean, 168–169, 172–173
    independent samples t-test, 173–176
    one-sample t-test, 168–169
    pooled variances, 174
    SPSS computation of, 183–186
    statistical assumptions, 167–168
    t-statistic, 167, 170, 174, 180
    types of, 167–180
two-tailed hypothesis test, 105–106
two-tailed nondirectional hypotheses, 101
Type I error, 103, 108, 212
Type II error, 108

U

univariate analysis, 12
unstandardized regression coefficient, 203

V

validity, 8–9
value

    categories, 19
    metric meanings, 19
variable, 18–19
    classification, 19–20
    confounding, 21
    dependent, 20
    independent, 20
    mediator, 21
    moderator, 21
    outcome or criterion, 20
    self-care, 57, 59
variance or sum of squares, 148
variance (SS^2), 57–59

X

x, y, and z symbols, 18

Z

z score, 77, 79–87, 181
    confidence interval using, 105–107
    directional (one-tailed or one-sided) hypothesis, 100
    effect size, 182
    formula for, 80
    rules converting z score to percentile, 80–84

CPSIA information can be obtained
at www.ICGtesting.com
Printed in the USA
LVHW050017090223
739027LV00009B/78